Transparency and Fragmentation

Books written or edited by Charles Sutcliffe

The Dangers of Low-Level Radiation

Banks and Bad Debts: Accounting for Loan Losses in International Banking

Stock Index Futures: Theories and International Evidence

Developing Decision Support Systems: A Study of Health Care Management

High-Frequency Financial Market Data: Sources, Applications and Market Microstructure

Management Accounting in Healthcare (editor)

Global Tracker Funds (editor)

Transparency and Fragmentation

Financial Market Regulation in a Dynamic Environment

John Board

Charles Sutcliffe

and

Stephen Wells

First published 2002 by
PALGRAVE MACMILLAN
Houndmills, Basingstoke, Hampshire RG21 6XS and
175 Fifth Avenue, New York, N.Y. 10010
Companies and representatives throughout the world

PALGRAVE MACMILLAN is the global academic imprint of the Palgrave
Macmillan division of St. Martin's Press, LLC and of Palgrave Macmillan Ltd.
Macmillan® is a registered trademark in the United States, United Kingdom
and other countries. Palgrave is a registered trademark in the European
Union and other countries.

ISBN 0–333–98634–2

This book is printed on paper suitable for recycling and made from fully
managed and sustained forest sources.

A catalogue record for this book is available from the British Library.

Library of Congress Cataloging-in-Publication Data
Board, John (John L. G.)
    Transparency and fragmentation: financial market regulation in a
    dynamic environment/John Board, Charles Sutcliffe, Stephen Wells.
        p. cm.
    Includes bibliographical references and index.
    ISBN 0–333–98634–2
    1. Securities—United States.   2. Securities—Great Britain.   3. Stock
    exchanges—Law and legislation—United States.   4. Stock exchanges—
    Law and legislation—Great Britain.   I. Sutcliffe, Charles, 1948–   II. Wells,
    Stephen, 1951–   III. Title.
HG4963 .B6 2002
332.64'241—dc21   2002025170

10   9   8   7   6   5   4   3   2   1
11   10 09 08 07 06 05 04 03 02

Printed and bound in Great Britain by
Antony Rowe Ltd, Chippenham and Eastbourne

Contents

List of Figures and Tables

Figures

Tables

Foreword

Financial market regulators everywhere have the maintenance of fair and orderly markets as one of their primary objectives. The UK is no exception. Recognition requirements for exchanges under both the Financial Services Act 1986 and its successor, the Financial Services and Markets Act 2000, require exchanges to ensure the orderly conduct of business and proper protection for investors.

Although not specifically defined in the legislation, an 'orderly market' is often held to be one exhibiting efficient price formation, as well as delivering fairness for investors. In its Guidance[1] on the present recognition requirements, the Financial Services Authority (FSA) focuses in particular on the need for exchanges to have reliable price formation and sufficient pre- and post-trade transparency – as well, of course, rules and procedures to prohibit abusive trading practices.

But even in a relatively straightforward world of floor-based, national and, generally, monopolistic exchanges, it was never particularly easy to determine just how efficiently a market was operating, particularly where an exchange offered several different methods of trading. In today's evolving market-place of electronic exchanges, of competing 'for-profit' exchanges, of non-exchange trading systems, of significant order internalisation, of increasing globalisation of trading, not to mention all kinds of new derivative products, the regulators' task of determining what constitutes a fair and orderly market has become increasingly complex.

At the same time, the 2000 Act has given the FSA new and much wider responsibilities in the markets area. In addition to its specific responsibilities for overseeing compliance with exchange recognition requirements, Parliament has set the FSA the much wider remit – as one of four statutory objectives – of maintaining market confidence. It was the prospect of this wider remit, together with the changes taking place in market structure, that persuaded us that it would be a timely moment to commission an independent, academic view of the direction in which the regulatory approach to market orderliness should be heading.

That was the genesis of the FSA commissioning the London School of Economics team to conduct a study of the key factors impacting on the operation of the financial markets, the findings and conclusions of which are set out in this book.

In addition to the report, the FSA also organised a conference in June 2001 that sought to take some of the main findings of the report and test them against the views of a broad constituency of market participants, financial regulators and other academics. Both the report and the output of the conference have provided the FSA with much to think about.

The number of policy initiatives connected to this work both domestically and internationally bears testimony to the importance of the issues raised and discussed in the book. Most significantly, the FSA is heavily involved in the consultation process for the revision of the EU Investment Services Directive, the key directive establishing a common framework for markets and their members across the EU. The present review of that directive focuses heavily on issues of market structure and the role and scope of transparency.

Similar issues are faced in the formulation of standards for the operation of alternative trading systems across Europe. This work, coordinated through the Committee of European Securities Regulators (CESR, formerly FESCO), aims to understand the nature of the relatively new forms of automated multilateral trading platform, and to determine the principles by which they should operate.

We therefore welcome this contribution to one of the most challenging areas of securities regulation. It will help to inform our thinking as we progress our work in determining where, and in what way, regulation needs to address the changing risks of the evolving market environment.

MICHAEL FOOT
Managing Director, Financial Services Authority

Note

1   FSA Handbook, *Recognised Investment Exchanges and Recognised Clearing Houses* (viewable at fsa.gov.uk).

Acknowledgements

Chapter 5 of this book was prepared by Owain ap Gwilym of the University of Southampton in collaboration with the authors of this book. Chapter 11 was written independently by James Angel of the University of Georgetown and formed part of his contribution to the FSA's 'Evolution of Market Regulation' conference at which this work was discussed.

In addition to those who have authored specific chapters, we wish to thank the following for their various contributions to this book: the staff of the Financial Services Authority including Matthew Elderfield, John Whitmore, Ed Davies, Simon Laughton, Gay Huey Evans, Michael Foot, Sir Howard Davies, George Frankland and Isaac Alfon; Sir Brian Williamson of LIFFE; Donald Brydon of the Fund Managers' Association; Jonathan Howell and Chris Broad of the London Stock Exchange; Benn Steil of the Council on Foreign Relations; Ruben Lee of the Oxford Finance Group; Alan Line of Foreign and Colonial Management Ltd; Stephen Wilson of Virt-X; William Fall of Bank of America; Markku Malkamäki of Evli Securities; Adam Austerfield and Gabriella Flores of Enterprise LSE; Julie Cardy of Southampton University; the participants in the Evolving Market Regulation conference in June 2001; the participants in the FSA seminar in January 2001; and the staff of the seven UK RIEs and Eurex whom we interviewed.

List of Abbreviations

ADR	American Depositary Receipt
AF	Authorised Firm
AIM	Alternative Investment Market
AMEX	American Stock Exchange
AMIR	Association for Investment Management and Research
APT	Automated Pit Trading
ASDA	Associated Dairies
ASX	Australian Stock Exchange
ATS	Alternative Trading System
BIS	Bank for International Settlements
BoBS	Board of Banking Supervision
BTP	Buoni del Tesoro Poliennali
CAC	Compagnie des Agents de Change
CATS	Computer Aided Trading System
CBA	Cost-Benefit Analysis
CBOE	Chicago Board Options Exchange
CBOT	Chicago Board of Trade
CEO	Chief Executive Officer
CFS	Committee on Financial Services
CFTC	Commodity Futures Trading Commission
CLOB	Central Limit Order Book
CME	Chicago Mercantile Exchange
COB	Conduct of Business
COMEX	Commodity Exchange, Inc.
CQS	Consolidated Quotations System
CSFB	Credit Suisse First Boston
CTS	Consolidated Tape System
CUNY	City University of New York
DAX	Deutscher Aktienindex
DGFT	Director General of Fair Trading
DTB	Deutsche TerminBörse
DTCC	Depository Trust and Clearing Corporation
DTF	Derivatives Transaction Facility
EASDAQ	European Association of Securities Dealers Automated Quotation system
EBS	Electronic Broking Services

ECN	Electronic Communications Network
EDSP	Exchange Delivery Settlement Price
EEA	European Economic Area
ERM	Exchange Rate Mechanism
EU	European Union
FESCO	Forum of European Securities Exchanges
FIBV	International Federation of Stock Exchanges
FSA	Financial Services Authority
FSMA	Financial Services and Markets Act
FTSE	Financial Times Stock Exchange
IBIS	Integiertes Börsenhandels und Informationssystem
ICE	Intercontinental Exchange
IDB	Inter-Dealer Broker
IMM	Inter Market Maker
IOSCO	International Organisation of Securities Commissioners
IPE	International Petroleum Exchange
IPO	Initial Public Offering
ISD	Investment Services Directive
ITS	Interexchange Trading System
JGB	Japanese Government Bond
LCE	London Commodities Exchange
LCH	London Clearing House
LIFFE	London International Financial Futures and Options Exchange
LME	London Metal Exchange
LTOM	London Traded Options Market
MATIF	Marché à Terme International de France
MBA	Master of Business Administration
MIP	Market Infrastructure Provider
MPC	Monetary Policy Committee
MTEF	Multilateral Transaction Execution Facility
MTS	Mercato Telematico dei Titoli di Stato
NASD	National Association of Securities Dealers
NASDAQ	NASD Automated Quotation system
NBBO	National Best Bid and Offer
NMS	National Market System or Normal Market Size
NYMEX	New York Mercantile Exchange
NYSE	New York Stock Exchange
OFT	Office of Fair Trading
OPRA	Options Price Reporting Authority
OSE	Osaka Securities Exchange

OTC	Over the Counter
PAL	Phase Alternate Line
PIP	Primary Information Provider
POSIT	Portfolio System for Institutional Trades
RFE	Recognised Futures Exchange
RIE	Recognised Investment Exchange
RNS	Regulatory News Service
RSP	Retail Service Provider
SBC	Senate Banking Committee
SEAQ	Stock Exchange Automated Quotations
SEAQ-I	SEAQ International
SEATS-Plus	Stock Exchange Alternative Trading System Plus
SEC	Securities and Exchange Commission
SECAM	Sequential Couleur Avec Mémoire
SETS	Stock Exchange Electronic Trading Service
SFA	Securities and Futures Authority
SFE	Sydney Futures Exchange
SGX	Singapore Exchange
SIAC	Securities Industry Automation Corporation
SIB	Securities and Investments Board
SIMEX	Singapore International Monetary Exchange
SIP	Secondary Information Provider
SOFFEX	Swiss Options and Financial Futures Exchange
SRO	Self-Regulating Organisation
S&P	Standard and Poors
TMU	Transactions Monitoring Unit
TSE	Toronto Stock Exchange
UBS	Union Bank of Switzerland
VHS	Video Home System
WPA	Worked Principal Agreement

1
Executive Summary and Policy Implications

A world in which markets are fragmenting and evolving in unpredictable ways presents three major risks to meeting the FSA's statutory objectives:

- the possibility of segmented trading of the same security in a number of venues, leading to low liquidity, price fragmentation, poor price discovery, difficulty defining an exchange, and the like
- best execution becoming hard to achieve and harder to monitor and enforce
- increasing risk of systemic risk and market abuse, as there is no single entity with an overall picture of trading activity.

This chapter outlines some of the major issues arising from these risks and our conclusions.

1.1 Fragmentation

There is now almost no functional difference between Recognised Investment Exchanges (RIEs) and Alternative Trading Systems (ATSs). The current UK regulatory regime is based on the RIE and it is implicit in much of the debate that there is one RIE per market. However, in a fragmented world, the single RIE might capture an increasingly small proportion of business and become less and less representative. As a result, monitoring only the RIE offers the FSA, at best, a limited view of the overall market.

Our analysis suggests that fragmentation is healthy and should not be regarded *per se* as undesirable, provided the various trading systems link together. To achieve this, real time information will have to be widely available on trading activity for each venue (i.e. transparency). Regulators will need to monitor the level of transparency achieved by each trading venue and be prepared to intervene where it is inadequate.

1.2 Best execution

In a fragmented world, the current regulations for best execution, which is at the core of the investor protection role for the FSA, cannot be sustained. The current rules are based on a single defined exchange, and brokers cannot be held liable if markedly better prices are available on other exchanges. Revised rules will have to recognise the complex nature of trading and will necessarily require a greater reliance on professional duties and competencies than at present. Such rules will be less tangible than the current ones, but the current ones no longer guarantee best execution. A key part of any such rule will be the ability to monitor, after the event, the performance of the broker/agent concerned. This can be achieved only with comprehensive trade reporting/publication across the relevant trading systems – a comprehensive transparency regime.

1.3 Market access

In a fragmented world, investors have the choice as to where they trade. Equally some trading systems may wish to restrict access (e.g. to institutions, large trades, retail traders) as part of their competitive positioning, and it will be difficult for the FSA to reject this unless it wishes to use an intrusive public interest criterion and withhold approval from all but public exchanges. However, there is a danger that, if price formation occurs in trading systems which restrict access, investors in the public trading systems will be systematically disadvantaged as arbitrageurs act to profit from the price differentials.

The solution is to ensure that those who are not eligible to trade in the restricted venues can at least see the prices and volumes being transacted in these venues. This will remove at least some of the information imbalance between the restricted and open venues, and requires all trading systems to be transparent.

1.4 Manipulation

The fragmentation of markets increases the risks of a failure to detect insider trading, market manipulation and the like. The RIEs can no longer effectively police markets because any RIE will see only part of the trading activity, while in other markets there is no RIE. Equally, we believe that, in a competitive world, RIEs will tend to withdraw from any supervisory role. Over the Counter (OTC) activity which accounts for significant proportions of trading in many markets also poses potential systemic risks to the financial system. A more comprehensive system of trade reporting and publication (i.e. transparency) will permit more accurate and effective policing of such behaviour.

1.5 Transparency

Regulators both in the UK and abroad accept that a high level of transparency is, other things equal, desirable. Arguing for high transparency does not, for example, mean that block trade facilities, which necessarily reduce transparency, should be forbidden – simply that they should be justified and implemented so as to have the smallest reduction in transparency consistent with achieving the facility's objective. Our analysis has shown no published evidence which supports the case that restricting transparency damages the quality of the market or drives business offshore. While traders can always evade any transparency regime, they will have little incentive to do so if the regime is sufficiently light.

In terms of publication, we regard both pre- and post-trade information as important. Post-trade information (time, price and quantity of each trade) is fundamental to investors' decision making, market supervision and best execution. Pre-trade information (such items as bid/offer prices, depth and the order book) is harder to mandate, and will probably be produced by each trading system as part of its business.

We therefore propose a more extensive system of trade reporting and publication, while allowing natural exchange transparency to produce acceptable levels of information at the lowest cost to market participants. It should be stressed that neither we nor other commentators propose revealing traders' identities. Anonymity is a fair requirement of markets and need not be compromised.

1.6 The future

These arguments suggest that the FSA has three choices in determining its future regime:

- *Status quo* – if new entrants do capture a significant share of trading, the existing approach will monitor an increasingly small part of any market's activity, be increasingly ad hoc, and runs the risk of breaching the FSAs statutory objectives.

- *Impose unity* – this regime of increased regulation would require in some way the consolidation of the market. One approach would be to prohibit non-RIEs, another would be to mandate a consolidated limit order book. We reject both of these as being over-intrusive, probably in conflict with the FSA's statutory objectives and likely to be unsustainable in the long run.
- A light but defensible regime based on the reality of the new market places. Such a regime is likely to be more acceptable to both regulator and industry than the others and should:
  - Abandon, for this purpose, attempts to distinguish between different types of exchange (e.g. RIEs, ATSs and others) and instead focus regulation on Authorised Firms.
  - Institute a more effective and complete system of trade reporting and publication than currently exists (i.e. transparency). This will effectively create a consolidated market from the various trading systems, allow comprehensive monitoring of breaches of market behaviour (reporting) and allow investors to make appropriate decisions themselves (publication).
  - Encourage and promote competition between trading venues by removing barriers to entry, facilitating the distribution of trade information and ensuring equal access where appropriate.

2
Introduction and Overview

2.1 Introduction and scope of UK market regulation

The Financial Services & Markets Act[1] (FSMA) has significantly extended the responsibilities of the Financial Services Authority (FSA) in the markets area. A central feature of the new Act is Parliament's establishment of four statutory objectives for the FSA. These have varying degrees of relevance to the orderliness and efficiency of markets but, potentially, broaden considerably the FSA's existing responsibility in this area, namely to ensure the 'orderly control of business' on RIEs. The four statutory objectives are as follows:[2]

1 *Maintaining confidence in the UK financial system*[3]
   The financial system includes financial markets and exchanges, regulated activities and other activities connected with financial markets and exchanges (FSMA, section 3).
2 *Promoting public understanding of the financial system*
   This includes promoting awareness of the benefits and risks associated with different kinds of investment or other financial dealing, and the provision of appropriate information and advice (FSMA, section 4).
3 *Securing the appropriate degree of protection for consumers*
   The FSA must have regard to the differing degrees of risk involved in different kinds of investment or other transactions, the differing degrees of experience and expertise that different consumers may have in relation to different kinds of regulatory activity, the needs that consumers may have for advice and accurate information and the general principle that consumers should take responsibility for their actions (FSMA, section 5).

4 *Reducing financial crime*

This involves reducing the extent to which it is possible for a business carried on by a regulated person[4] or in contravention of the general prohibition to be used for a purpose connected with financial crime.[5] The FSA must have regard to the desirability of regulated persons being aware of the risk of their business being used in connection with the commission of financial crime, and regulated persons taking appropriate measures to prevent financial crime, facilitate its detection and monitor its incidence, and regulated persons devoting adequate resources to these matters (FSMA, section 6).

The Act has occurred at a time of considerable change in market structure, creating a need for the FSA to take stock of the factors making for orderly markets and to determine how, in the changing environment, it should identify and address risks to those objectives. The FSA has commissioned this study to assist its consideration of this process, specifically in areas relating to the quality of price formation and the overall economic efficiency of the market, within its four statutory objectives.

In the context of markets and exchanges, there is a number of ways in which the FSA may fail to meet its four statutory objectives. (i) Confidence may be damaged if markets are opaque, open to manipulation, inaccessible to consumers, or consumers cannot be sure to get the best available price. (ii) Public understanding may be reduced if there is a lack of market transparency. This includes not just pre- and post-trade transparency, but also the way the market works (e.g. order routeing decisions, internalisation and payment for order flow). (iii) Consumer protection may be reduced if best execution is not achieved; and this requires transparency, access to markets and trade reporting. (iv) Financial crime may be enabled if markets are susceptible to manipulation, possibly due to the inadequate reporting of trades and positions in such a way that no single body has overall oversight. Finally, (v) there is the risk that trading through unregulated marketplaces has knock-on effects on regulated markets.

In discharging its general functions the FSA must have regard to (FSMA, section 2):

- the need to use its resources in the most efficient and economic way
- the responsibilities of those who manage the affairs of authorised persons
- the principle that a burden or restriction which is imposed on a person, or on the carrying on of an activity, should be proportionate

to the benefits, considered in general terms, which are expected to result from the imposition of the burden or restriction

- the desirability of facilitating innovation in connection with regulated activities
- the international character of financial services and markets and the desirability of maintaining the competitive position of the UK
- the need to minimise the adverse effects on competition that may arise from anything done in the discharge of those functions
- the desirability of facilitating competition between those who are subject to any form of regulation by the FSA.

The obligation on the FSA to maintain orderly markets is contained in section 4 of the FSA's Recognition Requirements[6] for investment exchanges and clearing houses. Therefore, the FSA must ensure that RIEs maintain an orderly market. As argued in chapter 4, 'the market' includes not just RIEs but also trading through Alternative Trading Systems[7] (ATSs) and over the counter (OTC) markets in particular instruments, the concept of orderly markets extends to the entire market, including ATS and OTC trading.

The major focus of this report is on factors which are likely either to promote or to compromise the efficiency of the UK financial markets and, so, undermine confidence in those markets. Many of these factors relate to a lack of competition, which usually results from barriers to entry, and can lead to excessive profits, restricted output, higher prices, and a lack of innovation. An important condition for competition to be effective is that information should be widely available at minimal cost, and its absence impedes the smooth functioning of markets.

A key issue is whether the markets are to be regulated for the benefit of the existing users or a broader constituency, which includes potential users. The first can be interpreted as the maintenance of the status quo in which an existing group of participants trade with each other and are content with the existing arrangements for trading (e.g. in terms of transparency and market structure). The problem is that those who are uneasy about the trading conditions will tend to withdraw from (or not enter) the market, thus reducing the number of discontented users. This means that, if regulation is for the broader constituency, assurances of market efficiency made by incumbent traders are not sufficient, and regulators should be concerned about potential users of the market. Of course, the theoretical difficulty is how wide should one draw the scope of potential users and the practical difficulty of measuring latent demand. However this distinction is important, and it has certainly been the case that practices and structures that were eminently accept-able to current users were deeply unattractive to new users. We believe that it is important that regulators consider market efficiency and confidence, not only in terms of existing users, but also in terms of potential users whose participation might further improve efficiency.

2.2   Fragmentation, convergence and divergence

A review conducted only a few years ago would have seen a much more varied landscape of trading systems than now. Exchanges had developed along their own evolutionary paths and there had been little to bring them together – except, of course, that they were all doing roughly the same thing in providing a venue for exposing interest and trading securities. These exchanges differed in a variety of ways with floor exchanges, electronic exchanges, trading crowds, dealer markets, exchanges with specialists of one kind or another, continuous markets and call-overs. Most of this diversity has gone, and the reviewer today would see a range of more homogeneous trading systems.

Twenty years ago exchanges operated in protected, segmented envir-onments with little intellectual or commercial challenge. They had grown out of essentially OTC trading arrangements in which intermedi-aries combined to regulate themselves. Regulation was primarily aimed at governing how they dealt with each other, rather than how they served investors or issuers. As a result, most exchange rule books started out largely to ensure fair play between brokers, and developed piecemeal over many years as the exchange rule makers tried to adapt their struc-tures to accommodate changes in the environment. The result was a complex set of rules within exchanges which produced unique trading systems which were the product of the interaction of local developments and existing trading systems. Each exchange claimed that its system, by ensuring fair play between its participants, produced the best possible price discovery and maximum liquidity.

This continuous evolution tended to produce systems that were quite flexible to incremental shifts in local trading needs, but which lacked an internal logic and were frail when larger, external challenges appeared. The systems also tended to have many intermediaries, often with highly specialised roles, and with restrictions that were argued to be essential for the continued functioning of the trading process. The systems were expensive, partly because of the artificiality of many of the restrictions, The need to preserve specialised roles added layers of cost to the trading system, but this was justified by reference to the high quality of price discovery and high liquidity.

Today there is far greater homogeneity of exchanges. Even the floor versus screen debate, which was conducted during the late 1990s, now largely seems a dead issue. Practically everywhere exchanges have moved to screen trading. Where floors persist, they largely reflect the resistance of floor brokers to abandoning their home, and often need to be supported by rules to ensure sufficient orders are routed there. Almost all the electronic, screen-based systems involve a public limit order book, and in many cases it is the sole or dominant method of trading on the system. All have priorities based on price and time. While some important differences between exchanges are highlighted by our survey results, the dominant impression is of similarity.

This convergence can be explained by changes in technology and the globalisation of investment. These two powerful forces have projected the market power of the international players into ever more distant markets, and these players have tended to favour trading systems that offer safe, transparent and cheap order execution. This is somewhat paradoxical in that the dominant cross-border investors tend to come from countries (UK and USA) that have not traditionally had public order books. But it would be a brave trading system that opted to introduce a trading mechanism based on competing dealers or a specialist-driven floor system. More recently, the formation of alliances, combined with transfer of some standard trading products, has accelerated the process of convergence.

The current dominance of public order book systems owes much to the combination of low set-up cost and high transparency. But despite the apparent convergence, trading systems still show significant variation – for example in their transparency and handling of block trades.

2.2.1 Emergence of contestability

Accompanying the trend towards the convergence of trading systems has been the emergence of competition in the supply of trading services. Exchanges in jurisdictions where there was no concentration rule have always faced some competition from brokers who could internalise business, but since the exchanges were monopolies and could enforce reporting rules without any restriction on reporting fees, this had relatively little effect. A number of recent changes have made the market for trading services more contestable, including the globalisation of investment, (which encourages the cross-border trading of assets or the creation of competing derivatives) and the impact of technology (which has sharply reduced entry costs and increased the reach of trading systems).

In consequence, there has been an increase in competition from a number of sources, for example:

- Exchanges have generally become more *commercially aware*, often accompanied by changes in governance, and are seeking to extend their trading into assets that were traditionally the province of other exchanges (e.g. the provision of trading in leading global 'blue-chips').
- Exchanges are extending their *product range* into new areas. The traditional example is the cross-border trading of equities (SEAQ-I and ADRs), but the introduction of individual stock futures is a more current example in the USA and UK.
- As broking business has tended to *concentrate*, so the scope for brokers matching orders from their clients has also grown. The recent changes to LIFFE's crossing rules are a response to this situation. These rules essentially compromise market centrality in the interests of keeping the business on-exchange. Business on equity markets and on the LME is substantially internalised,[8] with the 'central' trading system acting as a clearing house for proprietary positions.
- *New entrants*. This has been the most startling development for traditional exchanges (though possibly not actually the most threatening). Exchanges now face the possibility of direct competition in their market from exchange-like entities (ATSs) facilitated by technology and regulatory accommodation. Exchanges that trade generic products face the strongest challenge, while those with proprietary products (and, possibly, proprietary settlement) face less of a challenge from ATSs.[9] In addition, new exchanges (e.g. Tradepoint, which transformed into Virt-x, Coredeal and Jiway) have been established.
- The growth of the OTC markets, especially in derivatives, represents a competitive threat for traditional derivatives exchanges. Derivatives exchanges may be able to prevent the trading and settlement of their own products, but cannot stop the trading of contracts that are nearly identical to those on-exchange. Electronic systems are being established to conduct such OTC trades.

2.2.2   The UK RIEs

Our investigation of the UK RIEs has shown a pattern of convergence in trading methods, but with continuing diversity. Only two of the RIEs maintain floor trading; albeit only for a short period each day in one case, and for four contracts in another.[10] We expect the move towards electronic trading systems to continue, and that floor trading will continue to decline in significance. The benefits in terms of cost, information flow, access to analysis, transparency and control are such that floor systems do not generally survive long when electronic systems are on offer. Equally, there is no reason for regulatory intervention to hasten the transition to screen trading. The RIEs do retain significant differences in the areas of transparency, market centrality, exchange scope, liquidity support, protection of order priority and retail protection.

Our interviews with the RIEs and our examination of the trading systems used in these exchanges suggest no conclusive theoretical or empirical evidence either that one trading structure is absolutely better than others, or that some trading structures are naturally more suitable for trading particular products or for particular traders than are others. The microstructure of markets is a major focus of competition between trading systems, so that, where an existing structure is unchanging and unwanted, new trading systems without the undesirable features can be expected to open.

In particular, we found little evidence to support the proposition that different assets have inherent characteristics which require the application of a fundamentally different regulatory regime. This finding means that, although particular aspects of any market might justify a different intensity of regulation (for example, low liquidity might justify different levels of transparency or more intensive monitoring for market manipulation), the overall regulatory framework should be the same between markets. This means that attempts to couch regulation in terms of asset classes, other than for very specific purposes, are unlikely to be useful in the long run.

The nature of the traders who use a trading system will change over time as investor tastes change, and new marketplaces develop. As a result, instituting a system of regulation based on the current retail–wholesale divide may result in the anomalous treatment of different participants in the same trading system, or of the same participant in different trading systems. Thus, regulations based on historic client profiles might either exclude potential new institutional users because the rules were overly retail oriented, or fail to protect retail investors entering what were previously wholesale trading systems.

2.2.3 Conclusions

Our analysis suggests that, while there are criteria which an orderly trading venue should satisfy, these criteria can be satisfied by a number of different trading structures. Thus, the reduced cost of establishing new venues and the increasing ease of entry suggest that the current pattern of fragmentation, alliances, mergers and consolidation will continue. The outcome of this process is unpredictable and may itself change. This means that any regulatory stance which is based on a static picture of the market place will become increasingly inappropriate over time. Any useful regulatory position must be flexible enough to cover whatever market picture emerges, and should avoid being tailored to fit particular structures, dominant players or participant profiles. We believe that the proposals outlines below meet this requirement.

2.3   Regulatory options in diffuse markets

As trading fragments, it becomes increasingly difficult to distinguish between RIEs and ATSs. While, according to the current RIEs, the requirements for becoming an RIE are not unduly onerous, the RIE path does not, and will not, appeal to all trading system operators. Brokers operating in-house trading systems and some entities that could be classed as ATSs are already regulated as authorised firms and do not wish to take on RIE responsibilities. Such trading systems may, as in the USA, also reject the idea of being regulated by, and reporting through, an exchange that they see as a competitor. Equally, the increasingly commercial orientation of exchanges may encourage them to focus only on the business passing through their own trading systems, and become less interested in being a regulator for transactions negotiated away from the exchange's own system (essentially OTC transactions), unless it offers a commercial return.

OTC markets are growing and increasingly trading products that are similar to exchange-traded assets. Additionally they are, themselves, adopting trading through electronic systems so as to reduce the costs of trading standardised products. Many parts of the OTC market are therefore becoming more like exchange markets, while at the same time parts of some exchange markets are moving to being more explicitly OTC.

While the effects on the market of increased trading through any particular non-exchange trading system are likely to be small, the collective effect of many ATSs or other alternative systems may be large. Therefore basing a regulatory structure on the 'materiality' of individual trading systems, with small trading systems (those below a certain market share) being exempted from any regulatory responsibilities, runs the risk that a significant part of aggregate trading will be outside the regulatory structure, even though each part is judged not material.

Lastly, the definition of what is 'on-exchange' and what is 'off-exchange' varies between RIEs. For example, LME transactions involving non-members are executed on a principal basis and, while reported, are not published. In contrast, on the London Stock Exchange, such transactions are reported and published in the same way as trades through the electronic system. Much institutional business is conducted as principal business, as is retail business through Retail Service Providers. Finally, some derivatives exchanges, such as LIFFE, are able, through their ownership of the contract, to ensure that not only is business reported to them but is also actually transacted through their trading system.

Practice outside the UK varies. For example: in markets with a concentration rule, such as Italy, all orders must be brought to the central exchange and so there are no principal trades between an Authorised Firm (AF) and an investor. In those markets orders pass through routeing systems where they are handled as agency orders, whereas in other markets, there is a series of principal trades resulting in changes of ownership. SuperDot in the USA is an example of the former, while NASDAQ is an example of the latter. However, on the Deutsche Börse AF–investor transactions may be agent or principal, but principal client side trades are off-exchange and are not reported to the exchange or published. Our expectation is that the increasingly commercial orientation of exchanges will encourage them to focus on the business passing through their own trading systems, and they will become less interested in being a reporting mechanism for negotiated transactions that are essentially OTC.

Figures 2.1 and 2.2 show the traditional pattern of trading in which almost all participants trade on a single RIE, and the emerging model of fragmentation in which participants trade on a range on market venues and outside organised venues.

In both figures the rectangle represents the market as a whole, circles represent trading venues of one sort or another and symbols represent different market participants. Figure 2.1 shows a monopoly RIE, with almost all trading taking place on this exchange. The RIE is indicated in the figure by the large circle and it can be seen that most trades by retail customers, institutions and intermediaries are conducted using this exchange. Only a very small amount of off-exchange trading takes place, and this is indicated in Figure 2.1 by the two symbols outside the circle.

In Figure 2.2, there is no single trading system that is the clear focus of regulation. Trading system 3 might be the original RIE, while trading

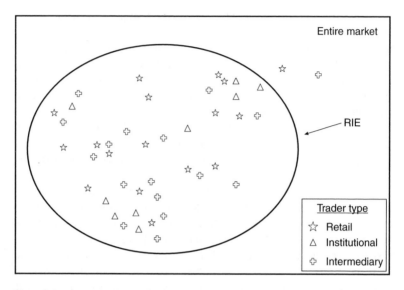

Figure 2.1 Market with a single RIE through which almost all trading is conducted

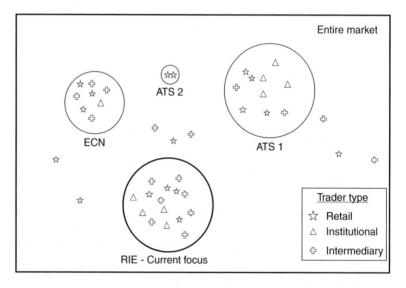

Figure 2.2 Market with trading fragmented between a number of venues

system 1 is a new ATS which has chosen to become an RIE, and trading system 2 is an ATS which continues as an AF only. Of these, trading system 3 may report its trades to either of the exchanges, so that exchange 3, the 'traditional' exchange, is no longer able to see a significant part of the market's activity. It is unclear whether trading system 4 is material enough to warrant regulation, and, in addition, there is a significant amount of OTC trading. The figures, and the preceding arguments, show that it is increasingly difficult to define a 'marketplace', let alone distinguish those which should be treated as RIEs from those which should continue as AFs, or even to determine the threshold for any form of materiality condition for regulation and supervision

2.3.1   Reliance on competition

As is apparent, we do not believe that security market fragmentation *per se* is a problem. A problem exists only if fragmentation results in worse execution (for example, a widening of the bid–ask spread). Provided the benefits of a consolidated market are preserved in a fragmented system (e.g. ease of execution and monitoring), we can receive the benefits of competition and the benefits of consolidation. In monopolistic markets, the task of the regulator is to ensure that monopoly power is not abused. In contestable markets regulators can distance themselves from the competing entities, relying on competition and new entrants to eliminate market defects. However it is unclear whether regulators can rely solely on competition to deal with all market imperfections. There seem to be three levels of regulation, all of which rely on competition to a greater or lesser degree:

No regulation except prohibitions on overt and demonstrable barriers to entry

In competitive markets if users do not like a trading system/broker or think they get a raw deal then they can always go somewhere else. If enough people think this way then new trading systems/brokers will emerge to serve them. Provided some traders can access both the old and new systems, there will be a bridge between old and new so, allowing some margin for the costs of arbitrage, prices will equilibrate across trading venues. For example, if an 'old' trading system is undesirably opaque, new trading systems will tend to be more transparent (if that is what users want), and the common access of traders to both markets will make it 'as if' the trading systems were one transparent and consolidated market (or nearly so). In the absence of regulatory intervention, a 'natural' level of transparency will emerge. There may, however, be barriers to entry (perhaps legacies of the monopoly exchange structure or obstacles created by the incumbents) which prevent the establishment of the new market. Such barriers will deter the emergence of genuine competition, and include such institutional rigidities as best execution rules defined in terms of one exchange, legal barriers to institutions trading outside the official exchange, and the definition of reference prices as equivalent to exchange prices. If only some traders can access both markets, there will be wealth transfers from those with access to those without.

Level 1 regulation plus more aggressive transparency requirements to enhance competition

Among the reasons why level 1 regulation might not ensure competition, good price discovery or high market quality is that significant differences in transparency might impede the efficient equalisation of prices between trading systems. Efficiency will be compromised if some trading systems are opaque and if commonality of membership is insufficient to align prices. Alternatively, incumbents may be able to obstruct new trading venues with covert barriers (e.g. by refusing to participate in a consolidated tape or to publish prices in real time[11]). As a result, competition may not arise, or promising new entrants may be immediately bought out by incumbents.

Level 2 regulation plus protection for retail clients

Retail investors face a potentially severe information asymmetry when trading with professional counterparties who have more information, and will therefore require protection even with competitive markets.[12] Regulatory approaches to providing protection include measures to address the information imbalance and to assure fair dealing, for example:

- reducing the information asymmetry before trade (*pre-trade transparency*)
- providing information about other trades (*post-trade transparency*)
- providing information to allow *assessment of trade quality*.

However, the nature of these participants may mean that simply publishing everything and allowing investors to make their own decisions about execution quality and the like may not be enough – they need to be protected by active monitoring of what is done to and for them. For example, there might need to be strict monitoring and enforcement of best execution by a regulator. The Securities and Exchange Commission (SEC) rule which mandates publication of execution summaries is an example that we discuss in Chapter 6. Best execution is a responsibility of the AFs that act for these clients, and the ultimate enforcement responsibility is with the regulator, though there may well be a market solution to the monitoring function. For example, specialist companies can summarise the information on execution quality provided by trading venues and brokers and make this aggregate information available to investors.

2.3.2   Regulatory impact of diversity

Trading systems in the UK are already fragmenting, and so a debate as to whether fragmentation is desirable is largely redundant. As this fragmentation continues, competition may lead to consolidation in some parts of the market; but, if entry costs are low, there should also be continuing innovation from new entrants, possibly aiming at niches or offering innovative systems.[13] Consistent with this, the evidence so far is that competition for trading services leads to innovation and a greater more genuine focus on user needs. For example, the willingness of some traditional exchanges to make their data feeds available at zero cost (albeit with some delay) over the Internet is one example of how competitive pressures have forced trading systems to respond to a user need. However, as trading fragments, it becomes increasingly difficult to define the concept of an exchange in a meaningful way.[14]

One consequence of competition is that trading systems will be unable to perpetuate inefficient rules and systems. In turn, this will allow regulators to step back from their traditional involvement in the micro-management of exchanges and their rules (for example, the RIEs currently act as if they are obliged to have changes to their trading rules approved by the FSA). However, the current regulatory focus is predicated on trading in any instrument being concentrated in a small number of venues, which can be clearly classified as exchanges. This approach works best when there is either a monopoly exchange or a dominant exchange. Since we do not expect this to be the pattern for the future, the issue becomes how best to modify the regulatory system to fit the new situation, rather than to discuss the maintenance of the single-exchange model.

These conclusions suggest that some significant rethinking of regulatory positions is required:

- *Fragmentation of trading across multiple venues is already a fact.* Given the Investment Services Directive (ISD) and the right of trading systems to be offered across the European Union (EU), fragmentation cannot be stopped. Regulators should welcome fragmentation, which is competition by another name.

- *Competition will tend to eliminate inefficiencies and structural weaknesses in trading systems*, and regulators can, therefore, withdraw from the detailed monitoring of trading rules. There will, however, be concerns about investor protection and barriers to competition that require regulatory intervention to set standards for all types of trading system, and a continued emphasis on the transparency of trading, which we discuss at length in Chapter 8.
- *It will become increasingly difficult to define an exchange*, and a regulatory structure based on exchanges will become increasingly unstable and inconsistent. This suggests that regulators should develop a focus based on AFs as the key building blocks for regulation. AFs are already the focus of Conduct of Business (CoB) rules, and are a natural focus for other aspects of regulation, including trade reporting.
- We recognise that inconsistencies in the UK regulatory structure, particularly in the treatment of OTC trading, are the result of long evolutionary processes and that reform should be approached with caution. However, regulators should address these as part of a review aiming for a structure that has consistency and resilience.

We have already discussed the reasons for the convergence in trading systems – largely cost and customer preference. But it is worth enquiring whether the remaining differences reflect underlying real differences in the markets concerned. This is important because market structure and regulation are intimately connected; indeed much current regulatory effort is devoted to judging the trading mechanism choices and proposals of RIEs. Our investigation of the UK RIEs found no grounds to support the adoption of fundamentally different regulatory standards between markets. In particular, we examined two possibilities – differences between asset class and one based on differences in client type.

Asset class

We have found little to suggest that 'metals are different' (i.e. that by their nature, some products are better suited to some regulatory structures than are others).

Although there are differences in the settlement arrangements for some products (e.g. the London Metal Exchange (LME) generally requires physical settlement, which involves complex warehousing systems), these could operate alongside any trading mechanism. Similarly, it is sometimes claimed that the specific features of physical assets require a different type of regulation because supply and demand are relatively inelastic, and this makes them particularly susceptible to manipulative tactics, such as cornering and squeezing. While commodity markets are more susceptible to some types of manipulation, all markets are vulnerable to manipulative tactics of one type or another. For example, stock markets may be more vulnerable to insider trading or fraudulent information than some physical markets. The fact that the manipulative tactics differ from market to market means that the thrust of the regulatory effort should also vary. But the overall requirement to operate clean markets (including, for example, prohibitions on actions designed to manipulate supply or misuse of private information) remains, irrespective of the type of asset. Clearly, the intensity of monitoring may vary with the perceived likelihood of such behaviour, but we do not believe that the overall regulatory structure should be different in these cases.

We do not see why a trading system's position as the market for principal price discovery (e.g. LME and, to an extent, the International Petroleum Exchange (IPE)) when the spot market is too diffuse to offer this function should dictate a particular trading mechanism. Nor is there substance in a related argument that a derivatives exchange like LIFFE is not a market for price discovery (since that was the function of the underlying market) and so deserves different regulatory treatment.[15]

Lastly, it has been argued that the complexity of many spread trading strategies means that they cannot be executed on screens. This might be true, but modern screen systems (such as LIFFE's Connect, and OM) support a number of complex trading strategies, and it is not clear why newer screen-based-systems will be unable to offer such facilities.

The most persuasive reason for the rejection of asset class regulation of markets is that new trading systems are likely to offer trading in several classes of asset, making regulation based on asset classes difficult to sustain.

Client type

The RIE with the largest retail element is the London Stock Exchange, while others, such as LIFFE and Jiway, have some retail involvement, and the other RIEs are almost entirely institutional. Although the importance of institutional trading has led to particular features of the trading process, notably block trade facilities, there is nothing to suggest that there need be fundamental differences in the regulatory treatment of retail and wholesale clients. Therefore, we are wary of suggesting that the regulation of trading systems should be differentiated on the basis of supposed differences in the client base, for a number of reasons:

- While the *current user base of most UK RIEs is mainly institutional*, there is no reason why this should always be the case. There is growing retail interest in equities, and no reason why retail investors should not diversify their portfolios further. It is also entirely possible that some trading systems are exclusively institutional because the structure of the trading system, through historical accident or intent, excludes retail participation (for example, the LME's contract size is too large for retail clients). The risks are that a regulatory split between wholesale and retail would either exclude retail clients from trading systems that they might otherwise enter or, more dangerously, allow retail clients to access professional systems at one remove.[16]
- There is a well-known difficulty of *defining groups of traders in an unambiguous way*. Traditionally this is done by size of transaction, but this is not entirely satisfactory – everyone knows that very large trades are almost certainly institutional and very small ones are retail, but there is always a substantial overlap in the middle. If users are allowed to self-select, then there is a strong possibility that they will all opt for the maximum protection. For example, few institutions have opted out of the protection offered by the best execution regulations.
- It is not clear that some of the possible *regulatory distinctions* often mentioned are actually supported by the particular user base. For example, it is often suggested that professional markets need less transparency than non-professional markets. While professional markets are often opaque to outsiders, this has been justified by the argument that, in a professional market, everyone knows what is going on anyway. However, it is noticeable that many of the new institutional entrants into the London equity market appeared to resent its lack of transparency and interpreted 'everybody knows' to mean that 'everybody except us knows', and that they were therefore disadvantaged. We conclude that a similar situation may exist in OTC markets. They operate with considerable efficiency for the current participants, but their exclusivity and opacity may tend to exclude new participants or competing trading systems.

While we do not believe that regulation should be fundamentally different for either types of asset or types of trader, there will be circumstances where it is appropriate to vary the weight of regulation (for example, block trade procedures, market opening and closing procedures or liquidity).

2.4 Regulatory issues in fragmented markets

This section considers a number of new problems for regulators that are created by the move to multiple trading venues for each market.

2.4.1 Investor protection and best execution

Where there is a single trading system offering a single method of execution, 'best advantage' is relatively easy to define, at least for retail trades. It is the best price on the single system. With multiple systems best execution becomes complex for retail trades, and extremely complex for institutional trades. The range of possibilities increases the scope for brokers to exercise discretion, even for retail trades, leading to the possibility of well-intentioned and well-informed misjudgements. A more complex best execution rule is required which recognises that brokers who operate in fragmented markets do not always make the right decisions, but should be required to justify their actions through enhanced disclosure. Multiple trading systems in the USA have led to complex systems of reward, including payment for order flow. This is controversial, and it is far from clear that investors have been the beneficiaries of this development in the USA, or that they will be if such practices are adopted in the UK. We note that the FSA has recently initiated a debate into the revision of the UK's best execution rules (e.g. FSA, 2001c).

2.4.2 Loss of efficiency (multiple trade prices)

In a fragmented market there is a possibility of loss of pricing efficiency because the price formation process may fragment, leading to multiple simultaneous trade prices.[17] This may have implications for investor protection, since it might imply that some investors were routinely forced to trade at a less advantageous price because they were unable to access some parts of the market. It also means that the economic signals which markets give to the real economy would be distorted, and investor confidence damaged.

While there is probably wide agreement that efficient pricing is desirable, there seems to be an emerging consensus, with which we agree, that attempts to enforce a single price through a Central Limit Order Book, CLOB, are undesirable (or unworkable). An alternative is to ensure that markets are transparent and that information on trading is widely available at appropriate cost. This will allow informal linkages to achieve the equalisation of pricing so that the costs of split liquidity (e.g. systems duplication, more executions and, maybe, arbitrage costs) are outweighed by the other benefits of a competitive market.

2.4.3   Access

The possibility that one class of investors might be routinely disadvantaged is particularly relevant where the available trading systems have different entry requirements, so that some types of investor are denied access to particular trading systems. For example, initially at least, ATSs in the USA were generally aimed at institutional traders, and some offered facilities to allow users to exclude professional intermediaries from matching their orders.

Provided access restrictions are imposed for a good reason (for example, that traders be members of a central counterparty or a clearing house), such restrictions and the consequent price differentials represent a real difference between traders and are defensible. However, it is hard to understand why trading systems that are run commercially (rather than as member clubs) would want to exclude potential users without an economic justification. This raises the regulatory question as to the criteria which could be used to justify restricting access to particular trading systems. Examples of an unsupportable difference might be the arbitrary denial of access to settlement for certain types of user, restrictions on access to information that effectively rules out some types of user, or arbitrarily high per-transaction charges that make it uneconomic for large orders to be matched by multiple retail orders.

2.4.4   Order priority

Trading systems always include rules governing the sequence of execution of orders, and almost always it is price and then time.[18] Priority rules are seen as crucial in attracting investors who are able to submit orders in the knowledge that these orders will not be traded through. Without priority there is less incentive for investors to submit limit orders as it increases the likelihood that such orders will be executed when the investor does not want their order filled (e.g. when the price has moved against them). Some trading systems have minimum tick sizes that are set above the minimum currency unit so as to ensure that users who want to jump the time priority queue by submitting an order with a better price incur a significant cost for doing so. However the recent trend is towards a reduction in tick sizes, so reducing the cost of buying priority.[19]

The existence of multiple trading venues raises the possibility that price and time priorities will not be maintained between different trading systems trading the same instrument. The limited evidence available for the UK equity market suggests that offering a better price on a different RIE does not necessarily guarantee execution priority. More generally, while a widely drawn best execution rule will tend to safeguard price priority, it does nothing for time priority since the broker executing an order will want the best price, but be indifferent to the time priority of the counterparty order.

Similarly, the existence of montage/order-routeing entities weakens time priority, while strengthening price priority, as they tend to highlight the best available price, regardless of time priority. Even if the time priority of order books was mandated through some kind of centralised limit order book, the possibility of OTC or telephone trading allows time priorities to be sidestepped. For example, it is not unknown for users to signal their willingness to trade with certain types of counterparty through the order book and then, if they can identify the counterparty, transact business OTC.

2.4.5 Negative externality

Individual trading systems are part of an overall market and a single price formation process. Thus the system and rules of one trading system may have an effect on the whole market and, arguably, may impair overall market quality, reduce confidence and damage the business of other trading systems (i.e. the trading system imposes a negative externality on other market participants). Since transparency is necessary for good quality price formation, the presence of a significant opaque trading system damages overall price formation. A test for materiality might be applied to judge whether the damage from opaque trading systems in aggregate was significantly serious to require regulatory intervention. Although it was feared that competition among systems might lead to a 'race for the bottom' in opacity and regulation generally, this has not happened, largely because the new entrants offered transparent systems and because major users do not generally wish to trade in unregulated venues.

2.4.6 Barriers to entry

Trading systems offer scope for network economies that give rise to a substantial first mover advantage. Incumbent trading systems are therefore in a strong position to see off competitors. Although cases where a challenger has dented an incumbent are relatively rare, they are not so rare as to make further inroads improbable. The LIFFE/Deutsche Termin Börse (DTB) competition, the movement of European equity trading from domestic markets to SEAQ-I and back, and the success of ATSs in the USA in capturing NASDAQ business are recent examples of sharp movements of trading between systems.

If regulators are to rely increasingly on competitive forces to ensure the quality of different trading systems, they need to be assured that there will be competition, and that incumbents will not prevent new entrants by erecting barriers to entry. Dominant trading systems will, of necessity, be the main arenas for price formation, and it seems unlikely that new entrants will be successful if the incumbent trading system restricts access to trading data. Unless new entrants and their users have access to the full set of trading information, business will tend to remain where it has always been – on the incumbent trading system. The incumbent trading system will likely argue that the new entrant is parasitic and that it is free-riding on the prices generated by the incumbent's investment. The regulator's task is to identify what is a fair advantage from investment, and what is actually a barrier to entry. This suggests that an immediate regulatory need is to monitor the prices charged for real time quote (and possibly trade) data so as to ensure that the high price of trading information charged by the incumbent trading system does not create barriers to new trading systems starting up.[20]

The natural barriers to entry are possibly stronger where trading systems own the brands for the assets they trade, as do some derivatives exchanges, or provide other services but with restricted access. For example, control of a clearing house gives the incumbent a barrier against newcomers who must not only set up a clearing house (or negotiate a deal with an existing clearing house), but also offer clearing in the full range of assets that the competitor wishes to trade. Indeed, a new entrant might find it difficult to attract business if it did not offer clearing in the full range of assets traded on the incumbent trading system so that traders can obtain the same cross-margining benefits as on the incumbent. Again regulators will need to judge whether the barrier reflects a fair competitive advantage gained by the incumbent through investment and effort, or if it represents a restrictive practice designed to obstruct new entrants.

Even if the barrier is a fair competitive advantage, the overarching need for effective competition in trading systems may mean that the interests of the incumbent have to be sacrificed to encourage competition. This raises the possibility that regulators may be required to disadvantage incumbent trading systems if competition is to have a chance, just as regulators in telecoms and utilities have been forced to do.

2.4.7 Manipulation

It is harder to pinpoint market abuse in a fragmented market, particularly at the level of an individual trading system. This is particularly true as abusive practice is increasingly likely to span more than one trading venue and to involve OTC activity. As a result, responsibility for preventing market abuse should rest with the regulatory authority, which is likely to need access to trade and position monitoring information. Although the FSA has responsibility for preventing market abuse, its regime is currently principally focused on exchange trading (where front-line policing is undertaken by the RIE itself) and there are limits to the transaction data it reviews. The ability and willingness of RIEs to engage in highly costly surveillance, including monitoring across trading systems, may well decline as commercial pressures mount. In consequence, the responsibility for preventing manipulation may well devolve to the FSA.

2.5 Transparency

Transparency refers to the ability of market participants fairly to observe current and recent levels of market activity. Pre-trade transparency refers to the ability to see current quotes or the limit order book, while post-trade transparency refers to information about recent trades (prices and quantities). It is important to note that the debate does not suggest the release of confidential information (e.g. the identities of the parties to a trade[21]). It is widely accepted that high transparency is desirable as it is associated with improved market efficiency and the absence of systematic disadvantage to particular groups of traders.

The debate about transparency has been long and there are arguments on both sides. However, our view is that transparency is generally beneficial and has an important role to play in achieving the FSA's statutory objectives. A clear summary of the reasons why transparency is beneficial was provided by the Securities and Investments Board (SIB, 1996, p. 17):

> In the SIB's view, the transparency of a market is a key factor in demonstrating its integrity because it:
> - permits the demonstration of market fairness;
> - is of fundamental importance to the price formation process;
> - enhances competition between market intermediaries; and
> - assists in the prevention and detection of a variety of abusive practices.

In spite of the arguments in favour of increased transparency (i.e. that transparent markets inspire confidence and so will attract liquidity), it is often claimed that increasing transparency will reduce the incentives for intermediaries to provide liquidity, or drive trading offshore, and that the costs of such effects will be sufficient to outweigh the benefits of increased transparency. We do not believe that this is the case because:

- There is no empirical evidence of which we are aware demonstrating that liquidity has been harmed by increased transparency.[22] In the cases where liquidity has shifted away from markets, a number of factors, other than transparency, has been responsible.[23]
- There is no evidence that business has been driven offshore purely because of increased transparency requirements. We accept that business has migrated in the past, however we are not aware of cases in which such movements have been caused by transparency requirements.
- Global best practice leans towards transparency – for example, Principle 27 of the International Organization of Securities Commissioners (IOSCO) Principles of Securities Regulation is that 'regulation should promote transparency of trading'.
- Many exchanges worldwide have voluntarily mandated high levels of transparency.
- Many regulatory authorities worldwide are insisting on increased levels of transparency.
- Users, and especially new users, are increasingly inclined to be wary of trading systems they see as opaque, and user pressure appears to be towards greater transparency.
- Even in opaque markets, dealers often share or exchange information with each other (e.g. through Inter Dealer Broker systems).

As suggested in Chapter 8, while the direct costs of moving business off-shore are low, the total costs may be non-trivial. It is interesting that although UK Stamp Duty is levied at the rate of 0.5 per cent on equity transactions, equity trading has not left the UK. This might suggest that the costs of moving offshore exceed those of paying Stamp Duty. In turn, this suggests that the costs of increased transparency would have to exceed 50 basis points before firms would make such a move. As the evidence surveyed in Chapter 7 shows, the costs of transparency are likely to be very significantly lower than this.

Once it is accepted that high transparency is desirable, the burden of proof shifts from the present situation in which those promoting transparency have to demonstrate the benefits of transparency, to one in which those wishing to retain opacity must demonstrate why transparency would be positively damaging to the market.[24]

In terms of the information to be disclosed under a high-transparency regime, the information that could be published in relation to executed trades (i.e. post-trade transparency) is relatively simple to define in terms of trade size, price, time and security traded. The pre-trade information that could be revealed differs with the type of market (e.g. dealer quotes or limit orders), requires more regulatory choice (e.g. top of the book only, the best five orders on each side of the book, order size) and offers more areas of potential ambiguity (e.g. any special procedures for block trades[25] and hidden orders). In addition, trading systems present their screen displays as part of their competitive advantage and, while they are similar in principle, there are important differences in detail,[26] and any mandated pre-trade transparency levels would need to accommodate such functions, making the system increasingly complex.[27] Despite these problems, the operation of trading systems naturally produces some pre-trade transparency. Dealer systems publish quotes, while auction systems publish limit orders, although there may be restrictions on who is allowed to see this information. Since both dealer and auction systems must reveal some pre-trade information if customers are to trade, there is likely to be considerable natural pre-trade transparency which regulators might wish to monitor before deciding on any regulation of pre-trade transparency.

2.6 OTC markets

OTC markets have developed to meet specific needs where exchange trading was insufficiently flexible or, because of the nature of the market, was deemed unnecessary by users. They have brought benefits in offering the flexibility of customised contracts, greater choice, product innovation and often lower costs. Sometimes they operate alongside exchange markets trading very similar assets, and sometimes in assets for which there is no close exchange market. Typically they are not subject to the regulatory requirements applied to exchange-traded assets. It is argued that OTC markets offer valuable trading opportunities and consequently have experienced rapid growth.

Presently, OTC activity in the UK is subject to prudential regulation through the application of capital requirements and to 'light touch' conduct of business standards, calibrated to the inter-professional nature of the business. What is at issue in this context is the absence in many respects of standards of market regulation; principally transparency requirements.

It is increasingly hard to argue that OTC markets, especially where they are large and organised around standardised products, have no influence on the exchange-traded markets and that they are purely price-takers. It is interesting that the International Federation of Stock Exchanges (FIBV) is in discussion with the Basle Committee on Banking Supervision on the acceptability of reporting and publishing OTC trades in instruments traded on their members' exchanges. If nothing else, the large volume of trading in OTC markets (estimated at over $94 trillion, compared to $14 trillion in on-exchange derivatives for the G10 countries in 2000) means that any inadequacies in the regulation of OTC trading creates a considerable risk that some or all of the statutory objectives of the FSA will not be met.

OTC markets are often opaque, and it can be argued that this might have an adverse effect on the related trading systems. Because the major participants in the OTC markets are usually also major participants in the exchange markets, their ability to observe large trades gives them information that is denied to other participants in trading on the exchange. This is analogous to the argument for regulating (and publishing) client-side, equity trades by dealers.

OTC markets have recently become increasingly organised around standard products, a process being driven by the high cost of trading and managing non-standard products and facilitated by legislative changes. Standard products are more amenable to electronic trading and management. So while customised products remain at the cutting-edge of the OTC market, the bulk of trading, which is in 'plain vanilla' products, is very much akin to the normal type of exchange trading. LIFFE follow this process actively so as to identify possible business opportunities. For some products the exchange and OTC markets are converging, with the exchange offering more customised products (e.g. FTSE flex options, and the OTC market standardising its products). Such developments blur the regulatory boundary between OTC and exchange trading and further weaken the justification for the current regulatory separation. Were OTC contracts to become traded through ATSs it would be hard to argue that they were not, in effect, the same as exchange-traded contracts. In the USA this has led to calls for regulatory changes.

In spite of these arguments, OTC markets are subject to different regulatory standards than are exchanges. This can lead to regulatory arbitrage between the exchange and the related OTC market, which possibly weakens the efficiency of the exchange markets. In addition, where there are no reporting requirements, different regulatory standards for OTC markets weaken regulatory control of market conduct. In the USA there has been repeated pressure for similar regulatory requirements to be applied to derivatives which are traded on recognised exchanges and regulated by the Commodity Futures Trading Commission (CFTC), and very close substitutes which are traded OTC (e.g. interest rate futures and interest rate swaps).[28]

A further consideration is that OTC markets are not currently accessible to retail investors. However, growing private wealth and investor sophistication along with the growing standardisation and ease of trading makes it likely that retail investors will be encouraged by intermediaries to diversify (either directly or indirectly) into the simpler types of OTC products. Retail investors may be more interested in some types of OTC market than others.

The benefits of bringing OTC markets into the transparency regime include enhanced price formation and market confidence, reduced scope for insiders to profit at the expense of outsiders, improved monitoring of best execution and manipulation and reduced opportunities for regulatory arbitrage.

Although we believe that transparency is both desirable and practicable, a number of arguments against increasing transparency of OTC markets is often advanced:

- Because OTC contracts are customised, there is little point in increasing transparency since the information gain would be slight. However, with the trend towards increased standardisation within the OTC markets there is, in our view, little justification for treating OTC replicas of exchange contracts and the corresponding exchange contracts differently.[29]
- Firms might object to reporting their OTC trades in exchange-traded or related instruments through RIEs. However, there are precedents for this (e.g. the London Stock Exchange used to act as a reporting agent for some Eurobond reports to the Securities and Futures Authority (SFA) through its SEQUAL system). Many OTC trades are already reported for transaction monitoring (i.e. enforcement) purposes directly to the FSA (e.g. equities, gilts, fixed interest), with OTC trades representing about 15 per cent–20 per cent of trades reported to the FSA.
- It would be costly. Reporting involves the one-off cost to firms of altering their in-house systems to generate the required reports, and

the continuing cost of a reporting charge for each trade. As the FSA currently charges 2p per trade for direct reporting, these costs do not appear onerous, particularly as all on-exchange trades must already bear the costs of being reported and published. We also note that some OTC traders voluntarily report their trades to the FSA, apparently because it is easier and cheaper to report all their trades than to separate those which must be reported from those which need not. Equally, OTC markets may be able to generate revenue from the sale of their trading information to data vendors.

- It is argued that OTC markets may move offshore if they are subject to greater transparency. However, moving offshore is rarely as simple as it sounds, and clients are suspicious of offshore entities. It has been threatened in response to many regulatory proposals, but has yet to happen in response to UK regulatory changes. For example, the UK OTC equity and debt markets have not moved offshore because they are required to report their trades for transaction monitoring purposes. However, the extent of this threat merits further discussion and it may be necessary for the regulatory authorities to address the question of OTC market transparency at a European or international level.

Notes

1 Financial Services and Markets Act 2000.
2 Under the FSMA, the FSA regulates trading in shares, debt instruments (debentures, bonds, certificates of deposit), warrants, options on securities, currencies, palladium, platinum, gold and silver, futures and contracts for differences (*Financial Services and Markets Act 2000 (Regulated Activities) Order 2001*, October, HM Treasury, http://www.hm-treasury.gov.uk/fsma/regulated_activities/regulation.pdf, part 3).
3 The financial system is the financial system operating in the UK, and includes financial markets and exchanges, regulated activities and other activities connected with financial markets and exchanges. This definition of the financial system in FSMA (2000, section 3) appears to include OTC markets within the scope of the FSA's statutory obligations.
4 A regulated person means an authorised person, a recognised investment exchange or a recognised clearing house.
5 Financial crime includes any offence involving fraud or dishonesty, misconduct in, or misuse of information relating to a financial market, or handling the proceeds of crime.
6 Treasury (2000) *The Financial Services and Market Act 2000 (Recognition Requirements for Investment Exchanges and Clearing Houses) Regulations 2001*, December, HM Treasury, http://www.hm-treasury.gov.uk/fsma/ recognition_req/annexa.pdf
7 In the USA and elsewhere, these systems are often referred to as Electronic Communications Networks, or ECNs.

8 I.e. with dealers executing customers' orders against their own book and subsequently closing their position in the market.

9 ATSs have made significant inroads in the USA, especially in NASDAQ stocks where they now have a combined market share of around 30per cent.

10 This seems likely to change in the wake of the recent developments at the IPE.

11 They would also have to prevent their own members/participants who have access to price data from offering competing trading services, as the NYSE effectively does. It is worth noting that the NYSE has largely managed to see off the ATSs.

12 It is significant that the need for protection arises from this asymmetry of information not the size of the investor, the asset to be traded, or the significance of the asset for their well-being.

13 Indeed, one interpretation of the investment in multiple trading systems by investment banks is that they see themselves as investing in a venture-capital portfolio of ATSs. The opinion of James Marks Credit Sursse First Boston, (CSFB) in January 2000 is that 'investing in an ATS is like purchasing an option against your worst rival controlling your business'.

14 The problem is compounded by the entry of montage/order routeing operations that have many of the external features of an exchange (display bids–offers and accept orders) but actually do not execute or settle business. Technology also makes it possible for companies that are essentially information vendors with order-routeing capabilities to offer services that look very similar to those of trading systems, but are, in fact, mere montages of information from trading systems. Such organisations present screens showing best prices, and route orders to the trading system offering the best price, but do not themselves conduct trading. In many ways these entities are undertaking the traditional role of brokers in seeking to identify the trading system offering the best opportunities, but the way investors use them suggests that they could be treated as if they are themselves trading systems.

15 For example, there is a substantial quantity of empirical evidence that derivative markets are markets for price discovery and often lead the spot market.

16 For example, the LME is introducing a commodities index product for use by retail oriented institutions, while LIFFE has introduced the 'mini-FTSE' contract.

17 A degree of price fragmentation has long been accepted as the norm in certain parts of the UK market, notably the equity market. It remains the case that institutional trades are conducted at prices that are different to, and generally better than, the prices for retail trades.

18 For example, some LIFFE short-term interest rate products have price and then pro-rata allocation.

19 For example the European Alliance model for stock exchanges has a tick size of €0.01 for all equities, and, since 9th April 2001, all US stocks have traded at a tick size of $0.01, rather than eighths or sixteenths of a dollar.

20 It could be argued that this represents a problem for the competition authorities rather than for the FSA. We argue that the concern to preserve and promote a competitive trading environment is at the heart of any successful regulatory regime. Even if it is argued that competition does not fall within the remit of the FSA, it will, at a minimum have to coordinate

very closely with the competition authorities to allow it to meet its statutory objectives. In particular, we believe that, if the FSA does not remove barriers to entry, their regulatory regime will fail.

21   Although there are those who argue for a 'sunshine' regime, in which full information, including trader identities, is disclosed, we do not believe that this is necessary or desirable.

22   An investigation by Board and Sutcliffe (1995a, 1995b, 1996b) of the impact of changes in transparency on the London Stock Exchange predicted that increasing transparency would have little impact on liquidity, and the follow up study (Board and Sutcliffe, 2000) revealed that no damage to the market had indeed occurred.

23   The Swedish equity market moved offshore as a result of a change in Swedish taxation, while the Eurobond market was created by the introduction of regulation Q by the USA.

24   For example, this would require venues wishing to retain opacity to quantify the costs, benefits and distributional implications of its proposed structure, rather than simply relying on assertion to continue long-established practices.

25   The existence of large orders is, in itself, valuable information and exchanges have found that attempts to mandate the exposure of large orders leads to a loss of business. Accordingly, most exchanges have, or are considering, some kind of block-trade facility whereby large orders can be arranged privately and brought to the market – perhaps with interaction, but not always. Since exchanges have not found it feasible to mandate the exposure of all orders, it is unlikely that a regulator would be any more successful.

26   An example is that some systems allow hidden or iceberg order functionality. Since this functionality merely automates the actions of a broker in monitoring the order book and feeding in tranches of a large order, permitting hidden orders is argued to make little difference to the market.

27   For example, if all trading systems were required to display hidden orders, how would a trading system be treated which has no hidden orders but which does have a facility to add pieces of a fragmented trade automatically as the previous piece is matched?

28   The introduction of exempt Multilateral Transaction Execution Facilities (MTEFs) meets this requirement by enabling interest rate futures to be traded on a similar regulatory basis to interest rate swaps. This voluntary code follows heated debate on the issue in the USA.

29   Conceivably increased transparency might be applied only to OTC replicas; but if only OTC contracts that replicate exchange-traded products are regulated, close look-alikes (e.g. the FTSE 99) also may have an effect on the market, even if they are not exactly the same as the exchange-traded product. As a practical matter therefore, most products traded on an OTC market should be included.

3
The Recognised Investment Exchanges

In this chapter we summarise and review the results of our discussions with the UK RIEs. These discussions took place in the early part of 2000 and therefore reflect the state of play at that time. We conducted extensive interviews with the RIEs, supplementing our understanding with searches of the literature, press coverage, reviews of RIE web sites, etc. The RIEs at the time were:[1]

- London Stock Exchange
- Tradepoint Stock Exchange
- LIFFE
- London Metal Exchange (LME)
- OM
- International Petroleum Exchange (IPE)

This study is focused on micro-structure issues, and we have tried to answer the question: What is the best structure for price efficiency or, if there is no single solution, what features should be present if a system is to be likely to deliver efficient price formation? Even a cursory glance at current micro-structures suggests that there is more than one way to skin the micro-structure cat. London's six RIEs display quite different trading mechanisms, despite the apparent convergence towards electronic order books. Looking outside the UK, the picture becomes more even clouded. An important question for the present study is whether these differences arise from:

- differences between assets – 'metals are different'
- different user bases – 'publication of trades is less important in a professional market where everyone knows what is going on'
- accidents of history – 'no-one has complained'.

The obvious corollary to that question is: Does this diversity matter – are some structures delivering less efficient price discovery than others?

Since it is practically impossible to measure the quality of price discovery as an absolute, the normal way to go about this is to identify certain features that seem indispensable for good price discovery and assess markets against those features. This, in itself, can be complex as often the features are seen as interchangeable – we are all familiar with the supposed liquidity versus transparency trade-off. Acknowledging this, the present study intends to follow the assessment of features approach and see how markets compare.

3.1   Critical features of orderly markets

Three specific features of orderly markets have been identified by the FSA:

1   Liquidity provision, which has two facets:
    (a)   Difficulties of providing orderly markets where liquidity is low. The issues include minimum liquidity requirements, segmentation of liquidity from less liquid instruments and safeguards to prevent illiquid products trading at manifestly wrong prices?
    (b)   Issues linked to decentralised price formation, including the effects on price quality and the effects of competing trading platforms.
2   Transparency requirements, which focuses on pre-and post-trade transparency, including the importance of real as opposed to processed information and reliance on indicative pricing.
3   Access requirements, which covers classes of participant able to access the market both in terms of information and trading.

While these are obviously critical, they are themselves the result of a complexity of market features. Initially therefore, we wanted to identify a wider range of trading mechanism features that were important in defining the attractiveness of a market to its users. These features would all be linked to the three identified features, but would be more amenable to discussion with market participants and to precise specification.

As well as meeting the RIEs, we were able to review a list of trading system features with the International Federation of Stock Exchanges (FIBV) and had these discussed at a meeting of their working committee comprising representatives from some 27 stock exchanges – including the major US and European markets. This discussion resulted in a list of 10 features that are seen as critical. Most of these do indeed link directly into the FSA's three features, but are expressed in a way that is more akin to the way the markets themselves see market structure. For example, in our view the question about when counterparties learn each other's identities is an important part of understanding price formation and transparency. However market participants tend to see this as part of settlement. The 10 features are:

1 *Supplementing liquidity and managing illiquidity* – covering specific features to supplement liquidity, minimum liquidity requirements, different trading procedures for liquid and less-liquid instruments and safeguards against illiquid instruments being traded at wrong prices.
2 *Protecting order priority* – generally and with specific reference to proprietary trading and multiple markets, tick sizes, hidden orders and their priority.
3 *Block trades*:
     (a) Order/quote display – hidden orders
     (b) Trade publication – immediate or delayed.
4 *Opening/closing* – special procedures for opening and closing, for example, special types of order that only execute at those times, or special algorithms for finding a clearing price.
5 *Volatility* – managing exceptional volatility in relation to special circumstances such as derivative expiry and uncertainty/disorderly markets. Also possible growth of speculative trading or retail day trading.
6 *Transparency*
     (a) Pre-trade transparency – publication and dissemination of quote and order data.
     (b) Post-trade transparency – publication of trade details – what, which trades and when?
     (c) Post-trade anonymity – counterparties' knowledge of each other's identity.
7 *Protecting/encouraging retail investors* – trading system features specifically designed for the benefit or protection of retail investors.
8 *Reference prices defined by the trading system* – these are widely used for pricing or monitoring in other markets and assessing execution quality.
9 *Fragmentation of price formation* – alignment of prices where there are multiple trading possibilities such as internalisation of business without exposure to the market.
10 *Fulfilment* – clearing and settlement operations, margining, central guarantee.

These 10 questions formed the basis for the analysis of UK RIEs.

3.2   RIE structures

With the exceptions of the IPE and LME, all RIEs had either moved to, or started out with, electronic trading systems. The IPE runs a hybrid system using a floor for some assets, and electronic trading for others. The London Stock Exchange runs an electronic system combined with telephone dealing and all RIEs permitted some measure of trading away from the central system. The LME has announced the introduction of a screen-based trading system which will run in parallel with the ring.

All the RIEs had either moved, or were in the process of moving their organisational and governance structure to a commercial, rather than a mutual, basis. The IPE is the exchange that has made least progress, following an abortive attempt in 1999. Tradepoint and OM have always been purely commercial entities, and OM is now practically a branch office of the parent, OM Stockholm.

The decision to operate as an RIE rather than as an AF seemed to be largely a question of historical accident or inclination. The London Stock Exchange, LIFFE, IPE and LME, as the dominant incumbents in their markets, seemed to be expressing a view that they really had no choice. None of the interviewees seemed to have strong views that RIE status conferred enormous advantage, but neither did they feel that the burdens of being an RIE, when other similar operations could operate as AFs, were important. The key advantages of opting for RIE status were:

- Exemption from Conduct of Business (COB) rules
- Exemption from capital adequacy rules
- Status among users – especially given the London location.
- Easier in that there was less ongoing monitoring
- Trade reporting revenue
- Stamp duty exemption
- European passport.

The last, passport, was very important to some RIEs, especially Tradepoint, but was presented to us as a happy accident that had not influenced their original decision to go for RIE status, but now fitted well into their business objectives.

3.3   ATSs

The representatives generally seemed sanguine about the emergence of competition from ATSs.[2] RIEs that offered proprietary products were very unconcerned, arguing that the proprietary nature of the products and associated settlement/margining made it hard for a competitor trading system to enter the market. They, of course, were more exercised by OTC trading, though LIFFE were more relaxed than the LME.

RIEs trading generic assets were also relaxed, seeing the ATS phenomenon in the USA as a special case driven by the peculiar inefficiencies in that market. They saw the issues in Europe as entirely different and considered themselves reasonably well placed to compete effectively with any new entrants.

There was little support for regulatory restriction of entry or for statutory consolidation. While this is likely to be a public posture, since any exchange would presumably prefer not to face competition, it did suggest that exchanges really are adapting to the commercial reality of operating in a world of multiple trading systems. There was little support for the proposition that the current divide between RIEs and others (e.g. ATSs) causes difficulty.

We did not ask ATSs whether the possibility of being regulated by a potential competitor caused them concern. However we note that Instinet has operated in London for a decade or more as a broker regulated by the London Stock Exchange. While it has been vociferous in its criticism of irksome London Stock Exchange rules, it has not raised the question of the London Stock Exchange's position as a competitor. Other ATSs may have a more hostile view, but the requirements on an RIE are not so demanding that they would, themselves, prevent new entrants.

3.4 Summary and analysis of RIE results

In the event, while we started out with 10 features, a number of them turned out to be less important, either because they showed little diversity and excited little controversy (e.g. settlement), or because they can be best viewed as competitive features of a trading system and not linked to orderliness of markets (e.g. opening procedures). The summary below and the analysis later focus on what appeared as the key features that were agreed to be important for market quality, but there was diversity of approach. These are:

- Access
- Liquidity support
- Illiquidity management
- Transparency

- Protection of priority
- Centrality
- Retail protection.

3.4.1   Access

RIEs now have relatively undemanding membership requirements and fees. There are no restrictions on the types of organisations that can be members. The major requirement is an ability to guarantee settlement of business, either by membership of a clearing house or a contractual agreement with a clearing house member.

With the exception of the London Stock Exchange, the RIEs have almost no retail business. Tradepoint, OM, IPE and LME have never sought to have retail business. LIFFE have tried, with no more than modest success, to recruit retail business onto its traded options market.

An examination of the membership (or equivalent) lists of RIEs shows that membership is largely confined to financial intermediaries. The IPE and LME have limited representation from producers of the commodities they trade but, otherwise, with the exception of Tradepoint, membership was all professional traders. Tradepoint has a significant number of institutional members – though as far as we could see no trading at the time of the survey.

Access is not limited in theory, but in practice appears restricted. In terms of retail access, four of the RIEs exclude retail participation, even through an intermediary. Therefore these assets are not available to retail investors. Contract size was given in some cases as something that, for practical purposes, excluded retail participation. It did not seem to us that LIFFE's traded options, which are available to retail users, were intrinsically less risky than LME options, which are not.

Where there are two RIEs trading the same asset with one open to retail investors and one not, there is a chance that retail investors will be denied access to better prices. This could happen, in theory, with Tradepoint and the London Stock Exchange and research has shown that Tradepoint does offer better prices at times (Board and Wells, 2001). It is probably more of a practical issue within the London Stock Exchange where, as has always been the case, institutional prices are frequently superior to retail prices. However, this has long been the case and there seems little anxiety about it. (Recent anecdotal evidence suggests that the narrower spreads on stocks traded on the Stock Exchange Electronic Trading Service (SETS) have alleviated this to some extent.) We suspect that the UK equity market has long been fragmented and there is no tradition of the 'single price' as there is in foreign markets. Therefore another example of price fragmentation excites little concern.

Of more immediate impact is the almost total concentration of trading in the hands of financial intermediaries. There are no formal barriers to participation by institutional investors, but it does not happen. This is also true in the USA where, until recently, the Exchange Act required members of exchanges to be registered broker/dealers. It is unclear to us why institutions have not joined exchanges, although a number of contributory factors have been suggested:

1 Institutions fear their anonymity will be compromised – more than they fear the possibility of front-running by intermediaries.
2 Large institutions have sufficient market power to drive down intermediation costs without the need to trade directly. But what of smaller institutions?
3 Intermediaries are able to punish institutions that trade directly. This is incompatible with point 2 above and implausible given the number of competing intermediaries.
4 Institutions wish to delegate responsibility for dealing and to keep their regulatory protection.
5 Intermediaries give services, including preferential access to good trades and/or Initial Public Offenugs (IPOs).
6 Regulatory and other costs are too high.
7 Inertia.

The answer to this, of course, is likely to affect the development of ATSs in the UK. In the USA, institutional concerns about front-running, for example, have fuelled the movement of business to ATSs. If UK institutions are voluntarily using intermediaries, they will not switch to ATSs in the same way.

3.4.2 Liquidity support

In general there has been a move away from formal liquidity support as trading systems have moved to electronic order books. The London Stock Exchange and LIFFE retain market makers in less-liquid asset types. Dealers in the most liquid stocks continue extensive proprietary trading activity, but on a 'fair-weather' basis – i.e. when, and with whom, they want.

As trading has moved towards electronic systems, liquidity has become more a function of the reach of those systems. RIEs have tended to move

away from reliance on specific liquidity providers supported by regulation. This has mainly been at the instigation of liquidity providers:

- Formal systems rely on an array of privileges (e.g. tax privileges, lower
  transparency) to compensate liquidity providers for their obligation
  to do something they would not always chose to do. The privileges
  have been eroded in various ways, tipping the balance towards the
  obligations, and against providing liquidity.
- Intermediaries acting as liquidity providers have realised that providing undiscriminating liquidity to all comers is less profitable than
  focussing their liquidity provision on selected users.
- Users have realised that provision of continuous liquidity is not cost-
  free. While they have not yet gone to alternative markets (as they
  have in the USA), they do negotiate fiercely and so limit the ability
  of liquidity providers to cross-subsidise bad trades from good. This
  has raised the cost of continuous liquidity provision, since that is
  mainly demanded by the 'bad' trades. The more liquidity providers
  are forced to charge the true price of liquidity, the more they will
  tend to be the market of last-resort, as they are in less-liquid assets.
  As such, they see a declining share of the business and are increasingly disadvantaged. Rules to enforce exposure of business to liquidity
  providers (such as market-makers) can only be a short-term solution
  as intermediaries increasingly resent having such obligations to
  competitors. A significant additional drawback is that retail clients
  tend to be priced in line with the bad trades.

The trend appears to be against formal liquidity provision, and RIEs
continue to face difficulties in enforcing obligations where they exist.
Provision now tends to be in less-liquid assets, but even there it is
increasingly difficult to maintain the balance of privileges and obligations.
The lack of competing market makers in most Alternative Investment Market (AIM) stocks illustrates the difficulty. Our expectation is that formal
liquidity support will vanish, even without competition from ATSs.

3.4.3   Illiquidity management – bad prices

The IPE and LME, which are both in transition from floor-based to electronic markets, have traditionally relied on the visibility of floor trading
to prevent trades in illiquid assets at 'wrong' prices, supplemented by
rules and powers of intervention. The London Stock Exchange (SETS)
and LIFFE have trade-to-trade price movement limits, but the London
Stock Exchange (SEAQ), where illiquidity is more likely, has nothing. The

SETS limits have been improved by introducing dynamic parameters – following the Xetra practice. Tradepoint and OM have no provisions to prevent trading at anomalous prices.

3.4.4 Transparency

The central trading mechanisms of the RIEs – screen or floor – are visible, and quotes are available pre-trade. Inevitably on the floor-based markets the quotes are less visible to all market participants, but we have no expectation that floor-based markets will persist in the longer-term. Generally the quotes are firm, though there are exceptions:

- London Stock Exchange SEAQ quotes are firm, but negotiation to improve the price is usual for institutional business.
- Although ring quotes and quotes on LME Select are firm, the LME permits its dealers to make indicative quotes on the telephone (but monitors that these quotes are justified by reference to actual trading).

Trade details are published immediately.

All of the RIEs have a block trade facility to allow larger orders to be executed away from the public arena, and some have delays to publication.

(a) *LIFFE* has a block trade facility. The qualifying block size is large (for equity index products, the amount corresponds to approximately 1,000,000 shares). There are no requirements for block trades to interact with the order book. The volume of such trades is significant – of the order of 10 per cent of market volume. Smaller crosses, etc. are possible, but must be exposed before completion.

(b) *OM* permits negotiated trades, but these must be exposed to the order book. There is no information on the extent of such trades.

(c) London Stock Exchange/*SETS* block trades are permitted 'off-SETS' and there is no requirement for interaction with the order book. Worked principal agreements may be used to delay publication of trades while a large block is being worked.

(d) London Stock Exchange/*SEAQ* trades are all intermediated and privately negotiated so that there is no need for a formal block trade arrangement. Publication of large, risk trades is delayed for 60 minutes (or more for the most illiquid stocks).

(e) *Tradepoint* has the equivalent of protected trades in which the block trade is concealed until the member has worked the trade through the book. It also has provision for the delayed publication of risk trades.

(f) The *LME* has no special facilities for block trades, but the structure of the market, with off-ring trades being negotiated between counterparties, makes this irrelevant.

(g) The *IPE* has a block trade facility in which blocks may be negotiated, but are required to be fully exposed to the order book and must be at prices no worse than the best prices available at the time of the exposure. IPE contracts traded on APT screens also have the facility for partly concealing large orders, so that the true size is revealed only when a counterparty receives a better than expected price on their order.

We draw a number of conclusions from this:

- *Trading systems where institutions are involved need some sort of mechanism for organising large trades.* The main reason is that the intentions underlying a large trade can be better understood in private negotiations. Therefore the price impact which would otherwise occur is mitigated. Institutions use intermediaries because of their skills in negotiating and placing such orders. Because of the price impact risk it is unreasonable to expect that large trades will be exposed as single orders on an order book.

- *It is likely that block trades will occur at prices different from those prevailing on the order book.* Where interaction is required, the market and block prices are brought into line, but only LIFFE and OM (both trading their own proprietary products) require interaction. Most of the issues concerning block trades are actually issues of market fragmentation. As we discuss elsewhere, this price fragmentation is accepted and expected among UK participants, although it causes some consternation among those from more concentrated markets. What is difficult to ensure through regulation is that the price at which blocks execute, while different to the 'normal' price, is not unfairly different. When asked about this issue, participants explain it in terms of long-term relationships. However, it is still difficult to see how those relationships, or indeed the wisdom of this particular trading strategy as opposed to working slices of the order through the book, are assessed without any formal measurement.

- *It is implicit in these arrangements that no publication takes place until both legs of the trade are complete.* Where the order is executed against the intermediary's book – a risk trade – there is an argument for delaying publication. The main thrust of the argument is that intermediaries would not commit their capital to risk trades if they were immediately disclosed to the market. While this argument is widely accepted, there is less agreement over how long a delay is optimal and at what size of trade. However, it seems this debate has become less heated than in the past. London Stock Exchange dealers accommodated a move to higher levels of transparency on SETS without undue problems and without significantly impairing institutional liquidity.

3.4.5 Protection of priority

All the electronic systems were based on the display of limit orders and all had price–time priority (with the exception of LIFFE's short-term interest rate products). However most of the RIEs have provision to allow trades executed away from the electronic system to be executed. Only LIFFE and OM enforce an interaction requirement on such trades.

Operators of trading systems make considerable play of the fact that their systems are fair in that they offer price and time priority. US commentators and regulators set great store by protection of order priorities – both price and time – and are surprised by the relative lack of concern for priorities in the UK and indeed, generally in Europe. To those commentators trade-throughs – trades at prices that could have been satisfied by public orders – are anathema, and exchanges also guard time-priority. As well as being 'unfair', failure to protect priorities is seen as damaging to market liquidity. Investors will submit limit orders – i.e. provide liquidity – only if there is a good chance that they will be rewarded by having their order executed. Allowing trade-throughs or the bypassing of time priority reduces the likelihood of execution and increases the likelihood that limit orders will become the market of last resort. The consequence, it is argued, is fewer limit orders.

The fact that ATSs may trade at prices worse than those available on public systems or bypass time priority is a serious concern. There has been a, largely inconclusive, discussion of a central limit order book as a way of addressing this failing. The consensus emerging seems to be that a mandatory central limit order book is unworkable and would also stifle innovation.

Among the UK RIEs, LIFFE and OM are the only ones that mandate interaction between off-system trades and the electronic system. On all other RIEs members may trade away from the electronic system and report the trades to an RIE for publication. Therefore, the effect on order priority protection of the possible entry of ATSs or other competitors into the UK market is less than it would be in more centralised markets. In a real sense, there is no protection of priorities on most UK RIEs. However, this is, in large measure, a consequence of two related UK features:

- *The wide definition of on-exchange business.* To a German, for example, the fact that the London Stock Exchange classes business done in telephone trading as on-exchange is anomalous. The argument of the Frankfurt exchange is that telephone business is off-exchange and therefore not the concern of the exchange. They impose price and time priority on on-exchange business (actually they do not – floor trades are not obliged to interact), and what happens in the OTC market happens.
- *The quest for revenue by RIEs.* The ISD and the FSA imposes a requirement to report trades, and the FSA has made it clear it did not want direct reporting. The RIEs therefore have a business opportunity to act as report collectors. Tradepoint's acceptance of off-system reports was, originally, purely a revenue device.

The ability of LIFFE and OM to enforce interaction derives from its ownership of the assets themselves – LIFFE contracts can only be traded on LIFFE. It is easy to imagine that OTC look-alikes could be traded at prices different to those on the RIE. The extent to which this happens depends on the ability to settle and cross-margin between OTC look-alikes and LIFFE contracts.

A related development involves service companies and information vendors offering access to montages of quotes from a number of trading systems, linked to an execution capability, of which Royal Blue is the best known in the UK. These systems bring together quotes and so guarantee price priority, but make it easy to bypass time priority. Again, since time priority is not protected, the emergence of montages makes little difference to order protection.

3.4.6   Centrality

The London Stock Exchange, LME and IPE have very significant upstairs business that is not required to interact with the order book. This business may be defined as on-exchange, but there is no notion of a single, central price in the market. Tradepoint has a similar structure to the

London Stock Exchange allowing reporting of upstairs trades, but its business volumes are low. LIFFE and OM enforce interaction for upstairs trades.

Centrality is, for the UK RIEs, the corollary of order priority protection. It is worth noting here that the UK market participants tend to attach little importance to the idea of a central price. For example, there is no widespread view that the price of small trades should correspond to that for large trades (at least among practitioners, though retail clients may see it differently). Therefore fragmentation, in the sense of simultaneous and otherwise identical trades being transacted at different prices, has long been a feature of UK markets and excited little domestic criticism. However, US participants have been less sanguine, and have been critical of this feature of UK markets. This, together with past lack of transparency, has led many US participants, especially institutions, to see the London markets as less clean than they would wish – similar to NASDAQ (before the recent order handling rule changes), which they tend to hold in lower regard.

3.4.7   Retail protection

With the exception of the London Stock Exchange's domestic markets, the RIEs have relatively slight or zero levels of retail business. With the exception of LIFFE, we found no evidence that the RIEs wanted more retail business, had any plans to handle such business, or had given it much thought.

The London Stock Exchange offers no special services for retail clients but has encouraged the setting up of Retail Service Providers (RSPs). They are the direct descendants of the proprietary networks set up by SEAQ market-makers to route retail business away from the institutional trading desks. They offer terminals (at no cost) to retail brokers who route business directly to the RSP. The RSP undertakes (on a contractual basis, since the regulatory responsibility for best execution rests with the broker not the RSP) to execute trades at the best SETS/SEAQ price (or better in some cases).

Initially SETS excluded small retail trades, but this limitation has been removed. However, for reasons of cost, most retail brokers treat retail orders as requiring immediate execution – either through an RSP or by phone.

The main protection for retail clients is the obligation to achieve best execution. This is defined as the best price in the chosen market (i.e. RIE). Compliance is monitored by the SFA, although in the past the London Stock Exchange was responsible for monitoring.

Two points stand out:

- *The SETS best price is markedly better than the old SEAQ price for the stocks covered by that system* (i.e. the bid-ask spread is narrower), but there are times of day when this is clearly not so. Spreads in the early part of the day remain wide despite continuing efforts by the London Stock Exchange to vary its system so as to attract more business at this time of day. Therefore market orders for retail investors submitted overnight are likely to be executed at wide bid–ask spreads. For less-liquid stocks the old problem remains – namely that the SEAQ prices are set by market-makers, and they set a bid–ask spread which protects them against adverse selection, although it is negotiable. Retail business – either RSP or telephone – is usually not negotiated, and so is executed at the (wide) bid–ask prices. It is debatable whether the current precise definition of best execution gives brokers sufficient incentive to improve. There is substantial competition for retail business but, as yet, this has not resulted in a search for better execution prices.
- *There is also the more general point about the possibility of growing retail interest in other asset types.* As we note elsewhere, there is no reason why the more sophisticated retail investors should not be attracted to a wider range of assets. To date, despite its efforts, LIFFE has not had much success, but retail interest in derivatives is high in foreign markets, and the growing interest in investment combined with easier access through the Internet may eventually tip the balance. It would seem unacceptable for other asset markets to exclude retail business just because it does not fit with their trading and regulatory regime. And it would be difficult to achieve anyway in the face of determined efforts by commercially minded intermediaries to offer the asset to a wider public. Such unilateral actions by intermediaries could result in a situation where the retail clients involvement was second-hand or derivative, and therefore less visible and less regulated.

3.5   Conclusions for UK RIEs

3.5.1   Market structures and scope

The UK RIEs displayed a range of market structures, though there has been a clear trend to converge on electronic, public limit order books. We expect that differences in what might be called the core trading system of the exchanges will be further eroded in London, just as they have been between equity markets across Europe.

However there remain differences in the handling of business trans-acted away from the core trading system (as is also true of European equity markets). These differences derive from the nature of the client base, the power of the RIEs over their members and the historical legacy of monopoly markets. UK RIEs who have proprietary control of the assets are more able to require traders to use their core trading system. But even these exchanges have been compelled to recognise the needs of their users to transact some business outside the core system.

We saw no particular reason to explain these differences – as we discuss below we do not feel that different assets or different client bases explain the differences. At the same time we did not see anything to suggest that one model was inherently better and that all RIEs should be encour-aged to converge on a particular trading mechanism. Indeed rather the opposite since competition has historically been a major driver of market improvements. Our sense is that the market users are forcing a measure of convergence, but that differences, largely resulting from historical differences in the way business is done, will persist. Additionally we expect that new entrants will introduce new trading mechanisms and ideas and this should be encouraged. Experience in the exchange busi-ness and elsewhere suggests that competition is the most powerful force for innovation and that diversity is a critical component of the competitive process.

RIEs that have been or are monopoly markets tend to have very broad scope rules such that all business by their members is deemed to be on-exchange. This was convenient in the past since it gave a home and a reporting path for such business. However emerging competition (combined with the ISD permission to report to any RIE) challenges this legacy. Equity traders already have a choice of reporting agent (though to date most continue to use the London Stock Exchange to report their off-SETS trades).

The nature of institutional trading suggests that there will continue to be a need for trading away from the public systems. If RIEs become more focused on the commercial business of running trading systems (i.e. they become more like ATSs) they may become less interested in regulating business transacted away from those systems. They may con-tinue to accept reports – as a commercial venture – but the monitoring of such reports is not a business where there is obvious commercial gain. In short, as current RIEs become more commercially oriented they may become less willing to fund market-wide surveillance activities. Aside from the reporting requirement, 'upstairs trading' may become entirely OTC in character and regulation.

3.5.2   Asset type regulation

We have found nothing to suggest that 'metals are different' – i.e. that by their nature some products are better suited to some trading systems than are others; nor that the regulatory framework should vary between assets:

- There will, of necessity, be differences in the *settlement arrangements* for some products (e.g. LME settlement involves bulky physical assets and so requires complex warehousing systems), but these could operate alongside any trading system.
- There is no reason why a *trading system's position as the venue for principal price discovery* (e.g. LME and, to an extent, IPE) when the spot market is too diffuse to offer this function should dictate a particular trading mechanism. Nor is there substance in a related argument that a derivatives trading system like LIFFE is not a venue for price discovery (since that was the function of the underlying market) and so warrants different regulatory treatment. Clearly derivative trading systems are venues for price discovery and usually lead the spot market.
- It is sometimes claimed that the *specific features of physical assets* require a different type of regulation because the fact that supply and demand are relatively inelastic makes them particularly susceptible to manipulative tactics – cornering and squeezing. This is true at the level of enforcing and monitoring regulations, but all markets are susceptible to manipulative tactics of one type or another. For example, stock markets are likely to be more vulnerable to insider trading or fraudulent information than physical markets. The fact that the manipulative tactics differ from market to market means that the thrust of regulatory effort should also vary. But the overall requirement to operate clean markets including, for example, prohibitions on actions designed to manipulate supply or misuse private information, remains irrespective of the type of asset.
- It is argued that the *complexity of many spread trading strategies* means that they cannot be executed on screens. This might be true, but

  - LIFFE's system, Connect, and OM both claim to support a number of complex trading strategies
  - It is unclear why some markets require these strategies while others do not
  - It is unclear why future screen based systems will be unable to offer such facilities.

Recent history suggests that screen trading can compete effectively and offer more attractive trading venues.

3.5.3 Client-based regulation

We did not find anything to support the suggestion that the differing user bases requires different market and regulatory structures. Only the London Stock Exchange has a large retail element, with the other RIEs being almost entirely institutional. We did find that the importance of institutional trading has led to particular features – notably block trade rules – but saw nothing to suggest fundamental differences in the sort of things regulation should be concerned with.

We would therefore be wary of suggesting that the regulation of markets should be based heavily on supposed differences in the client base for the following reasons:

- *While the current user base of UK RIEs is mainly institutional there is no reason why this should always be the case.* There is growing retail interest in equities and no reason why they should not diversify further. It is also entirely possible that some markets are exclusively institutional because the structure of the market, through historical accident or intent, excludes retail participation. The LME is a case in point, where the contract size is too large for retail clients. The risks are that a regulatory split would either exclude retail interest from markets that they might otherwise enter or, more dangerously, encourage OTC involvement for retail clients to access the market at one remove.
- *There is a well-known difficulty of defining the group of customers in an unambiguous way.* Traditionally this is done by size of transaction, but this is not entirely satisfactory. Everyone knows that very large is almost certainly institutional, and very small is retail; but there is always a large overlap in the middle. If users are allowed to self-select then there is a strong possibility that all will opt for the maximum protection – e.g. few institutions have opted out of best execution.
- *It is not clear that some of the possible regulatory distinctions often mentioned are supported by the wishes of the particular user base.* For example, it is often suggested that professional markets need less transparency than non-professional markets. While this has often been true, and is supported by the argument that in a professional market everyone knows what is going on anyway; many of the new institutional entrants into the London equity market have bemoaned its lack of transparency. They interpreted the 'everybody knows'

argument to mean that everybody except them knew, and that they were therefore disadvantaged.

- *The main features we have discussed here bear upon the quality of the markets.* For example, more transparency, other things being equal, means better prices and more liquidity. Price quality and liquidity are important to all users, and so there is nothing to suggest that an institutional market would not (subject to perhaps a limited restriction for block trades) be better for greater transparency.

Notes

1 Subsequently Jiway and Coredeal became RIEs, while Tradepoint joined with the Swiss Stock Exchange to create the RIE Virt-x.
2 In their evidence to the SEC (1994, A VI p.35) the London Stock Exchange view was that ATSs gain an advantage over recognised exchanges because they avoid regulatory costs, and may pose a threat if they are unregulated.

4
Fragmentation and Consolidation

4.1 Introduction

This chapter considers the changing structure of the securities industry. In particular, it analyses the centripetal forces pushing the trading of securities to consolidate on monopoly exchanges, and the centrifugal forces driving securities trading to fragment. 'The tension between centrality, on the one hand, and competition, on the other, is probably the oldest of all market structure issues' Arthur Levitt, Chairman of the SEC, Senate Banking Committee (SBC), 1999), and the current market structure reflects the present balance between these two opposite effects. 'Today's technology may afford us the opportunity to better achieve these goals [to garner the benefits of centrality without stifling competition] – once thought to be mutually inconsistent' (Arthur Levitt, 1999).

Section 4.2 of this chapter outlines the structure of securities trading, and this includes a brief description of the evolution of securities exchanges, the increasing concentration of exchanges on the trading function, the cost advantages of screen-based trading, the demutualisation of exchanges and the possible consequences for corporate governance, a brief description of the role of brokers, and the rapid growth of ATSs. Section 4.3 defines fragmentation for the purposes of this chapter, and sets out the industrial economics approach towards market structure that will be used in subsequent sections. Section 4.4 details the main economic forces for the consolidation of exchanges – economies of scale and network effects, coupled with listing restrictions. Section 4.5 sets out some reasons why markets may fragment, and section 4.6 considers the effects of market fragmentation, relative to a consolidated market.

4.2   Securities market structure

Before considering the fragmentation – consolidation debate, it is helpful to outline the structure of securities trading, and how it has developed over time. This will provide the context for the subsequent analysis of the forces which are currently driving markets to fragment, while other forces are pushing trading systems to consolidate.

Trading systems may be categorised along five main dimensions:

1   Type of *security* traded – e.g. spot, futures, options
2   Type of *underlying asset* – e.g equities (small companies and large companies), bonds, foreign exchange, commodities
3   The *geographical area* served – e.g. region, country, continent, etc.
4   The type of *customer* – e.g. institutional, retail
5   Screen-based or floor-based *trading systems*.

This five-way categorisation is helpful in classifying trading systems. Much of the analysis below deals with trading systems that trade shares, and derivatives trading systems that trade futures and options on equities, interest rates and foreign exchange.

4.2.1   A very brief history of trading systems

Exchanges lower the search costs of finding a counterparty. Initially regional stock exchanges were created using open outcry, and these gradually consolidated into national stock exchanges, still using a trading floor.[1] These exchanges developed as member institutions with brokers acting as intermediaries, rather than allowing the public direct access to the trading floor. This was for a number of reasons. First, there were space restrictions on the number of people who could physically be present on the exchange floor. Second, there was a need to ensure that trading was conducted in a *proper* manner.[2] Third, there were the costs to traders of travelling to the exchange and then waiting while a suitable counterparty emerged. Finally, there was a need to make sure that traders were credit worthy.

Separate (national) exchanges were created in futures and options well after the creation of equity markets. Indeed, derivatives exchanges are still being formed, and over 80 currently exist. While the early derivatives exchanges were open outcry, virtually all exchanges (derivatives and otherwise) formed in the last 10 years have been screen-based. Screen-based trading means that many of the arguments for the use of inter-mediaries in the trading process have been weakened, or cease to apply.

The problem of limited space on the exchange floor is no longer relevant when trading in cyberspace. Observance of the exchange rules can be ensured by well-designed software that prevents traders from breaching the regulations. Travelling to the exchange is irrelevant, while the trader need not wait around until a suitable counterparty arrives, but can simply submit a limit order. The only problem that still remains is the credit worthiness of the trader. In consequence, day-traders can now submit orders via the internet in real time. At present, because of the credit worthiness problem, exchanges require orders to come from brokers.

Currently national stock exchanges are consolidating into international stock exchanges, e.g. Paris, Amsterdam and Brussels forming Euronext,[3] Norex (Sweden, Denmark, Norway, Iceland and, possibly, Latvia and Lithuania), Tradepoint and the Swiss Stock Exchange merging to form Virt-x, the failed merger between the London Stock Exchange and the Deutsche Börse to form iX (in conjunction with NASDAQ)[4] and the hostile takeover bid for the London Stock Exchange from OM Group of Sweden. There is also the proposal to form Gem (NYSE, Tokyo, Toronto, Euronext, São Paulo, Australia, Hong Kong and Mexico). There have also been mergers between derivatives exchanges, e.g. New York Mercantile Exchange (NYMEX) and the Commodity Exchange (COMEX), LIFFE, London Traded Options Market (LTOM) and the London Commodities Exchange (LCE), and some international mergers of derivatives exchanges, e.g. DTB and the Swiss Options and Financial Futures Exchange (SOFFEX), and the takeover of the IPE by the Intercontinental Exchange (ICE). Finally, there have been mergers and takeovers between stock and derivatives markets in Finland, Sweden, France, Germany, Hong Kong and Singapore.[5] There has also been the takeover of LIFFE in the UK by Euronext. In addition, some derivatives exchanges are starting to move into trading the underlying asset, as well as derivatives on that asset, e.g Eurex announced that as from 6th October 2000 they will trade government bonds, as well as futures and options on government bonds. This consolidation process demonstrates the power of the centripetal forces at work on securities exchanges, leading to the amalgamation of both exchanges trading similar products (e.g. shares), and exchanges trading different types of security (e.g. shares and derivatives).

At the same time as mergers and takeovers between existing exchanges are taking place, new (screen-based) exchanges are being formed.[6] Some of these are targeted at new markets, e.g. the pan European equity market, while others offer a centralised screen-based market where previously there was only an informal telephone market, e.g. bonds, forex, etc. The important attractions of pan-European stock exchanges are (a) trading shares from across Europe under a single set of rules and (b) using a single clearing system to permit netting of transactions.[7] Some of these new markets have targeted specific market segments, e.g. AIM, EASDAQ and Neuer Markt trade small companies, while Jiway has targeted the retail investor wishing to trade foreign equities within Europe.[8]

So, on the one hand, there is a general movement towards consolidation of existing exchanges trading similar securities, while there is also a move towards the creation of exchanges specialising in a particular market segment not previously served by a screen-based exchange.

4.2.2   Specialisation on trade execution

Exchanges have traditionally supplied a range of services as a bundle, and trading has not been the paramount source of income as shown in Table 4.1. This shows that only 20 per cent of NYSE revenues came from trading fees, while listing fees were twice as important. Table 4.2 shows that in 1998 US exchanges derived only 30 per cent of income from trading fees, while they derived substantial income from regulatory fees, listing fees and the sale of trade and quote data.

However, in recent years there has been a trend to unbundle the services provided by exchanges (Macey and Kanda, 1990; Macey and O'Hara, 1999a, 1999b). For example, price and quote distribution is now commonly handled by outside contractors (e.g. Reuters, Bloomberg) rather than by the exchange itself; clearing and settlement is often handled by a separate company, e.g. Crest, London Clearing House (LCH); the dissemination of company news announcements (e.g. the

Table 4.1   Sources of NYSE income, 1992

Item	%
Listing fees	40
Trading fees	20
Sale of price and quote data	13
Regulatory fees	11
Facilities fees	8
Investment income	6
Membership fees	2
Total	100

Source: SEC (1994).

Table 4.2 Sources of US exchange income, 1998

Exchange	Regulation %	Trading %	Listing %	Information %	Other %
New York Stock Exchange	14	23	41	15	7
NASD	33	18	20	22	7
American Exchange	8	41	7	37	7
CBOE	15	67	0	14	4
Pacific Stock Exchange	4	71	3	17	7
Chicago Stock Exchange	0	54	0	44	2
Philadelphia Stock Exchange	0	69	0	16	15
Boston Stock Exchange	13	57	4	21	5
Cincinnati Stock Exchange	8	45	0	45	2
Total	**19**	**30**	**23**	**21**	**8**

Regulatory News Service, RNS) may be contracted to a separate company and rules governing the trading process are increasingly set by other organisations, e.g. EU, etc., rather than by a self-regulating exchange. Indeed, as exchanges become profit maximizing companies, they are tending to lose their regulatory powers. The National Association of Securities Dealers (NASD) has offered to provide regulatory services to exchanges who wish to out-source this function. While most exchanges retain the listing function,[9] the quality of companies can be signalled in other ways than by being listed on an RIE, e.g. by investment banks who agree to underwrite share issues and by brokers recommending shares to their clients. In consequence, exchanges are increasingly focussing on the provision of liquidity as their main function. This change, coupled with the demutualisation of exchanges, means that operating an exchange is shifting from being a relationship business to a commodity business (Macey and O'Hara, 1999b). It also means that it has become much easier for new trading systems to enter the market as they do not need to offer listing, clearing and settlement, the dissemination of company news announcements, price and quote distribution, etc.

4.2.3   Lower costs of screen-based trading

In addition to many other benefits, screen-based trading systems provide important cost savings, and this is a major factor driving the restructuring of financial markets. The Sydney Futures Exchange (SFE) estimated it would achieve savings of at least 40 per cent by switching from open outcry to screen-based trading (*Financial Times*, 6th April 1998). In addition to the savings from running the exchange (which are passed on to the users), the users of the exchange can make substantial cost savings from a switch to screen-based trading. Domowitz and Steil (2000) conducted an empirical study which compared the costs of trading via a broker on an intermediated market with those of disintermediated trading on a screen-based market. They studied data from a large US mutual fund manager who used 35 traditional brokers and four ATSs[10] over the four years 1992–6. Trading costs included the realised spread and fees, but no allowance for trading delays or non-execution of an order. After allowing for trade difficulty (proxied by trade size, market capitalisation of the company, stock beta, return volatility and share price) they found that trading via the ATSs was clearly cheaper. They also found that the trades routed via the ATSs were the 'easier' trades (i.e. small trades in large companies whose shares have low values for beta, volatility and share price).

4.2.4   Corporate governance of exchanges

Currently, exchanges organised as membership organisations are converting to companies with shares listed on an exchange (possibly themselves) (see Domowitz and Steil, 2000 for a list of 11 exchanges that have demutualized and 13 exchanges that are in the process of demutualization). Pirrong (1999) shows that mutual exchanges tend to restrict the number of members, which increases the profits of member firms. The economic rent from being an exchange member is then reflected in the price of a seat on the exchange. Hart and Moore (1996) demonstrate that, as the interests of small exchange members diverge from those of large members and the exchange faces more competition, a demutualised exchange becomes relatively more efficient than a mutual exchange. Both of these situations have occurred in recent years with the growing role of investment banks in equity and derivative markets, and the creation of new trading systems to challenge existing exchanges. Demutualisation facilitates innovation and competition by changing the power and incentive structure of an exchange, and this is widely seen as strongly desirable. For example, floor traders in an open outcry exchange are no longer able to block conversion to screen-based trading (as at LIFFE, Chicago Mercantile

Exchange (CME) and Chicago Board of Trade (CBOT)). Demutualisation also enables exchanges to raise additional funds on the capital markets, and to enter into joint ventures with other companies more easily.

As exchanges move from being mutual organisations to profit maximising companies, the corporate governance issues change as they swop one set of governance problems for another. Increasingly exchanges are owned by a few large players in financial markets (e.g. the major investment banks). These owners tend to be the main users of the exchange, and the same banks have large shareholdings in a number of different (possibly rival) trading systems. This raises a number of regulatory issues – e.g. it has been claimed that the London Stock Exchange merger with Deutsche Börse was driven by a few large American banks, against the wishes of the smaller shareholders in the UK exchange. (George Cox, *Financial Times*, 19th May 2000). Once an exchange is owned by its major users, they have both the incentive and the means to change the way the exchange operates to suit themselves, possibly to the detriment of smaller users of the exchange (Di Noia, 1999). In this context, OM (the Swedish derivatives exchange) passes reports on the activities on any member who also owns 10 per cent or more of OM shares to the Swedish regulator. This tends to act as a check on large shareholders receiving preferential treatment from the exchange. The major users may also decide on restructuring a number of exchanges to benefit themselves – e.g. creating iX, blocking competition between exchanges they largely own, declining to enforce exchange rules against themselves, initiating policies for the exchange which directly benefit its largest customers at the expense of exchange profits, etc.

The demutualisation of exchanges also means that for-profit companies regulate other for-profit companies, who may be their rivals for order flow – e.g. recognised investment exchanges (RIEs) may regulate ATSs. This could easily lead to conflicts of interest.

4.2.5 A very brief history of brokers

The nature of the role performed by brokers is changing radically. With just one exchange, brokers received client orders and executed them on this exchange (or filled the orders themselves). This process is illustrated in Figure 4.1 for a multi-dealer market with one exchange, where the broker has to select the market-maker offering the best price.

With the fragmentation of markets, brokers receive client orders which they then execute on one or more of a number of rival trading systems, or fill themselves at prices currently quoted on the trading systems. Brokers now provide two services for clients – they guarantee their credit worthiness, as before, and they route orders to the trading

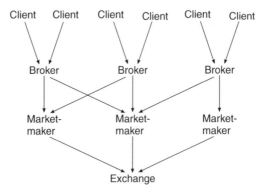

Figure 4.1   Structure of securities trading in a monopoly dealer market

system where the best execution is available. This is illustrated in Figure 4.2 for a multi-trading system market.

Brokers offer advice to their customers, and this process may reveal the customer's reasons for trading, e.g. hedging. In consequence, brokers have a better idea than other market participants of whether the order flow from their clients is informed (Hagerty and McDonald, 1996). Brokers can benefit from this knowledge by either acting as the counterparty themselves (internalisation), or selling this information to others (payment for order flow). This behaviour is analysed further in section 4.6.4.

At present, the order flow to market-makers and trading systems is directed by brokers, rather than customers. In an attempt to encourage order flow in a fragmented market, trading systems may move to allowing traders (subject to some credit worthiness check) to trade in their own names, rather than via brokers. This will prevent the order flow being diverted elsewhere by brokers or ATSs (see section 4.6.5).

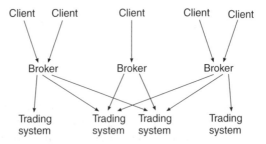

Figure 4.2   Structure of securities trading in a fragmented market

1 *ATSs.* The first ATS (Instinet) was founded in 1969, and in America there are some nine recognised ATSs – Archipelago, Attain, Brut, Instinet, Island, NexTrade, Market XT, GFI Securities and Redibook (Strike has recently merged with Brut), while three ATSs operate in Canada (Instinet, Tradebook and Versus Brokerage). The change in the US SEC order handling rules in January 1997 was the main stimulus for the development of ATSs.[11] It is commonly argued that the reason for their success in the USA is the inefficiency of the US market, notably its use of a $0.125 tick size. This made it easy for the ATSs to accept and display quotes in smaller increments, and so show narrower prices.[12] If this is the only benefit offered by ATSs, then the decimalisation of US equity trading may drive out the ATSs in the USA and, in addition, they may not succeed elsewhere.

In December 1998, the SEC passed rule ATS which allows alternative trading systems to apply to become securities exchanges.[13] ATSs (chiefly Instinet and Island) accounted for 29 per cent of NASDAQ turnover in November 1999 (Benhamon and Serval, 2000). The size of orders on ATSs is small, being well under 1,000 shares, while only about 5 per cent–10 per cent of orders submitted to ATSs are executed internally (NYSE, 2000). ATSs in equities may be largely an American phenomenon because Europe already has order-driven screen-based stock exchanges – e.g. SETS and Virt-x, while America does not. ATSs are not involved in listing securities, and may free ride on the price discovery process of recognised exchanges – i.e. are passive pricing systems. In the US the regulations on transparency and access vary with the level of volume of the ATS, with higher volume, e.g. 5 per cent and 20 per cent, leading to greater obligations.

2 *Differences Between ATSs and exchanges.* In many countries securities exchanges are subject to different regulations from brokers. ATSs look rather similar to exchanges, and so this distinction between exchanges and brokers poses problems for regulators in determining which set of rules to apply to a particular entity. Both ATSs and exchanges execute trades and require customers to route their orders via brokers. All exchanges, and some ATSs engage in price discovery. However, there are some important differences between exchanges and ATSs (which are regulated as authorised firms in the UK[14]):

- ATSs do not list securities (e.g. companies, futures contracts, etc.) as do exchanges, and ATSs trade in securities which are currently listed on at least one exchange.

- ATSs generally do not disseminate widely their trade and quote information, while this is an important source of revenue for exchanges (Domowitz and Steil, 2000, quote a figure of 17 per cent for European exchanges, while it was 13 per cent of NYSE revenue in 1992).
- US ATSs generally charge ½ to 1½ cents per share for access to their quotes while US exchanges are prohibited from making such charges (Cecin, SBC, 2000).
- An ATS may route some of their orders to an exchange, while exchanges generally do not route their orders elsewhere.
- In Europe, ATSs must report their trades through an RIE, and the RIEs charge for providing this service.
- ATSs are often owned by a single company, or a small group of companies, while exchanges are either mutuals, or have a more widely dispersed ownership.
- Screen-based systems such as ATSs provide anonymity for clients. Floor-based exchanges may not preserve client anonymity.
- Exchanges are themselves regulators who establish rules governing the conduct of their members, and both monitor and enforce compliance with these rules. Exchanges have to bear the cost of this regulatory overhead. ATSs do not have such powers, and are subject to rules made by others, e.g. the FSA or SEC.
- Under the ISD, recognised exchanges qualify for a EU passport, and can operate in any EU country while being regulated in their home country. This does not apply to ATSs.
- In the UK an exchange can only trade securities in which there is a *proper* market, while this restriction does not apply to authorised firms, such as ATSs.
- UK exchanges are not required to have any arrangements for compensating users, while authorised firms (e.g. ATSs) must have a compensation scheme of up to £48,000 for retail investors.
- Exchanges have greater flexibility, in that they must meet high-level recognition criteria, while authorised firms (e.g. ATSs) must meet more prescriptive rules.
- In the USA, exchanges must go through a lengthy procedure to change their rules, while non-exchanges, e.g. ATSs, can change their rules much more quickly, SEC (1994).[15]
- Some investment funds must conduct all their trades through a recognised exchange, and so cannot trade via an ATS.
- When an authorised firm trades via an ATS they may be subject to more onerous capital requirements than if they trade on a recognised exchange.

- In the UK the exemption to market-makers from paying stamp duty only applies to the trades of registered intermediaries on a recognised exchange.
- Being an RIE gives the trading system a clear label which enables customers to understand the nature of their function, as well as some degree of status and respectability. For example, 'we believe that there is a significant brand value associated with having the ability to use the term *exchange*' (Putnam (Archipelago), SBC, 1999, emphasis in the original).

The FSA (2000a) suggested that non-exchange trading systems (mainly ATSs) might be classified into four categories:

1 *Price-makers*. At least one side of each trade has submitted a price with their order and the prices at which securities are traded are, at least in part, determined by the interaction of the buy and sell orders received by the system. Such ATSs participate in the price discovery process.
2 *Price-takers*. The system matches unpriced orders using an externally determined price, e.g. the mid-price on the primary trading system.
3 *Indication of interest*. Orders posted on the system (e.g. a bulletin board) are not firm, but may lead to the negotiation of trades.
4 *Dealer system*. A dealer posts prices at which he or she is willing to trade with customers.

The FSA suggested that indications of interest and dealer systems may be viewed as different from price-makers and price-takers. The later are executing trades between traders without themselves acting as principal, and this is a major part of the activities of recognised exchanges.

4.3   Fragmentation

This section sets the scene for the subsequent analysis. It introduces the idea that the market for the trading of securities is a market in services, and can be examined using the tools of industrial economics. It also sets out the definition of market fragmentation to be used in this study.

4.3.1   Industrial economics and securities exchanges

An exchange can be viewed as a firm that produces a range of services (trade execution, price and quote distribution, firm listing, the rules of the exchange, trade monitoring, clearing and settlement, company news announcements, etc.). With this view of the exchange as a company, if it is a profit maximiser, the theories of industrial economics can be deployed, e.g. monopoly, competition, barriers to entry, economies of scale, entry and exit of firms, etc. The analysis of mutual exchanges is more difficult as they may not be seeking to maximise profits. However, there is currently a move for mutual exchanges to convert to companies, while new exchanges tend to be part of the profit maximising sector.

The trading of financial securities involves two related markets: (a) the market for the financial securities themselves, and (b) the market for the service of trading these securities on behalf of investors. In consequence, every trade involves two prices: the price of the security and the price for executing the trade. Securities exchanges are in the second type of market – the market for trading services – and do not buy and sell financial securities on their own account. Of course, in a dealer market, market-makers buy and sell the underlying securities as part of the process of suppling trading services to customers, while some brokers may, on occasion, act as counterparties. Participants in financial markets who only supply trading services are not exposed to the price risk of the underlying security, and so are not directly concerned about the information impounded into the current price, e.g. low transparency or asymmetric information. They make their money from commissions and fees, and so wish to maximise the order flow. Therefore, they are willing to accept any arrangements on transparency or insider trading that customers want. However, in dealer markets, market-makers are concerned about these issues, e.g. the desire of market-makers in London for the delayed publication of large trades to allow them time to unwind their inventory. On such exchanges the trading rules are a compromise between the desire to maximise the order flow, and to protect market makers from price risk on their inventory.

Cohen, Maier, Schwartz and Whitcomb (1986) and Schwartz (1991) argue that there may be a conflict between the markets in the underlying securities and trading services. Competition in the market for trading services may adversely affect the quality of pricing of the underlying securities by fragmenting trading. Alternatively, consolidation of the market for financial securities reduces the degree of competition for trading services. In which case, investors may have to make a trade-off between lower transactions costs and possibly a worse mid-price. This issue is at the centre of the subsequent analysis in this study.

4.3.2 What is fragmentation?

The definition of the market

Whether a market is fragmented or not depends on the definition of the market, and there are a number of alternatives. For example, a stock exchange may be viewed as a single market for shares in which every stock listed on the exchange is a very close substitute for every other stock, and so they effectively constitute one market. In this case fragmentation of trading between exchanges is impossible as every exchange corresponds to exactly one market. This argument could be taken a bit further and used to argue that all stock exchanges throughout the world effectively constitute a single market in equities; or even that every trading system which trades financial securities (equities, bonds, foreign exchange, futures, options, etc.) is part of a single giant market in bundles of risk and return. In this case fragmentation (i.e. trading of the security on a number of trading systems) is very hard to avoid.

Some theoretical papers define fragmented markets in a different way, with transparency playing an important role in the definition. For Biais (1993) and Madhavan (1995) a fragmented market is one such as NASDAQ or SEAQ where there are bilateral trades by telephone involving many different market-makers, while a consolidated market is one where all orders are addressed to the same location, and market participants can observe all quotes and trades, e.g. CBOT and NYSE. Both these authors analyse the effects of transparency because the key difference between consolidated and fragmented markets under their definition is transparency. Consolidated markets are transparent, while fragmented markets are not. With this definition of fragmentation, markets where everyone trades on the same RIE in the same way are regarded as fragmented if there is not full transparency. Thus, under this definition NASDAQ trading in Microsoft shares is highly fragmented because it constitutes thousands of separate bilateral markets and, with this definition, fragmentation and transparency are essentially the same thing!

The analysis in this study takes a somewhat different view of the market from the various possibilities mentioned above. It defines the market as being all trading in a particular security (and its very close substitutes) irrespective of the trading systems on which they are traded, e.g. all trading of shares in company X.[16] Such a market may be consolidated on a single trading system, or fragmented across a number of trading systems. A particular trading system may have both an upstairs and a downstairs market in the same security, and this could be regarded as market fragmentation; but not in this study. Even if trading involves bilateral deals (as on NASDAQ) this will be regarded as a single trading system for these purposes. Note that a particular trading system may trade two securities Y and Z, and trading in Y may be consolidated on this trading system, while trading in Z is fragmented across a number of trading systems.

Time fragmentation

As well as trading being fragmented between trading systems, trading can also be fragmented across time on the same trading system. Even when trading is consolidated on a single trading system, unless all trading occurs at a single moment in time, there is temporal fragmentation. Most trading systems now operate continuously during the trading day, and so the order flow is spread out during this period. As trading systems lengthen their trading hours (which is increasingly the case), temporal fragmentation increases.[17] Call (or batch) markets operate at particular times, but still involve time fragmentation because the order flow is fragmented across different call sessions (e.g. the call session this morning and the call session this afternoon). Time fragmentation gives traders who do not desire immediacy the opportunity to choose when they trade, and there is a considerable theoretical and empirical literature on the resulting intraday patterns in volatility, spreads, depth, volume, etc. In their evidence to the SEC (2000b), Schwartz (CUNY) and Wunsch (Arizona Stock Exchange) stressed the problem of time fragmentation, and advocated a switch to call auctions. Such auctions would prevent one trading system free-riding on the price discovery process of another trading system, Schwartz (1991). They argue that continuous trading encourages the fragmentation (or fracturing) of orders over time, i.e. one big order is chopped up into many small orders.[18] Call auctions prevent this.

In the next two sections the tools of industrial economics will be used to analyse the forces encouraging and discouraging the fragmentation of securities markets.

4.4 Forces for the consolidation of markets

There are two main forces for the consolidation of securities markets – increasing returns to scale and network effects. In addition, the listing function can be used by exchanges to prevent fragmentation. Large trading systems provide a better service to traders than do small trading systems, for two reasons. First, there are traditional economies of scale in the provision of the trading function – the more trades, the cheaper is the cost to the trading system of conducting an additional trade. Second, there are network effects from having many trades and traders using a trading system which mean that customers receive a superior service. This has two potential consequences – (a) the emergence of a monopoly exchange, and (b) this winning exchange may well be the first mover, rather than the most suitable trading system (e.g. low cost), with society locked into an inferior outcome to what could have been attained if a different exchange had been the first mover.

4.4.1 Economies of scale

Financial trading systems exhibit economies of scale, although these are probably smaller for screen-based than for open outcry trading systems.[19] An open outcry trading system requires a trading floor with sufficient ancillary space for members to have office space to receive and transmit orders. Exchange members must provide floor traders. There must also be a mechanism for inputting completed trades into the clearing system. An electronic trading system requires a central computer, the requisite software, and electronic links to member firms, who must provide staff and screens in their own offices. Exchanges also engage in listing securities, the distribution of quote and trade data and regulation, and stock exchanges are involved in the release of company information. In addition, all trading systems will incur an administration overhead.

If the fixed costs per period of running the trading system are FC, the variable cost per trade is VC and the number of trades per period is n, then the average total cost of a trade is $FC/n + VC$. As the number of trades increases, the average total cost declines at a decreasing rate towards a minimum of VC. Since the variable cost for each trade, particularly a screen-based trade, is very low, the average total cost per trade becomes very small as the number of trades becomes very large. This is illustrated in Figure 4.3.

Malkamäki (2000) looked for economies of scale in the two main functions he identified as performed by an exchange (a) trading, and (b) listing companies and releasing company-specific information. He found considerable economies of scale in trading, but much smaller-scale economies for activities related to the number of firms listed. He also found that the economies of scale are bigger for the larger exchanges. This reveals that it is only in the trading function that exchanges benefit from economies of scale. These results indicate there is an incentive for exchanges to merge their trading activities, but not to merge the other functions of an exchange, e.g. listing.

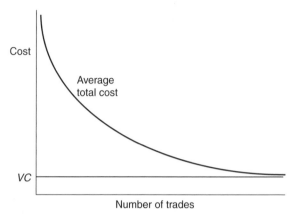

Figure 4.3   Average cost per trade

4.4.2   Financial markets as networks

Financial markets can be viewed as networks (Di Noia, 1999, 2001; Domowitz, 1995; Domowitz and Steil, 2000; Economides, 1993; Jochum, 1999). In this context, the network is interpreted as the trading opportunities in a particular security provided by a particular trading system. If two rival trading systems both trade the same security, they constitute two separate networks, and the market for that security is fragmented. These distinct rival networks (trading systems) may be linked together to form a network of networks, i.e. an internet of trading in a particular security.[20] A particular trading system trading a number of different securities can be viewed as a collection of separate networks, where each network is the trading in a particular security.

Figure 4.4 illustrates how a financial trading system connects together a network of traders in a particular security, e.g. shares in firm *Z*.

Some types of network require the provision of an expensive physical infrastructure, e.g. railways, water, gas, electricity, cable television and telephones. In consequence, they have substantial economies of scale, and a single network is much cheaper than creating (say) two rival rail networks. Such industries have been called natural monopolies because of the prohibitive cost of creating competition between rival networks.[21] Financial trading systems do not involve an expensive physical network, although they do have economies of scale, as reported in section 4.4.1. Therefore, the natural monopoly argument based on economies of scale does not apply to trading systems. However, they are still networks.

Figure 4.4 A financial trading system as a network

In the context of financial trading systems, Economides (1993) iden-tified two categories of trader–buyers and sellers. Each offer to buy is complementary with each offer to sell, and may be matched either according to the rules of an order-driven market, or intermediated in a dealer market. While in a telephone network all subscribers are complementary, i.e. can be connected to each other, this is not the case for financial markets since a pair of buy (or sell) orders cannot be matched with each other. Financial trading systems require that traders submit their orders in a compatible manner, e.g. the order is submitted according to the protocols of the trading system. However, in comparison to other types of network, issues like compatibility and complementarity are not major problems for financial networks.[22]

4.4.3 Network effects

A network effect occurs when a rise in the number of users of the network increases the benefits received by existing network users.[23] For example, the benefits from owning a telephone are increased as additional people buy telephones.[24] For someone contemplating subscribing to a telephone network, the network benefits are related to the *expected* number of other subscribers when they are connected to the system.

This section considers the interaction between the size of the network and liquidity, price discovery and segmented demand. It also examines the use of standards or adapters to link networks, the move towards a network of networks, and the possibility of getting locked into a sub-optimal network.

1 *Liquidity*. For a trading system, additional buy and sell orders increase the quality of the market. The greater is the order flow, the more liquid is the market. Increased liquidity is associated with

greater depth (e.g. larger orders can be executed at the bid and ask prices), greater resilience (i.e. reduced market impact), a smaller bid–ask spread and greater immediacy (i.e. a shorter time lag before an order is executed).[25] It can also be shown that the variance of market prices decreases as the number of traders participating in the market increases, i.e. price volatility drops as liquidity rises. Note that these network effects relate to the market for a particular security.[26]

The network effects relate to the order flow at the time a trader wishes to trade. Therefore, as well as consolidating the order flow on a single trading system, the network effects are also increased by concentrating a given order flow into a short time period, e.g. by the use of a call or batch market to reduce time fragmentation. While call markets have been advocated by academics for this reason, there are few if any examples of a move towards call markets. Rather, trading systems using a call trading system have converted to using a continuous system. Mendelson and Peake (1994) have criticised call markets because they prevent traders from immediately acting on information. Informed traders must wait until the time of the next call market, and this reduces the incentive for traders to collect information.

2   *Price discovery.* A particular form of network effect in financial markets is price discovery. Trading impounds information into the price, and so additional traders create a benefit – additional price discovery. The value of the trading information is an increasing function of the number of traders. Exchanges have captured this benefit by selling the trading information for the benefit of the exchange. This may indirectly benefit traders as exchanges can use this revenue to reduce transaction charges. In addition to any such revenue benefits to users of the exchange, Schwartz (1991) argued that price discovery by an exchange creates a public good.

3   *Segmented demand.* If the merger of two trading systems creates no additional order flow, there are no additional network effects from such a merger. Thus, if investors in Belgium and the Netherlands are not expected to trade French shares (and vice versa), the only benefit from a merger of the French, Belgian and Dutch stock markets is the economies of scale in running the new large exchange. This argument implies that, if traders can be segmented into N distinct groups, with members of each group wishing to trade a separate set of securities, there are no additional network effects from consolidating N separate trading systems serving each of these groups. The only force for consolidation is the economies of scale in operating the trading systems, and provided these are modest, the equilibrium outcome may be N

trading systems. However, if segmentation of traders is not possible, there will be additional network effects from consolidation into a single monopoly exchange.

The extent to which markets are segmented appears to be changing rapidly. A key factor driving the consolidation of exchanges, particularly in Europe, is changes on the demand side as users are rapidly becoming less segmented. Previously, investors in (say) France, wished to invest largely in French companies. Therefore, the demand was for a trading system offering the possibility of a liquid market in French stocks. However, with the introduction of the ISD and the euro, investment in Europe is moving from a country perspective to European industrial sectors. This has created the demand to be able to trade Europe's major companies in euros on the same trading system with the same regulations and the same clearing system.

In addition to geographical segmentation, demand may also be segmented by type of company, e.g. size of company (large–small firms), high technology–low technology companies, etc. and separate trading systems are emerging for different types of stock. There is also some segmentation of the order flow between institutional and retail investors, and this is considered below in section 4.6.5.

4 *Standards and adapters.* Katz and Shapiro (1985) demonstrate that the total output of a network good (e.g. video recorders, where more machines using a particular format stimulates the production of more videos to watch on these machines) is greater when all suppliers produce a compatible good. Since compatibility maximises the network effect, this creates strong pressure for the creation of a single industry-wide network (e.g. every video recorder can play every tape). Katz and Shapiro (1985) go on to argue that there are two main ways of achieving compatibility between different networks: the joint adoption of a standard by the rival networks, and the construction of an *adapter* by one or more networks which allows the customers of one network to use another, e.g. the translation of English books into Japanese (enabling books available to the English network to be enjoyed by the Japanese network). Domowitz (1995) pointed out that the use of standards in securities markets (e.g. a specification of the way the trading system works), facilitates the merger of screen-based trading systems as this permits the interconnection of networks, but tends to stifle innovation. Domowitz suggests that compatibility between trading system networks can be better achieved by the use of *adapters* which allow the users of one trading system to access another. Domowitz and Steil (2000) define adapters in the context of

financial trading systems as providing a standardised interface across different trading systems – i.e. adapters are companies who are members of a number of trading systems, and offer their clients a standardised order entry system for trading on any of the specified trading systems. With the increase in demand to trade on many trading systems, there has been rapid growth in the provision of such services, e.g. Instinet and Jiway.

5 *Internets.* If there is a network of networks (e.g. the US ATSs are building a private network to link their order books), then:

(a) new trading systems joining this network can benefit from the common network effects, even if there is only a low level of trading on their trading system

(b) every additional trading system joining the internet most probably increases the size of the common network effects enjoyed by all trading systems in the internet

(c) traders will be attracted to the lowest cost trading system, unless a trading system can offer some other benefit which differentiates them from the rival trading systems in the composite network.

Given technological developments and the fragmentation of markets, a network of networks is becoming more and more relevant as trading systems merge, form alliances and create implicit mergers. The concept of implicit mergers is discussed in section 4.5.7.

4 *Path dependence (or lock-in, or history matters).* History may matter for networks when there are high costs in switching to a rival network (Arthur, 1989; Economides, 1993, 1996).[27] In switching, the economies of scale and network effects from the present network are lost, while those for the new network may be small because it has few customers. There may also be one-off costs to customers of connecting to the new network. It has been argued that, where there are network effects, history matters and the possibility exists of a lock-in at some Pareto inferior solution[28] (e.g. the QWERTY, not Dvorák, keyboard; VHS, not Betamax, videos; the US PAL, not SECAM, colour TV system; narrow guage, not broad gauge, rail track; etc.). Hence there may be a first mover advantage to the first network to be established. Such arguments have been applied to the major financial trading systems.

However, Liebowitz and Margolis (1994) have questioned whether the quoted examples of lock-ins are, in fact, correct. They claim that there is no evidence that the QWERTY keyboard and VHS video format are inferior to the Dvorak keyboard and Betamax videos, and that there are no generally accepted examples of society getting locked into inferior networks. There are several reasons why lock-ins have not happened. Where the network (e.g. a financial trading system) is owned by some economic entity, they can internalise the network benefits by charging higher fees for using a large network. If the owners think a new network is potentially superior to the existing large network, they can subsidise the initial user fees in order to increase the size of the new network. Having established a large network with substantial network effects, they can then increase their fees to recoup their earlier losses.

An alternative solution applies to networks that have no owner (e.g. the English language), as well as to owned networks. Potential users of the new network, or its owners, can co-ordinate the switch to using the new network so that the initial scale of the new network is sufficiently large to generate worthwhile network effects (Witt, 1997). This may involve publicising expectations concerning the number of customers who are about to switch. New trading systems will benefit from expressing their intention to expand rapidly, so that potential customers expect the network effects to increase rapidly.

Both strategies can be followed simultaneously, i.e. special low prices for early users of the new network, and co-ordination of the switch of a number of users. Much order flow to financial networks is routed by intermediaries, who can choose the trading system to which their orders are routed. So trading systems need to attract financial intermediaries, rather than customers. Domowitz (1995) argues that, if market participants expect screen-based trading systems to attract most of the order flow, then this is what will occur – a self-fulfilling prophesy. The available evidence is that such mechanisms have insured that society has not been locked into demonstrably inferior networks.

At one stage it was claimed that financial markets were stuck with the existing trading systems, which would continue to use floor trading and open outcry. However, this is now seen not to be the case. For example, Pagano and Steil (1996) document the fragmentation of trading in European shares when SEAQ-I was introduced and captured a substantial share of the order flow in German, French, Italian, Spanish, Dutch, Swiss and Swedish stocks from the relevant home exchanges. This competition stimulated the reform of these European exchanges, and much of this volume then flowed back to the home country exchanges. The only way a lock-in is likely to occur in financial markets is by regulatory action, e.g. prohibiting rival trading systems, or banning screen-based trading. Thus it is important that regulators do not, perhaps inadvertently, create a lock-in by creating some rule which prevents innovation and competition between trading systems.

Given the presence of economies of scale in trading, network effects for financial trading systems and the one-off costs of connecting to new networks, it is to be expected that new trading systems will initially price their services at below cost in order to compete with existing networks, followed by a rise in price as the network expands. For example, in 1997 the DTB offered a fee holiday on bund futures traded on their exchange to win order flow from LIFFE.

4.4.4 Listing restrictions

If a security can be traded only on a particular exchange, this is a powerful force for consolidated markets. In derivatives markets, contracts are devised, created and owned by the exchange on which they are traded and are fungible only against identical contracts traded on the same exchange.[29] Therefore, the order flow for a particular derivatives contract cannot be fragmented, unless it is with the agreement of the initial exchange (and its clearing house). However, another exchange can list a very similar contract, e.g. the bund on LIFFE and the DTB which, in effect, fragments the order flow. For index derivatives, the owner of the copyright on the underlying index may only licence a particular trading system to trade derivatives on their index, although there are a number of examples of futures on the same index being traded on different exchanges, e.g. FTSE 100 in London and Chicago, Eurotop 100 in New York, Amsterdam and London and the Nikkei 225 in Osaka, Chicago and Singapore.

Some exchanges have rules preventing members of the exchange trading elsewhere, such as NYSE rule 390. This 1976 rule prohibited members of the NYSE from trading NYSE-listed securities away from a national securities exchange.[30] In 1980, the NYSE adopted rule 19c-3, under which rule 390 did not apply to stocks listed on the NYSE after 26th April 1979. Rule 390 was rescinded on 5th May 2000 and this has allowed NYSE members to trade all NYSE listed securities outside the national market system, and to internalise their order flow in all NYSE listed stocks.

A proposal has been made concerning listing which would tend to restrict fragmentation. Amihud and Mendelson (1996) argued that the arrangements for trading a company's shares affect the liquidity with which they are traded, and the more liquid is the market, the higher the share price. Therefore, the way in which its shares are traded is a matter of legitimate interest for a company. Amihud and Mendelson (1996) proposed that each company be allowed to decide the exchange on which its shares are traded. Companies will choose to list on the exchange which maximises the value of its shares, and may refuse to allow their shares to be traded on other exchanges or ATSs. Implementation of this proposal should reduce the need for detailed regulation of markets and exchanges because exchanges now have an incentive to create rules and trading procedures which are beneficial to shareholders. Since the rules and procedures which maximise the share price may vary from share to share, uniform rules governing all exchanges may be inappropriate, and the company concerned can use its knowledge of its shareholders' interests to select the most appropriate exchange. Competition between exchanges for listings is also suggested by Beny (2001) and Cohen, Maier, Schwartz and Whitcomb (1986).

Foucault and Parlour (2000) have also considered the effect of listing shares on competition between exchanges. They constructed a theoretical model in which rival exchanges compete for listings by varying their trading rules and fees. The outcome is that each exchange caters to a different set of shares, where companies may be differentiated by market capitalisation, size of the issue, liquidity of trading in the shares etc. This is consistent with the views of Amihud and Mendelson (1996). Foucault and Parlour then go on to argue that competition between exchanges for listings can produce a result that does not maximise social welfare because each exchange, in effect, is the only supplier of listing services to a particular type of company, and so has some market power. However, in a contestable market, such power is strictly limited by the threat of new entrants.

4.4.5   Empirical evidence on the causes of fragmentation

Fong, Madhavan and Swan (1999) conducted an empirical investigation of what causes markets to fragment. For the Australian equity market they obtained data on all trades in Australian Stock Exchange (ASX) listed stocks from January 1993 to December 1998 (25 million trades) which included data on whether the trade was conducted on or off the ASX. For the 1,771 stocks in the data set, the proportion of trading that was off-exchange varied between stocks and over time for the same stock, and the researchers sought to explain this variation using a range of variables. They found that off-exchange trading increased when the trading volume of a share was high, the share's quoted bid–ask spread was wide, the share was included in the All Ordinaries index, the share's market depth (the daily median of the dollar value of the best two limit bid orders plus the best two ask orders) was low, no option was traded on the share and there was no closing call market in the share.

4.5   Forces against market consolidation

While there are powerful forces pushing markets towards consolidation, there are also powerful forces against consolidation and towards fragmentation, and these will now be considered.

4.5.1   Heterogeneous trading services

Trading a particular security is not a homogeneous service as the characteristics of the trading process differ between trading systems. Different trading systems offer traders different trading environments, and these may appeal to different sets of traders.[31] Some traders may prefer to use a trading system with a high level of transparency, while other traders (or the same trader at different times) may prefer to use a trading system with low transparency. Trading systems may differ in the access they give to traders, and some traders may be denied access to information or trading facilities by some trading systems, e.g. not allowed to be a floor trader and so get floor information, Harris (1993). Most exchanges offer an 'upstairs' market for large trades, which facilitates 'an audit of trading motives'. Other possible dimensions along which there can be differences in market design include anonymity, order-driven or dealer market, central counterparty, the clearing and settlement arrangements, margins, tick size, opening hours, contract size, etc. For such reasons, traders may be prepared to support a number of rival trading systems. The heterogeneity results in differences between trading systems in terms of spreads, depth, immediacy, resiliency (market impact). In essence, while they are trading the same security, trading systems are offering a slightly different type of service and attract their own clientele (like buying the same products from either Harrods or ASDA).

In a competitive market for trade execution, traders will move their business to what they perceive to be the 'best' trading system. If the long-run equilibrium is to be other than a monopoly, the surviving trading systems need to offer a different mix of attributes, each appealing to a different market segment. The idea that the nature of trade execution differs between trading systems, making the concept of 'best execution' problematic, is discussed in section 4.6.8.

4.5.2   Heterogenous regulation

There may be differences in the regulatory regime as between trading systems. For example, there may be a split between trading systems for retail investors and trading systems for professional investors, with the former subject to more stringent regulation. The Commodity Futures

Trading Commission (CFTC) has recently introduced different regulations for exchanges servicing retail and professional investors (CFTC, 2000d).

Previously, the CFTC applied a single regulatory framework to all US futures and options exchanges, even though they differ greatly, i.e. a 'one size fits all' policy. The CFTC (2000a, 2000b) view is that regulations should differ according to the nature of the products traded and the market participants, and proposed three alternative types of trading facility:

1 *Exempt Multilateral Transaction Execution Facility* (MTEF). This is the least regulated category, and is available for the trading of non-manipulable derivatives by institutional investors only. These facilities have approximately the same regulatory freedom as an OTC market, e.g. the swaps market.
2 *Recognised Derivatives Transaction Facility* (DTF). This is available for trading non-manipulable derivatives by institutional investors. Non-institutional investors are permitted to use a DTF, but only if their trades are intermediated, and they are provided with enhanced disclosure. A DTF is a recognised exchange, and is more heavily regulated than a MTEF.
3 *Recognised Futures Exchange* (RFE). There are no restrictions on the type of underlying asset, nor on the type of trader. This type of exchange is subject to the greatest level of regulation and corresponds to the existing recognised derivatives exchanges.

It appears the CFTC initiative is to allow the creation of an MTEF in swaps trading to compete with the OTC swaps market.[32] However, permitting three alternative types of derivatives exchange could lead to the same security (e.g. US Treasury bond futures) being traded on three different derivatives exchanges under different regulations appealing to three different sets of users. Section 6.3.1 discusses the problems that result from a policy like that adopted by the CFTC – market distortions, multiple regimes, loopholes, instability and lack of scrutiny.

Similarly, market fragmentation may result in trading systems in different countries trading essentially the same security, but subject to different regulation (e.g. UK and Germany). Such regulatory differences will tend to promote fragmentation and prevent consolidation into a single exchange. The European Commission (2001) has proposed that, if a financial instrument is traded on what the EC calls a 'regulated market', no trading in that instrument be permitted on organised, but non-regulated, markets. This proposal is to prevent instruments being traded on different trading systems under different sets of rules.

4.5.3   Heterogenous types of security

The preferred trading arrangements for some securities may differ from those for other securities. For example, small companies have a much lower liquidity, and so may be better served by different trading arrangements, e.g. a dealer market rather than an order-driven market. This implies separate arrangements for trading, if not separate trading systems for these different types of stock. The listing requirements for large companies are often more onerous than those for small companies. Therefore, unless a trading system has different arrangements for trading different stocks, there will be a demand for separate trading systems; permitting the small company trading system to have different trading arrangements and listing requirements. Since the network effects relate to the particular security being traded (at least for screen-based trading systems), it is possible for trading system Y to consolidate the trading of share A, and for trading system Z to consolidate trading in share B. For these reasons separate trading systems for large and small companies have developed. Once established, this situation may prevail (although particular stocks can move from one type of trading system to another as the companies grow in trading volume; as was intended for iX).

4.5.4   New entrants

Technological progress means that new low-cost trading systems, probably offering a different choice of trading characteristics, are constantly being created to challenge the dominant trading system, so preventing consolidation. The contestability of financial markets has increased greatly in recent years. This is because the costs of acquiring a screen-based trading system have fallen, and off-the-peg systems can be tailored to the particular requirements of the trading system. It has been estimated that the cost of establishing a new electronic trading system is only about $10 million (Domowitz, 1995). In addition, screen-based trading allows the trading system to service customers located anywhere in the world, rather than just those located close to the trading system. The use of screens also helps new entrants to benefit from the available network effects (see section 4.4.2).[33]

4.5.5   Links between trading systems

If a well functioning system linking together the various trading systems can be created, there may be little to be gained from consolidation, as the system will already offer the aggregate network benefits, although not the economies of scale in trading. (Linking trading systems is considered in section 6.2.1). Hence, a good linkage system facilitates the creation of new trading systems.

4.5.6 Clearing and settlement

The arrangements for clearing and settling the transactions of a trading system are an important consideration, and their effects on the consolidation of trading are not straightforward. If each trading system has a different clearing and settlement system then the effect on fragmentation depends on whether traders use a single trading system or many trading systems. In the former case the clearing and settlement arrangements create an important barrier to traders (or their agents) switching their order flow from one trading system to another, so helping to preserve fragmentation. In the latter case clearing and settlement can be a force for consolidation by encouraging a trader who trades on a number of trading systems (and clearing and settlement systems) to concentrate their trading on a single trading system (and clearing and settlement system). This will both simplify the administration of dealing with a variety of different clearing and settlement systems and permit positions to be netted.

Irrespective of whether traders use one or many trading systems, if all trading systems use a common clearing and settlement system (as in the USA), this removes a problem for new trading systems who wish to enter the market, so facilitating fragmentation.

4.5.7 Implicit mergers and alliances

Another way of obtaining network benefits without consolidation is what have been called 'implicit mergers'. They can be defined as an agreement between two trading systems that securities listed on one trading system can be traded on the other trading system. For example, Eurex has 5,000 screens in 16 countries, and the CBOT-Eurex alliance announced in 2000 would enable these customers to trade both Eurex and CBOT products using the same (Eurex) network connection and software (David Brennan (CBOT), SBC, 2000). Domowitz and Steil (2000) presented a list of 47 exchange mergers or alliances over the three-year period from 1997 to March 2000. The implicit merger is a form of alliance between trading systems which captures the benefits of economies of scale in trading and the network benefits (for the securities covered by the alliance), while allowing the trading systems to continue to conduct the company-specific functions separately. There are a number of reasons why exchanges trading systems have tended to use alliances, rather than mergers or takeovers, for this purpose.

Until recently, exchanges have been mutual organisations, and this has prevented hostile takeovers because the bidder could not buy the shares of the target in the market. It has also made exchanges hard to value as their shares are not traded, and made it difficult for exchanges to raise additional capital to finance a takeover or engineer a 50:50 merger. Alliances have a number of advantages over mergers. They are quicker and easier to implement, e.g. a 75 per cent membership vote is not required, one exchange can have alliances with a number of different exchanges, alliances are flexible in that they can be structured in many different ways to suit the circumstances, and can be reversed or lead to a full merger. For example, an exchange can form an alliance with another exchange in a different continent under which there is a mutual offset agreement for futures on security X, and they can also form an alliance with another exchange to offer one of the other exchange's futures on their trading system. Since economies of scale do not appear to exist for the company-specific functions performed by exchanges of listing, information release, compliance, etc. there is no incentive to merge exchanges to save money on these activities. (Domowitz (1995) argues that implicit mergers or alliances are possible only for screen-based exchanges.)

Although an implicit merger or alliance preserves the number of exchanges, exchanges who have implicitly merged are no longer rivals, but collaborators, at least for some of their products. This possibility brings into question simple measures of fragmentation based on shares of the order flow. What matters from the point of view of the customer is not whether exchanges form alliances, rather than mergers, but the quality of service provided.

4.5.8   Segmented demand

Demand may be segmented, with users of (say) the Shanghai Stock Exchange wishing to trade only Chinese stocks. In which case there are no network benefits from a merger with (say) the Tokyo Stock Exchange (TSE), and so only economies of scale would be gained from such a merger. Similarly, the demand to trade small companies may be only a local demand, and so there are no network effects from listing on a national or international exchange. In which case, the forces for con-solidation are weak.

4.6 Effects of fragmentation

If any view is to be formed on the desirability, or otherwise, of market fragmentation, an understanding of the effects of such fragmentation is necessary. This section sets out the main economic effects of market fragmentation. While these effects are both good and bad, it will be argued that the fragmentation of securities markets is, on balance, beneficial when coupled with the appropriate regulatory measures. Schwartz and Steil (1996) report that only 4 per cent of the 59 large European fund managers surveyed thought that the fragmentation of the market in French stocks (e.g. Paris Bourse and SEAQ-I) was a bad thing, while most thought it was a good thing.

4.6.1 Competition

Charles Schwab (Schwab) suggested to the SBC (2000) that fragmentation is just a pejorative term for competition.[34] Fragmentation results in competition for the order flow between trading systems and, in the longer run, this is likely to lead to an improvement in their trading systems and liquidity (e.g. SEAQ-I and Europe) (Amihud and Mendelson, 1996). The SEC view is that the increased competition associated with market fragmentation has led to (a) faster trade execution, (b) cheaper trade execution, (c) more choice and (d) greater market capacity to handle the enormous increase in the volume of order flow (SEC, 1994). Existing trading systems will naturally be opposed to changes which result in the creation of additional competitors, i.e. fragmentation. But such a self-interested view does not mean that fragmentation is bad from a social point of view.

4.6.2 Costs

The innovation and competition associated with fragmentation can lead to cost savings. Bradley (American Century) informed the SBC (2000) that their use of ATSs and other electronic trading technology had saved American Century (a US mutual and pension fund manager) $110 million per year for the last 10 years. However, fragmentation can also lead to an increase in some costs. These include the extra costs of running the rival trading systems and the costs of linking them together. Systems for the linkage of trading systems are considered in section 6.2.1, and they inevitably have operating costs. In addition there is the cost of inter-trading system arbitrage, and the cost of unnecessary dealer intervention, e.g. when customer orders interact only indirectly via dealers

(Mendelson and Peake, 1994). However, on balance it appears that the cost savings greatly outweigh the extra costs.

4.6.3   Reduced order flow to existing trading systems?

It appears to be generally accepted that, in the absence of good links between the various trading systems (which are discussed in section 6.2.1), fragmentation tends to reduce the network benefits, with the same order flow being spread across more trading systems. However, this need not be the case as a new trading system may create additional order flow, such that order flow to the old trading systems is not reduced. This may be for a variety of reasons, e.g. arbitrage trades between the two trading systems, the new trading system has a trading process which differs from that previously available and this attracts new business, the new trading system is in a different time zone which generates additional orders, etc. Pagano and Steil (1996) summarised the empirical evidence of the effect of Italian and Belgian stocks being traded in London on SEAQ-I which finds that trading volume in Italy and Belgium *increased* when SEAQ-I began competing with these European exchanges.

4.6.4   Price matching

Fragmentation facilitates various practices that have been controversial in the USA – price matching (or 'step up and match') and the associated behaviour of internalisation, payment for order flow and preferencing. The first priority rule used by trading systems for matching orders is invariably 'price', and this is often reinforced by a regulatory requirement for 'best execution'. The second priority rule for use when two or more orders or quotes are at the same price is usually time priority. These rules provide a strong incentive for traders to improve the current best prices by placing new limit orders or quotes at improved prices because this behaviour guarantees them priority, and this stimulates the price process. Price matching can occur when time priority is not enforced, and traders are allowed to be the counter party to an order if they match the best price currently available. As with front running, this behaviour damages the incentive to post aggressive quotes or limit orders, and may lead to a widening of the bid–ask spread.[35]

By posting a quote or limit order a trader is, in effect, giving a free option to the market. For example, in a dealer market the market-maker's bid and ask quotes represent free put and call options, amounting to a bottom vertical combination (or bottom strangle) (Copeland and Galai, 1983). If new information arrives to move the equilibrium price, one of these options may be in-the-money. For example, if a market-maker has an ask quote of 25p, and then information arrives which justifies paying 28p, this free option is 3p in-the-money. Similarly, in a continuous auction market, a trader who places a limit order to sell at 25p when the market price is 24p is writing a free call option. The value of these free options is affected by the volatility of the share price and the speed with which the writer can cancel their limit order.

Writing free options is more costly when price matching is allowed. This is because attractive order flow will tend to be executed via price matching, while the unattractive orders will be executed against the outstanding limit orders or published quotes. In consequence, limit orders to sell (buy) are more likely to be executed only when the equilibrium price has risen (fallen). This adverse selection is to the disadvantage of those who provide quotes or limit orders, and may well lead to poorer prices being offered, to compensate for these adverse selection costs. The resulting reduction in the quality and quantity of quotes and limit orders damages price discovery and widens the bid–ask spread.

Price–time priority is enforced on individual trading systems, but not between trading systems. As Blume (University of Pennsylvania) (SEC, 2000b), has argued, this price–time priority within trading systems currently gives sufficient incentive to investors to submit limit orders, and so no regulatory action is required.[36] However, the introduction of decimal prices in the USA may make placing limit orders less attractive (SEC, 2000e). Before decimalisation, to step ahead of a limit order on the same trading system, a trader had to offer a price improvement of at least 1/16th of a dollar (or 6.25 cents). If prices can be improved by as little as 1 cent, it is much cheaper to gain price priority over a limit order, thereby reducing the incentive to post such orders.

While price matching can occur within a consolidated market, the possibilities for price matching are greater in a fragmented market because price matching can take place between trading systems.[37] While the rules of a particular trading system may require price–time priority, there may be no enforcement of time priority as between trading systems. In which case, price matching is possible only because of market fragmentation. For example, Harris (1993) points out that time priority is often not enforced across a system of related markets. The existence of price matching can mean that price discovery occurs very largely in the primary trading system, with peripheral trading systems largely price matching.

In his evidence to the SBC (2000) Paulson (Goldman Sachs) asked for price matching to be banned in the USA, as did Buck (NYSE), Peterffy *et al.* (Interactive Brokers) and Lamb *et al.* (Association for Investment Management and Research, AMIR, SEC, 2000b) in their submissions to the SEC.

Overall, secondary precedence rules need to be enforced in all markets if the negative externalities of price matching mentioned above are to be avoided. Price matching is particularly likely to occur in fragmented markets. The main proposal for achieving price–time priority across markets is a mandatory consolidated or central limit order book (CLOB), and this is considered in section 6.2.1.

Fragmented markets increase the opportunities for price matching, and such price matching may occur in a number of ways:

(a) *Internalization*
The order flow is passed to a market-maker who is under the same ownership as the broker.

(b) *Payment for order flow*
A market-maker or trading system pays a per share amount to a broker for directing its customers' orders to that market-maker or trading system.[38] The order flow to trading systems and market-makers comes via brokers, and so trading systems and market-makers need to attract brokers not the clients of brokers. Brokers route orders to the trading system or market-maker that provides *them*, not their customers, with the best deal. Hence the success of payment for order flow.

(c) *Preferencing*
This occurs when, for example, broker *A* directs their order flow for stock *X* to broker *B*, while broker *B* directs their order flow for stock *Y* to broker *A*.

In each case, execution occurs at the best publicly available price, i.e. price matching; although the concern is that the customer does not get the best price. If there is a monopoly exchange, internalisation, preferencing and payment for order flow can occur only if it is a dealer market, unless traders in an auction market are able to match orders without submitting them to the order book (as is the case on the NYSE and London Stock Exchange). However, if there is market fragmentation and multiple trading systems, internalisation, preferencing and payment for order flow can occur in both dealer and auction markets. For example, in the USA the regional exchanges offer payments to brokers who route order flow to their exchange.

Brodsky (CBOE) (SBC, 2000) is opposed to payment for order flow, although it has not become established in US options markets, Bradley *et al.* (American Century), Buck (NYSE), Richhelm (AGS Specialist Partners) and Peake (University of Northern Colorado) (all SEC, 2000b) are opposed to both internalisation and payment for order flow, while Lamb *et al.* (Association for Investment Management and Research, AMIR) (SEC, 2000b) are opposed to just internalisation.

Internalisation means there is no opportunity for price improvement as the order is filled by price matching. It has been argued by the NYSE (2000) that a consequence of internalisation is that order flow never reaches the floor of the NYSE, and this damages price discovery. This is a simplistic argument as the dealer is just an intermediary and so, instead of the customer trading on the exchange, the dealer trades these shares on the exchange (probably with a slight delay). If the trade is crossed with another offsetting order, then both demand and supply are reduced by the same amount and net demand is unchanged.

Despite the disadvantages of price matching in its various forms, it is still permitted in the USA and does have some advantages:

1 The SEC (1994) view is that fragmentation of US equity trading increased the costs to brokers of routeing small orders to the trading system currently offering the best price. The need to avoid such additional transactions costs was partly responsible for the development of the automatic routeing of orders to a pre-specified market, and the associated payment for order flow.
2 Colker (Cincinnati Stock Exchange) argued before the SBC (2000) that internalised order flow encourages broker – dealers to provide liquidity to their customers. Thus, at the current best available quotes, the market is very deep as price matching will occur. If price matching were banned, very few orders would be executed against the small number of orders at the best available price, and subsequent orders would move up the queue to be executed at inferior prices, Miller (Orrick, Herrington and Sutcliffe) (SEC, 2000b).
3 When the order flow is routed to a particular market-maker the execution will be speedy and certain, allowing the customer to be sure of execution at the stated price.
4 Levin (NexTrade) (SEC, 2000b) argued that payment for order flow enables new trading systems to build volume on their systems. In effect, it is a price discount that helps increase the network effects of new trading systems, and may be an important part of the competitive process in an industry with network effects (as suggested in section 4.4.3).

Thus, price matching increases market liquidity, depth and speed of execution, and, since transactions costs are reduced, may well lead to cheaper net costs for customers. It also facilitates the contestability of securities markets.

Some US market participants wish to see internalisation permitted only when the customer is offered an improvement on the best available price, e.g. Grasso (NYSE) and Bachmann (Edward Jones Investments) in their evidence to the SBC (2000). However, as Downey (Interactive Brokers) (SBC, 2000) pointed out, requiring price improvement breaches pre-trade transparency (the trade is executed at a price that was not previously disseminated).

The problems of internalisation, payment for order flow and preferencing can be addressed by removing the principal–agent problem inherent in brokers deciding where to route customer orders. Screen-based trading and a well-developed information system displaying the current dealer quotes and limit orders could permit customers to route their own order flow. Such disintermediation would largely end the role of brokers. For example, the NYSE now offers both 'XPress routeing' and 'NYSe Direct'. The former allows institutions to route orders for 15,000 + shares anonymously to the NYSE SuperDot system, while the latter permits customers to submit limit orders via the internet for 1,099 shares or less to the NYSE. The NYSE (2000) expressed the hope that most member firms will empower their informed customers to make their own routeing decisions.

4.6.5   Categorisation of the order flow

The order flow for a particular security is not homogeneous and differs in various ways, e.g. size, immediacy, informed–uninformed, etc. These differences mean that the costs of executing these trades also differ, e.g. trading with an informed customer will, on average, be more expensive than trading with an uninformed customer. Small retail traders are seen as uninformed, and therefore, it is advantageous to attract such order flow. Previously, trading systems have allowed cross-subsidies between various types of trade. For example, Domowitz and Steil (2000) argue that small trades have subsidised large trades, wholesale trades have subsidised retail trades, and trades on the exchange 'floor' have subsidised 'upstairs' trades. However, with the recent reduction in barriers to entry, the trading of securities has become much more contestable and cross-subsidies have become unsustainable in a fragmented market.

If a particular type of trade can be provided more cheaply, new trading systems will enter the market to offer just this type of trade. Since there is no cross-subsidy in these new trading systems, they can undercut the existing trading system. Therefore all trading systems must price each type of trade in line with the costs of that type of trade. It is already observable that almost every exchange has a special mechanism for executing large orders. This is usually some form of 'upstairs' dealer system, even when the 'downstairs' market is order-driven. Trading systems are emerging which cater for just a particular type of order flow, as did the inter-dealer broker (IDB) systems in the UK equity market, and Jiway (which has only retail business). The development of specialised trading systems may run into the same objections as did the IDB systems – lack of transparency and lack of access.

An example of the development of specialised trading systems creaming off the attractive order flow is crossing networks, where there is little need for immediacy for large uninformed trades. For example, E-Crossnet is a multilateral crossing network which deals in equities from 14 European countries four times per day, and has been operating in London since 23 March 2000. It has 32 institutional members who submit their orders via Bloomberg terminals. E-Crossnet passes the matched trades to Merrill Lynch, who then execute, report and settle the trades. Trades take place at the mid-price. There are two advantages to institutional traders from using a crossing network – the transactions costs are substantially reduced, with a cost saving of about 0.5 per cent of the value of each trade, and the crossing network permits anonymous trading in size. In the first eight weeks of operation, E-Crossnet traded shares worth over £1 billion. POSIT has been operating a crossing network in the USA since 1988 and crossed 6.5 billion shares in 1999 at the mid-price. It has over 500 institutional and other clients, and matches orders seven times per day. In 1991 the NYSE initiated two after-hours crossing sessions for institutional investors.

Crossing networks are clearly highly attractive to institutional traders owing to their very low transactions costs and anonymity. Such networks remove a substantial part of the order flow from the main market. Since these trades are very probably informationless, this fragmentation of the order flow should not do much damage to price formation, although it will mean a considerable reduction in revenues for trading systems (unless they offer crossing services, as may SETS). Crossing networks are open only to institutional traders and so retail traders are excluded from the reduction in transactions costs.

If the order flow in securities markets is disaggregated in such a manner, some investors will get worse execution than others, e.g. wider spreads, and will be unhappy about being excluded from participating in those trading systems where spreads are tighter. However, if their trades are more costly, traders should pay a higher price. It may be difficult for regulators to distinguish between situations where a particular class of trader is excluded by a trading system on grounds of cost, and when a trading system wishes to deny a group of trades access for some other reason. However, provided the market is contestable, any exclusion of traders on grounds other than cost will create an incentive for other trading systems to enter the market and provide access for the excluded traders.

4.6.6   Price discovery

In their evidence to the SEC (SEC, 1994, A VI pp. 23–4) Instinet, Lattice Trading and the College Retirement Equities Fund argue that fragmenting a market by removing large orders from the downstairs market to an upstairs market improves price discovery. This is because it reduces the price volatility in the downstairs market that would be caused by the arrival of large orders. Accepting for the moment that this situation represents market fragmentation, the debate over the immediate publication of block trades in the UK has centred on the information content of these trades. Chapter 7 has a summary of the empirical evidence, which supports the view that these large trades are informative and that delaying their publication harms price discovery.

4.6.7   Transparency

In a fragmented market a lack of transparency (and access) may be used by a primary exchange as a way of preventing competitors from sharing in their network effects. Suppose a new trading system is established to execute large trades, and the existing exchange is left with mainly small trades. If trades on the new trading system are published with a 24-hour delay, this may have negative consequences for traders executing small trades on the old exchange who are unable to observe the price and volume information from the new trading system while it is still valuable. Thus, there could be a 'race for the bottom' in terms of transparency, particularly for large trades, as such trades move to trading systems with low transparency requirements. In which case, regulators may choose to set minimum disclosure standards for all trading systems.

As markets become global, the transparency of trading conducted overseas becomes more important. The SEC (1994) suggested that such trades be subject to domestic reporting to ensure that the transparency of the market is not circumvented. There may also be a need to ensure pre-trade transparency for foreign quotes or limit orders. When trading after hours (possibly overseas), the level of transparency may be much lower than during the trading day as the regular information sources have shut down. Again, there may be a need to ensure transparency.

The transparency systems in the USA and UK identify the best available quotes that have been entered into the various trading systems. However, they may not be the best prices that could currently be obtained by a broker for their client, e.g. the NYSE claims to offer price improvement on its published quotes. The NYSE (Buck of the NYSE, SEC, 2000b) suggested that dealers be required to publish their real quotes, i.e. the prices and size they offer to their private customer base.[39]

One study suggests there may be no need to set transparency standards for a fragmented market. In a survey of 59 large European fund managers, Schwartz and Steil (1996) found that most were content to have post-trade transparency levels set by the exchange concerned. However, large European fund managers may not be typical of all investors, and mandatory disclosure standards may be necessary.

It is generally accepted that high levels of transparency are desirable, and that if transparency is set at a low level this will result in various costs (although there is little empirical evidence to support this position). However, high levels of transparency have been argued to carry the risk of damaging the market (e.g. reducing liquidity). The extent to which greater transparency damages the market is an empirical question. Since every market can be argued to be unique in some way, it is not possible to demonstrate conclusively that greater transparency will, or will not be harmful before any such change is made. A review of the available empirical evidence reveals no documented cases of increased transparency being harmful, while Board and Sutcliffe (2000) show that the substantial increase in transparency for UK shares on 1 January 1996 had no detectable harmful effects. It should be noted that this study included stocks from the FTSE Small Cap index which have a low level of liquidity. Subsequently, when SETS was introduced in October 1997, transparency was increased further in the UK.

In a fragmented market, if one or more trading systems is permitted to offer a low level of transparency this could have a damaging effect on the price discovery process for the market. In such a situation, a key role for regulators is ensuring a high level of transparency. There is always a possible risk that high transparency could damage liquidity, but there is no empirical evidence to support this view; and a substantial quantity of evidence to the contrary, particularly for liquid securities. If a high level of transparency is not required, there is a real possibility that opaque trading systems will be established, and this will both damage price formation and create an advantage for those who are able to see the trading activity on this opaque market.[40]

It may be thought that there is a conflict between promoting both competition and transparency. Transparency might be expected to create a regulatory burden for potential entrants, so discouraging competition; but this unlikely to be the case. Indeed the contrary is likely to be the result, and transparency and competition are quite compatible. Transparency brings a range of benefits to a trading system at a fairly small cost. The requirement to publish quotes and trades may be seen as a way of publicising the quality of trading available on the new trading system. Transparency may increase confidence in the new trading system leading to higher volumes than otherwise. Information asymmetries between traders will be lowered leading to narrower bid–ask spreads, and cross-subsidies between market-makers and traders eliminated. While it is possible that some entrants may wish to run an opaque trading system so damaging the price formation process, transparency is an important aspect of market quality and should not be compromised to allow entrants to run opaque trading systems.

4.6.8   Best execution

It is easiest to ensure best execution in a consolidated auction market, as orders are just submitted to a single market. In a consolidated market with rival dealers, the performance of a broker is still reasonably easy to measure. Every rival dealer is offering the same trading characteristics, e.g. clearing and settlement system, transparency rules, anonymity, etc. because all trades go through the same trading system. The only difference between dealers for a given trade size is price. Therefore brokers simply have to identify the dealer offering the best price. When several dealers are offering the same price, the customer will be indifferent as to which dealer is chosen by their broker. However, if not all available quotes are publicly disclosed, identifying best execution can be a problem, even in a monopoly dealer market. For example, the NYSE claims to offer improvement on its publicised quotes. This is also the case for market makers under the SEAQ system in London, in which case a better price that the current best quotes may have been available, but this is hard to ascertain. There is evidence that a small percentage of US orders receive execution that is outside the national best bid and offer at the time the order is received, i.e. price disimprovement (SEC, 2000e). This may occur because of quote exhaustion (multiple orders try to hit the same quote with insufficient depth to satisfy them all), the order exceeds the size up to which market-maker quotes are firm, or because of a mistake by the broker in routeing the order.

Best execution is an ambiguous concept in a fragmented market, for two reasons. First, the identity of the lowest cost trading system (i.e the price of the trade, net of all transactions costs) may differ between traders. For example, the main costs for a retail investor may be commission and bid–ask spread, while the main element of cost for an institutional investor may be market impact. Therefore the lowest cost trading system may differ as between traders. Second, some traders may desire anonymity, immediacy, etc. rather than the best price. Again, best execution differs as between traders. Without a detailed knowledge of the trader's transactions costs and preferences, it is not possible to determine whether a broker has obtained best execution for their client.

If brokers receive payment for order flow, they may route orders to trading systems other than those offering the best deal. The use of brokers creates an agency problem between client and broker, and this may mean that 'best execution' does not occur, and that the trading systems are not well linked. The client's protection is the requirement for best execution, but this is difficult to measure and enforce. The more the market fragments, the more difficult it becomes to define and enforce best execution. Some market participants argue that best execution in the USA is viewed in aggregate, rather than looking at each individual order or each customer (Downey (Interactive Brokers), SBC, 2000; Peterffy *et al.* (Interactive Brokers), SEC, 2000b). In which case, particular orders may receive poor execution, provided that, on average, customers receive 'best execution'. Peterffy *et al.* (Interactive Brokers) (SEC, 2000b) argue that an individualistic view should be taken of best execution.

Market fragmentation increases the importance of supplying the customer with sufficient information for them to be able to judge the quality of the execution they have received. Since brokers receiving payment for order flow are able to offer lower commissions, they may attract order flow, even though they are not getting good prices for their customers. Levitt (SEC) (SBC, 2000) argued that, if customers could not measure the quality of the execution they received, they might select brokers purely on the basis of commission rates. This blunts the forces of competition. The SEC (1994) proposed increasing the information available to US investors, including the disclosure of any payment for order flow. This view was supported by Pasternak in his evidence to the SBC (2000) and has recently been implemented by the SEC (see Chapter 6).

4.6.9   Regulation and supervision

The fragmentation of a market has a number of very important implications for the nature of regulation and the role of regulators:

1   *Regulatory arbitrage.* Under the ISD a regulated exchange in any EU country has a 'single passport' and can operate in any EU country while being regulated in its home country. A likely outcome in a fragmented market is that rival exchanges will be based in different countries, and so operate under different sets of rules. For example, Dorsch (Derivatives Net Inc) cautioned the SBC (2000) that, unlike physical exchanges, ATSs are internationally footloose, and can easily relocate to a more sympathetic jurisdiction. In addition, fragmentation of trading between exchanges and non-exchanges means that there are two sets of regulations governing trading in the same security in the same country. The development of rival trading systems in different jurisdictions, and rival trading systems in the same country subject to different regulations, offers the possibility of regulatory arbitrage. For example, there are suggestions that some European stock exchanges have waived their listing requirements to attract particular companies. However, there is some evidence that this need not lead to a 'race for the bottom', e.g. the desire to have iX regulated in London because the UK regulatory system gives confidence to users of the exchange; coupled with a desire for trading to be subject to a single regulatory system. Thus, it is possible that, while markets may fragment, regulation may consolidate (hopefully on a high-quality regulatory system).

2   *Discipline of the market.* The contestable nature of the market should restrict any abuse of market power by a monopoly exchange, as there is always the threat that a new or existing trading system will start trading the securities (or a very close substitute) presently traded only on a single exchange. Similarly, in a fragmented market, if a trading system introduces unwelcome trading rules customers have the option of voting with their feet and moving their order flow to a different trading system. Even if two trading systems are not trading exactly the same security, there may be competition between trading systems when the degree of substitution between securities is very high, e.g. bond trading on one trading system may be a very close substitute for different bonds traded on another trading system. As competition between trading systems increases, the nature of regulatory intervention changes. There is a decrease in the need to control

the conduct of individual trading systems, but an increase in the need to ensure that there is a level playing field, e.g. setting transparency and access standards. This idea is considered further in section 6.3.2.

3 *Compliance.* Securities markets require someone to look out for insider trading and market manipulation. Individual exchanges in a fragmented market have less incentive to spend money on these activities than a single exchange because these activities generate a public good which benefits all trading systems, while the costs fall only on those exchanges who look for such abuses. In addition, in a fragmented system, spotting such behaviour probably requires information from several trading systems. Therefore, responsibility for preventing market abuse is best placed with the regulators. This view is reinforced by the arguments of Pirrong (1995) that self-regulation of manipulation by exchanges will not work.

4 *Price stabilisation.* Specialists on the NYSE are charged with price stabilisation, in return for being given various privileges. However, in a fragmented market such a public good may cease to be provided. The UK has not placed any such obligations on market-makers, and so will not suffer the loss of this service.

5 *Supervise competitors.* In a fragmented market, the recognised exchanges end up supervising the ATSs, and this puts the ATSs in a very uncomfortable position (Putnam (Archipelago), SBC, 1999). Therefore, Archipelago is applying to be an exchange and escape supervision by the National Association of Securities Dealers (NASD).[41] This may become an increasingly important issue as competition 'hots up' in securities markets, and it is difficult to justify one profit maximising firm supervising another profit maximising firm with whom they are competing.

6 *Manipulation.* Manipulation (e.g. corners and squeezes) can be a problem for markets with a limited supply of the underlying asset, e.g. crude oil, natural gas, gas oil, aluminium, aluminium alloy, zinc, lead, nickel, copper, tin, silver, wheat, sugar, cocoa, coffee, barley and potatoes.[42] In principle there is a fixed supply of the shares in any particular company and in any issue of bonds, but, given the current regulations, cornering and squeezing equity and bond markets has generally not been a problem.[43] While futures and options contracts are in unlimited supply, manipulation of the underlying spot market can affect the related derivatives markets, particularly where there is physical delivery. Exchanges with physical delivery are vulnerable to corners and squeezes, while cash settled contracts are vulnerable to manipulation of the Exchange Delivery Settlement Price (EDSP). Manipulation in markets where there is no physical asset often

involves manipulating trading to give a false impression of the underlying supply or demand. Markets have developed trade reporting systems as a way of monitoring attempts at market manipulation.

If there is physical delivery, traders with a short position are obliged to produce the requisite quantity of the underlying asset at delivery, irrespective of the price. If a trader owns most of the available supplies of the physical asset and refuses to sell, holders of short positions in derivatives who do not themselves own the underlying asset must bid up prices to obtain the supplies they require to meet their contractual obligations under the derivatives contract. To ensure there are plenty of short positions, a manipulator will establish large long positions in the futures and call options markets. In markets where the value of the underlying asset available for sale is very large, corners and squeezes are much more difficult. Thus the market in US Treasury bonds is very unlikely to be cornered or squeezed. However, some metals and soft commodities are vulnerable to such tactics.

While index futures or options cannot be cornered or squeezed because they are cash settled, there have been allegations that the value of the index has been altered by share trading (or quote alteration) at the time the EDSP is computed. The main beneficiaries of such behaviour are those with large positions (short or long) in the futures or options markets in the appropriate direction.

In view of these potential dangers for derivatives with both physical and cash settlement, it may be sensible for traders with 'large' positions in a particular contract month (spot, futures, options and OTC markets combined) to be required to report them to the regulatory authorities.[44] A 'large' position can be defined with respect to the available supplies of the underlying asset, and so a modest number of contracts may be reportable for an obscure metal, but would be a long way short of the threshold for most interest rate products. It may also be sensible for regulators to have the power to require traders to unwind large positions if this is judged to be having an adverse effect on the market. Provided the threshold for reportable positions is high, very little reporting will actually take place, so minimising the regulatory burden.

If the same reporting requirement were to be applied to all markets, it is likely that reportable positions would arise much more often in some markets than in others, e.g. small illiquid markets, and markets with just a few large traders who between them control most of the supplies of the underlying asset and most of the open interest in the derivative markets. It is suggested that reporting be required in markets where manipulation looks unlikely because attempted manipulation is always a possibility, and on a number of occasions very large positions have been associated with other problems in which there is a regulatory interest, e.g. Sumitomo, Codelco, Metallgesellschaft and Barings.

7 *Insider trading.* Some assets are more susceptible to insider trading than others. For example, there may be substantial inside information about equities, while that relating to interest rates is limited to a small group, e.g. the members of the Monetary Policy Committee (MPC) and civil servants. For some securities, inside information is even harder to obtain, e.g. stock market indices or futures on a pair of floating exchange rates. For annual crops, inside information is also rare, but can occur in the form of government crop forecasts (as featured in the film *Trading Places*). However, there is no reason why the same rules on inside trading should not be applied to all types of asset, with the rules biting more in some markets than others.

4.6.10 Price data

Mulherin, Netter and Overdahl (1991) argue that trading systems produce prices, and have established legal rights to the ownership of these prices.[45] This trade and quote information can be sold by the trading system to interested parties.

In the USA, the system is that an agent collects and distributes the consolidated trade data from all trading systems for a specified group of securities, e.g. the NYSE and the Securities Industry Automation Corporation (SIAC) perform this function for NYSE listed stocks, NASDAQ for NASDAQ stocks, and the Options Price Reporting Authority (OPRA), SIAC and CBOE for exchange listed options. In each case the net revenues from selling the consolidated data are shared between the contributing exchanges in proportion to their volume. The consolidated data is sold to data vendors, who may add value to the data before they sell it to users. Alternatively the consolidated data may be sold direct to subscribers. As shown in Table 4.2 (p. 55), in 1998 US exchanges derived 21 per cent of their total revenues ($411 million out of $1,970 million) from the sale of data, SEC (1999).

Levitt (SEC) informed the SBC (2000) that transparency may be threatened if exchanges charge high prices for access to their price and quote information, and that the US Congress had decided that such fees must be reasonable. The SEC regulates the prices which can be charged for the consolidated data, and ensures that they are roughly in line with the costs of providing this information. Since transparency is important in a fragmented market, regulators may need to control the prices which trading systems are able to charge for price and trade information see section 6.2.2.

If the market fragments with several trading systems generating price data, this may have a negative effect on the value of the price information generated by the primary trading system, as they are no longer monopoly suppliers. The SEC (1999) pointed out that the value of a trading system's trade and quote data is related to the quality of the price discovery performed by the trading system. For example, if the trading system sometimes ceases trading owing to technical problems, or its prices are tainted by fears of manipulation, this information will be worth less than if the trading system did not have these problems. However, if consolidated data from all trading systems is produced, with net revenues shared according to volume (as in the USA), a particular trading system may simply seek to maximise their volume.

4.6.11   The dynamics of fragmentation

Economists tend to think in terms of comparative statics, i.e. one long-run equilibrium versus another long-run equilibrium. However, the long-run equilibrium will never be reached, and the dynamics of how the system moves in response to a change may be important to policy-makers. In his evidence to the SBC (2000), Greenspan of the Federal Reserve Board suggested that the fragmentation of markets (following the earlier move towards the consolidation of markets) may only be temporary as competitive pressures foster the consolidation of liquidity. This leads to a cycle of competition, fragmentation and then consolidation.

The process of fragmenting a market may lead to a range of short-run problems:

1   During the fragmentation process there is a danger of many new trading systems entering the market, some of which may then experience financial distress, and possibly liquidation. During this process the proper functioning of the failing trading systems may be compromised, e.g. some regulations may cease to be applied. While the clearing house system has been developed to mitigate counterparty risk (particularly for derivatives exchanges), less attention has been given to 'trading system risk'.

2   The creation of many new trading systems (or existing trading systems entering new markets) is argued to reduce the order flow to each trading system, possibly to unsustainably low levels. If these trading

systems are linked together well (see section 6.2.1), what matters is aggregate liquidity in the market, and not the order flow to any particular trading system. However, at least initially, it is possible that such links may not function well, leading to a reduction in the liquidity available to investors. Indeed, a dominant trading system has an incentive to block the creation of any such links as the greater liquidity of the large trading system gives them a strong competitive advantage.

3 As a new trading system succeeds in taking order flow away from existing trading systems, there may be 'tipping', where the order flow suddenly tips from one trading system to another (e.g. bund trading on LIFFE rapidly shifting to the DTB). The successful trading system may initially have insufficient capacity to handle such a surge in order flow, and offer poor execution until capacity can be increased.

4.6.12 National exchange

Fragmentation permits every country to have a national stock and derivatives exchange, while consolidation may not result in such an outcome. The Swiss Stock Exchange has moved the trading of blue chip Swiss stocks to London; the Scandinavian exchanges have formed Norex, Belgium, France and the Netherlands have merged their stock exchanges, the Spanish and Italian stock exchanges wished to join iX, and the New Zealand stock exchange was contemplating a merger with the Australian stock exchange. While a country's firms need access to a healthy stock exchange on which to raise capital, there is no particular advantage in having a national stock exchange.

4.6.13 Measured volume

The fragmentation of a market can lead to an increase in the reported trade volume, purely because traders in one trading system are offsetting their positions on another. In addition, fragmentation may generate arbitrage trading between the various rival trading systems, and this will raise total volume.

4.6.14 Theoretical models of the effects of fragmentation

A number of papers have examined the effects of fragmentation on the bid–ask spread and price volatility. Biais (1993) concludes from his theoretical model that bid–ask quotes and spreads are the same in both consolidated and fragmented markets, and that the bid–ask spread is more volatile in a consolidated market. Madhavan (1995) finds from his model that, if there is less than full transparency, a fragmented market need not consolidate, and that fragmentation leads to increased price volatility (because only a varying sub-set of the information is impounded into each price). Hagerty and McDonald (1996) found that increased fragmentation (brokers acting as the counterparty for their clients) gives better prices to some customers, and no worse prices in the primary market. The conclusions of these theoretical papers depend crucially on the specification of the model. Chowdhry and Nanda (1991) conclude that fragmentation will lead to large orders being broken up and submitted as small orders to many trading systems to reduce the price impact. This will create positive correlation in the volume of the order flow across trading systems. They also argue that trading will tend to consolidate on one trading system. If information is valuable for more than one time period, Chowdhry and Nanda show that market-makers on each trading system will choose to publicise the information content of the order flow to other trading systems. This is to deter informed traders from initially exploiting their information on that trading system by reducing their profits from subsequently exploiting this information on other trading systems.

Notes

1   In the USA in 1850 there were 250 stock exchanges, Macey and O'Hara (1999b).
2   A *proper* market is when there are adequate forces of supply and demand, effective means of settlement and availability of adequate information (FSA, 2000a).
3   Lisbon joined Euronext on 6 February 2002.
4   The proposal was for iX to constitute five exchanges – pan European blue chips, pan European high growth, domestic UK, domestic German and the AIM. The Italian and Spanish stock markets expressed a desire to join iX in 2001.
5   In September 2000, LIFFE proposed to the London Stock Exchange that they link their trading systems, although the London Stock Exchange rejected this suggestion, while in October 2000 the Tokyo Stock Exchange and the CME agreed an alliance which could lead to the interconnection of their trading systems.
6   It is also worth stressing that most existing exchanges are switching to screen-based trading (e.g. London Stock Exchange, LIFFE, MATIF).
7   LIFFE began trading futures on 15 individual shares from Finland, France, Germany, Netherlands, UK, USA on 29th January 2001. This trading uses a single rule book, regulatory regime and settlement and clearing system, although there are three different currencies.
8   From May 2001, the London Stock Exchange has offered trading in 111 European and US stocks listed on 10 different exchanges as part of its International Retail Service.

9   In May 2000 the FSA took over the role of listing authority from the London Stock Exchange.

10 Instinet continuous order matching system, Instinet crossing network, POSIT (Portfolio System for Institutional Trades) and the Arizona Stock Exchange call auction.

11 Market-makers and specialists were required to inform the market of any better quotes they had placed on an ATS. This could be accomplished either by improving their quotes displayed on the exchange, or the ATS concerned could provide the information to the relevant exchange for public display. Note that this did not mean that all orders placed on an ATS are displayed to the market.

12 The fact that Instinet trades as a broker not an exchange is often claimed as evidence that ATSs do not really threaten exchanges. However, Instinet's continuance as a broker is a matter of choice and it is naive to suggest they are not able to exploit their position as a major threat to NASDAQ.

13 Regulation ATS also requires ATSs with 5 per cent or more of the volume in a security to publicly display their quotes for exchange-listed and NASDAQ securities, and to allow members of the registered exchanges to hit these quotes. ATSs with 20 per cent or more were required not to unfairly deny investors access to their systems, and to meet various capacity and security standards.

14 The UK also has service companies, which carry out various functions including order entry, order routeing, post-trade matching, trade allocation and settlement instructions.

15 For example, the Chicago Stock Exchange cannot change their fee for processing member ID badges without first submitting it to the SEC, Robert Forney (Chicago Stock Exchange) (SBC, 2000).

16 Therefore, OTC trading in the shares of company X, and its close substitutes, constitutes part of the market.

17 A number of the witnesses before the SBC (2000) supported longer trading hours for US markets, (Charles Schwab (Schwab), Alan Wheat (CSFB) and Frank Zarb (NASD)).

18 An order for 1,400,000 shares was chopped up into over 600 orders which were then submitted over a 10-minute period at the rate of one order per second, Steve Wunsch (Arizona Stock Exchange) (SEC, 2000b).

19 This is an empirical question on which there appears to be no evidence.

20 If two trading systems agree to link their networks this constitutes an implicit merger and is considered in section 4.5.7.

21 The current UK solution to this lack of competition in such network industries is periodic competitive tendering for the franchise to operate the network for a fixed period, coupled with regulation during the period of the franchise.

22 For an explanation of the economics of network industries see Shy (2001).

23 While many authors call these benefits network *externalities*, Liebowitz and Margolis (1994) point out that they are externalities only if they remain untraded. Since traders can be excluded from the network by the trading system, these benefits can be priced in the various fees changed to users by the trading system. Therefore these benefits will be called *effects*, not externalities.

24 However, these network effects are minimal in some network industries, e.g. water, gas and electricity, and may be negative in some, e.g. railways, where congestion can occur.

25 A buy order is more likely to execute at a good price, the larger is the flow of sell orders to the trading system; while a buy order is less likely to execute, the larger is the flow of other buy orders. So orders on the same side of the market create a negative effect. However, while there may be short-term variations in the size and direction of the net order flow; without a reasonable expectation of execution, traders are unlikely to continue submitting orders to a trading system. Thus buy and sell orders are joint inputs, and a trading system with a large imbalance between the volume of buy and sell orders is unlikely to prosper.

26 There may be network effects from the trading of share A for traders in share B. On a floor or open outcry trading system, it is possible for traders to rapidly move between the markets in different securities, and this has a number of benefits. However, moving between trading systems is more difficult. With screen-based trading it is possible to move with the same ease between markets in different securities and between trading systems. Thus there might be some network benefits from trading other securities on the same trading system for physical trading systems, but less so for screen-based trading systems. Di Noia (1999) argues that the liquidity of firm A which is traded on a trading system is increased if many other firms are also traded on the same system. This may be due to the trading system attracting many intermediaries, greater investor knowledge of the firm and the quality signal of being traded on such a system. The evidence of the large number of co-operative agreements in the last few years between trading systems trading related but different securities supports this view (see Domowitz and Steil, 2000, for a list of such agreements), although there are other reasons for such agreements and these are considered in section 4.5.7.

27 A related empirical question is the ease with which traders can switch their business to new trading systems. What are the costs (fixed and variable) of using a new trading system? How much switching goes on?

28 A Pareto inferior situation exists when it is possible to make at least one person better off without making anyone else worse off.

29 There are a few agreements which make identical contracts traded on different trading systems fungible, e.g. in 1984 the CME and Simex (now the Singapore Exchange, SGX) agreed to trade Eurodollar futures (and subsequently Euroyen futures) on both exchanges and to allow mutual offset, the Japanese Government Bond (JGB) is traded on both LIFFE and in Tokyo, and Brent crude futures are traded on the IPE and SGX).

30 Mulherin, Netter and Overdahl (1991) argue that rules against off-exchange trading are to minimise transactions costs, rather than to create a monopoly. As well as discouraging off-exchange trading, exchanges also have rules which make it hard to delist securities. NYSE rule 500 required that at least two-thirds of the shareholders of an NYSE listed stock vote in favour of the decision to list on another exchange, with not more that 10 per cent of the shareholders opposing this decision. This rule was amended on 21 July 1999 to allow delisting on the approval of the company's audit committee and board of directors.

31 As Demarchi and Foucault (1998) point out, most trading systems offer different trading rules for different securities, depending on the liquidity of the security; as well as different rules for different-sized trades.

32 As well as creating the three new types of exchange, the CFTC has announced that the OTC swaps market will be allowed to trade standard contracts which will be cleared and fungible. This makes OTC swaps very similar to futures, although swaps are not regulated by the CFTC. The creation of exempt MTEFs means that the same instruments traded among the same participants have the same oversight, Dennis Dutterer (President and CEO of the CBOT) (CFTC, 2000c, p. 82).

33 However, the existence of large network effects also creates a barrier to entry which prevents new trading systems from entering the market, unless new trading systems are able to enter with a large number of trades or plug into some existing network.

34 Stephen Wilson (Virt-x) has pointed out that fragmentation and competition are not synonymous – a market can be fragmented, but the participants are not competing.

35 Trade crossing by brokers also violates time precedence.

36 A recent survey by the SEC (2000c) has found that limit orders constitute two-thirds of all orders on the NYSE and NASDAQ.

37 The move to decimal pricing of US equities will allow smaller price improvements, and this may reduce the extent of price matching as the cost of offing a price improvement will be lower.

38 The recent move to a tick size of 1 cent for US equities traded on NASADQ and the NYSE has resulted in a substantial narrowing of the bid–ask spread and a reduction in order size, (John Labate, *Financial Times*, 28th June 2001). In consequence market-makers have less revenue from which to make payments for order flow.

39 There is evidence for the UK that some market-makers engage in fair weather market-making, and appear willing to offer better prices to their favoured customers (Board, Sutcliffe and Vila, 2000).

40 In essence, a group of traders forms their own private club where they can see both the trading information generated by their fellow club members, and trading information from the transparent trading systems used by everyone else. As a result, club members are better informed than non-club members, and make profits at the expense of non-club members. Such behaviour could be interpreted as a cartel against the public interest, and it is not surprising that members are very keen to preserve such non-transparent clubs.

41 Island and NexTrade have also applied to become exchanges, SEC (2000d).

42 There have been claims of market manipulation in silver, copper, zinc, nickel, aluminium and natural gas.

43 For example, in the UK any stake of 3 per cent and above in the shares of a company must be disclosed, while a stake of 30 per cent and above triggers an offer for the remaining shares. The CFTC reported in October 1999 that they had encountered only two minor cases of attempted manipulation of financial futures in the last 20 years.

44 Since it is proposed that a reportable position be defined with respect to a trader's net position across all trading systems and instruments; the

appropriate person to receive and monitor these reports is the regulator, rather than the various exchanges.

45   A US Supreme Court decision in 1991 (*Feist Publications, Inc.* v. *Rural Telephone Service Co., Inc.*) cast doubt on whether market data can be owned. In response, the US exchanges have been advocating legislation that would grant them property rights over market information, e.g. Richard Bernard (NYSE) and Richard Ketchum (NASDAQ) (CFS, 2001b). Carrie Dwyer (Charles Schwab) argued that no-one has ownership of the market data because 'the facts' are created by the investors and broker–dealers, not the trading systems, and that exchanges should not be granted ownership rights (CFS, 2001a). A similar point was made by Hardy Callcott (Charles Schwab), Cameron Smith (Island) and Marc Lackritz (Securities Industries Association) (CFS, 2001b). However, they did not propose that exchanges be required to supply such data for free; merely that new legislation should not be enacted to grant them property rights over such information.

5
Evidence on Trading Mechanisms

Owain ap Gwilym
University of Southampton

This chapter is divided into three main sections. Section 5.1 addresses the question of whether the FSA should require trading systems to use a particular trading mechanism (e.g. dealer or auction, floor or screen); or ban the use of specified trading mechanisms. In particular, it investigates whether different assets or types of client require different trading mechanisms. If this is the case, the FSA might require that a specified trading mechanism be used (or banned) for trading certain types of asset, or for trading by particular types of client. Apart from some empirical evidence on floor versus screen, this section is largely theoretic. The answers to these questions have implications for the issue of fragmentation because rival systems trading the same security may be using different trading mechanisms. Such differences in trading mechanism may cause variations in the quality of trading services provided in parts of a fragmented market.

One specific issue concerns the effect of the choice of trading mechanism on the bid–ask spread; and section 5.2 examines this question. The theoretical determinants of the bid–ask spread are presented; followed by a consideration of the effects of preferencing, internalisation and collusion on the bid–ask spread. The empirical evidence on the effects of different trading mechanisms on the bid–ask spread is then summarised. These empirical studies have not used the same securities traded on different systems, but samples of similar securities traded on different trading systems. Finally, the empirical evidence on intra-day patterns in the bid–ask spread on different trading mechanisms is discussed.

Section 5.3 of this chapter goes on to consider the empirical evidence on fragmented trading. If trading in a security is fragmented across two or more exchanges, the security is cross-listed. Such securities present a direct way to study the effects of fragmentation on various aspects of market quality, e.g. bid–ask spreads, liquidity, volume, volatility, price discovery. This section summarises the available evidence on cross-listed futures and equities.

5.1 Trading mechanisms

The aim of this section is twofold. First, we review the theoretical and empirical evidence on the design of optimal trading mechanisms for financial assets and commodities. Secondly, we investigate whether there is any evidence that some trading mechanisms are more suitable than others for different products or trade types. The academic literature recognises that market structure influences price formation. However, in anticipation of our conclusions, we find that this literature does not provide unequivocal evidence for the superiority of any particular trading mechanism and thus does not justify any prescriptive regulatory influence in this regard.

Madhavan (2000) briefly surveys the relevant academic literature with particular focus on the implication of market structure upon measures of market quality such as spreads, liquidity and volatility. There is a particular emphasis in the literature on the debates surrounding floor versus electronic trading and auction versus dealer systems, and this section is primarily structured around these two themes. In practice, there is a wide divergence in trading systems ranging from automated limit order book systems which offer continuous trading with high levels of transparency, to markets (e.g. in foreign exchange) which are heavily reliant on dealers and offer very little transparency.

Madhavan (2000) questions whether such differences affect price formation and trading costs, and concludes that there is no unequivocal recommendation on what structures offer the greatest liquidity and least trading costs. The author states that 'ultimate decisions on market structure are likely to be decided by the market place on the basis of factors that have less to do with information than most economists believe' and identifies the need for automation and electronic trading to handle the increasingly high volumes of trading as a factor of utmost importance. Further, he concludes that 'what ultimately matters is not the medium of communication between the investor and the market but the protocols that translate that order into a realized transaction'.

5.1.1 Auction (order driven) versus dealer (quote driven) systems

Madhavan (2000) notes that both theory and supporting empirical evidence suggest that periodic multilateral trading systems (e.g. single-price call auctions) can be efficient mechanisms, particularly in situations where there is a large degree of uncertainty over fundamentals and market failure is a possibility. However, trading is far more commonly organised around continuous bilateral (or dealer) systems. The demand for this type of trading is possibly surprising given its reliance on dealers to supply liquidity (discussed later).

Within the class of continuous trading systems, there is a choice between auction and dealer systems. Briefly, a dealer market consists of market-maker(s) (either a single dealer with market power or competing multiple dealers) who post bid and ask quotes at which they are ready to buy and sell. In an auction market, orders must wait to be matched with each other, meaning that prices are established from the incoming buy and sell orders.

There are the following important differences between these systems:

- *Information asymmetry* is more of a problem in dealer markets. In an auction market, all traders can see orders arrive, whereas in a dealer market each dealer sees only their own order flow (until the trades are published). Dealers will require compensation for their lower level of information.
- *Execution risk* refers to the possibility that prices may move between the time an order is initiated and executed, and this risk is greater in auction markets. In a dealer market, the trader should achieve the price as quoted by the market-maker, but in an auction market the trade price depends on the random order flow from other traders.

Tonks (1996) notes the following. In dealer markets, liquidity is supplied by the authorised market-makers who typically provide competing price quotes. In auction markets, any trader can supply liquidity by submitting a limit order. In both cases, investors should face a competitive price schedule, which ultimately should ensure that liquidity traders do not earn excess profits. Tonks (1996) also argues that there is no fundamental difference between screen-based auction and screen-based dealer trading systems, because both result in the same set of equilibrium prices.

Madhavan (2000) identifies the dealer puzzle whereby, although pure limit order books are feasible in most settings, many markets (e.g. foreign exchange) rely upon dealers as intermediaries. The puzzle consists of two related questions: what functions do these dealers provide that make their presence valuable; and why cannot auction markets provide the same functions? These issues are now discussed in turn.

Among the key functions of dealers are price discovery, provision of liquidity (immediacy) and continuity, and price stabilisation. Competition between dealers can also generate positive outcomes. First, given a fixed number of market participants, inter-dealer trading reduces bid–ask spreads by allowing dealers to move towards desired inventory positions (see Reiss and Werner, 1998). Secondly, dealers will typically be competitive on only one side of the market, with the consequence that actual market spreads will be narrower than quoted spreads.

In an auction market, all orders can be viewed as limit orders. Market orders are limit orders where the limit prices are based on the prevailing bid or ask prices as relevant. The literature on limit orders has identified a basic trade-off whereby the limit order trader's expected profit (loss) depends on whether the trade initiator is uninformed (informed). In equilibrium, competition among limit order traders will fulfil existing orders. At higher prices, the probability that the limit order was initiated by an uninformed trader is lower, but the profits from executing against such a trader are higher. Further, Madhavan (2000) states that 'if there are shocks that cause changes in values, a limit order provider is offering free options to the market that can be hit if circumstances change. Consequently, the limit order trader needs to expend resources to monitor the market, a function that may be costly. It is perhaps for this reason that dealers of some form or other arise so often in auction markets.'

Madhavan (1992) takes a theoretical approach to comparing continuous dealer and continuous auction systems. If the latter is not anonymous, price competition eliminates the difference between transaction price and the expected value of the asset. However, strategic behaviour can distort prices and induce inefficiency. Pagano and Röell (1990) make a direct empirical comparison between a pure dealer (SEAQ International) system and a pure auction (Paris Bourse) system using data on French stocks traded on both. They find that the Paris exchange has both narrower spreads and is deeper. The paper also discusses various merits of each type of system.

It is often argued (e.g. Pagano and Röell, 1992) that large orders obtain a better price in dealer markets than in auction markets. An example where this could arise is if an electronic system has narrower bid–ask spreads, but is more price sensitive to large orders than an auction system. In this scenario, small orders get a better price on the auction system and large orders get a better price on the dealer system. However, some empirical evidence contradicts this.

An exception to the view that no trading system is generally superior, is the paper by Mendelson and Peake (1991). They argue that dealer systems are inappropriate for trading large blocks of very active stocks. They suggest that the example of SEAQ indicates that such systems result in fragmentation and, most importantly, a lack of transparency. They argue that order-driven systems can provide better liquidity and more efficient and economical market-making, whether the security is heavily or lightly traded.

5.1.2 Floor versus screen trading

The above discussion is also relevant to the debate on floor versus screen trading since many floor systems considered here are continuous dealer-driven systems, and most electronic systems are continuous auction systems with automated order matching.[1] As an example of the growth of electronic trading, volume on automated systems used by futures exchanges more than doubled between 1989 and 1996 (Sarkar and Tozzi, 1998). Electronic systems are increasingly viewed as a means of competing more effectively and boosting trading volumes. Further, in the USA, ATSs have made a big impact on equity markets (see McAndrews and Stefanadis, 2000 and Chapter 3 in this volume). To many, the eventual dominance of electronic trading seems inevitable (e.g. Glosten, 1994; Ross, 1992).

There are a number of key characteristics which differentiate screen-based and floor-based execution of trades, including transparency, trade publication, trading procedure, and costs:

(*a*) *Transparency*. The computer system operating a screen-based trading system contains full information on the trading process, including the price and quantities of all the bids, offers, limit orders, trades, trader identities and possibly principal identities. This potentially allows a very high degree of transparency. However, in practice, trading systems usually restrict the set of information which is publicly released. For example, Domowitz (1993) reports that only 5 per cent of screen-based systems for futures and options trading displayed personal identifiers for quotes, and no identities of traders were publicly released. However, screen-based systems typically provide information on the limit order book which is not available under floor-based systems. With floor trading, the exchange has less information on the order flow. However, the process of open outcry necessitates the availability of some information, including the price and quantity of all trades and the identity and behaviour of the floor traders involved in the bids, offers and trades.

(*b*) *Trade publication*. Because the screen trading process is automated, dissemination of trade prices and quantities can occur far more quickly than in floor-based trading. With floor trading, the information needed for recording trades and disseminating prices needs to be entered into a computer system manually, with the consequences of unmatched trades, potential errors and higher costs.

(*c*) *Trading procedure.* Screen trading can incorporate trading rules and procedures that may be difficult to implement with floor trading, e.g. the way in which orders are filled. Also, information on trading in other markets should be more easily available to a screen trader, which can be advantageous, e.g. in making futures spread trading easier to implement. Since all trading information is captured electronically under a screen-based system, out trades are prevented and erroneous trades are less common than in a floor-based system. The differences between the two forms of trading imply that different trading skills are required under the two types of system. Screen traders can be located anywhere, and this may avoid the need for brokers to maintain a presence in a given financial centre. Locating the trader in the firm's office rather than at the exchange permits the trader to be integrated into the firm's operations.

(*d*) *Costs.* For screen trading, one person can conduct the tasks which would require an office broker, floor broker and floor trader under a floor-based system. This one person will also tend to command a lower salary than a floor trader. Further, a screen trader can switch between trading a number of different securities, while a floor trader tends to remain in the same location trading the same security. A screen-based system avoids the costs of a building to house the trading floor, but requires investment in both hardware and software together with office space to accommodate screen traders and the central computer system. Introducing a new product or security (e.g. a new contract on a derivatives exchange) simply requires modification of the software on a screen-based system but requires trading space in a floor-based system.

Table 5.1 provides a useful comparison of open outcry and electronic trading.

There has been widespread recent debate in the financial press and among regulators and policy-makers regarding the relative merits of screen and floor trading. A particularly pertinent example is the success of Eurex (formerly Deutsche TerminBörse, DTB) in securing a dominant role in the trading of German bund futures via electronic trading, which is seen by many as evidence that floor-based open outcry systems are antiquated. In sub-section 5.3.1 of this chapter there is a review of the empirical evidence of LIFFE and the DTB in trading bund futures. Lower costs are frequently cited as the crucial factor giving the advantage to

Table 5.1 Open outcry and electronic trading

Item	Open outcry trading	Electronic trading
Main suppliers of liquidity	Locals	Large institutions; market-making firms
Primary costs	Upkeep and staffing of trading floor; back-office tasks	Upgrading of software and hardware; tele-communications costs
Information sources	Traders' observations of market activity	Order book; outside news sources
Operating efficiency	Large time and labour investment; potential for errors	Speed, accuracy and transparency
Possible sources of trading abuse	Lack of precise trade records; lack of anonymity in trading	Manipulation of orders prior to entry

Source: Sarkar and Tozzi (1998).

screen-based trading. The fixed costs of running an electronic traded market are lower than for floor trading (see Harris, 1990), which in a competitive environment should translate into lower trading costs. For example, in relation to the bund futures contract, Buckle and Thompson (1998) note that in 1997 the cost of a round trip on the DTB was $0.66 compared with $1.50 on LIFFE. These developments have hastened the introduction of electronic trading at LIFFE and other exchanges. Nevertheless, given the mixed evidence discussed below, the question remains whether electronic trading is really so superior that there is no future for the floor-based structure that has served the derivatives and commodities exchanges so well.

5.1.3   Theoretical comparisons of floor and screen trading

Beyond the cost arguments in favour of electronic trading, the theoretical literature highlights advantages in both floor- and screen-based trading systems. A key advantage of floor-based trading is cited as being a high level of liquidity, especially in active periods. This can be attributed to various factors, e.g. the greater willingness of locals trading on their own accounts to provide liquidity (e.g. Massimb and Phelps, 1994), and the ability of dealers to distinguish more accurately between informed and liquidity traders (Benveniste, Marcus and Wilhelm, 1992). With regard to the former, Khan and Ireland (1993) suggest that there is less activity by locals in screen-based markets because of the high set-up costs, an inability to get in and out of positions quickly, and an inability to see orders coming as they would on the floor. Benveniste, Marcus and Wilhelm, (1992) demonstrate that, under certain conditions, floor trading is superior to anonymous screen trading because it is easier to distinguish between informed and uninformed traders. A market-maker obtains this knowledge through interaction in an open outcry environment, and can use this to offer better prices to liquidity traders. This should imply that the open outcry market is more liquid, and although bid–ask spreads will be narrower, the market maker is compensated by higher volume.

The advantages of screen-based trading include low trading costs, fast order execution, fast information dissemination, anonymity, and the possibility of trading remotely and thus possibly in several markets simultaneously (e.g. Grunbichler, Longstaff and Schwartz, 1994; Harris, 1990; Massimb and Phelps, 1994; Miller, 1990; Pieptea, 1992). These factors should lead to greater liquidity. Kempf and Korn (1998) note that it could be argued that screen-based trading systems perform well under normal market conditions but not so well in periods of high volatility. In the latter case, there is a tendency (where this is possible) for traders to prefer to put business through a floor market or a broker system. One explanation is tied to the fact that most electronic systems ensure anonymity of the trader. This could be a problem during periods of high volatility when knowledge of the counterparty may be more important (see Franke and Hess, 1996). An alternative explanation may be that posting limit orders in an electronic order book provides a free option to other traders, which is especially valuable in volatile periods (Copeland and Galai, 1983). This does not apply in floor-based trading, where quotes are typically valid only 'as long as the breath is warm'.

Order books and their structure are a key factor in the differences between systems (e.g. Bollerslev and Domowitz, 1991).[2] The existence of an open limit order book tends to reduce adverse selection costs because traders acting as market-makers will have information on future order flows and can thus protect themselves. It can also be argued (Harris and Hasbrouck, 1996) that information on future order flow may reduce competition among potential liquidity suppliers and thus reduce market liquidity. The existence of a limit order book in electronic markets provides depth even in very quiet periods. However, in very busy periods, the limit order book can have the disadvantage of delays in the replacement of old quotes with new. In contrast, under open outcry, a simple hand signal is sufficient to change quotes, thus providing this system with an advantage in price discovery during fast-moving markets. This is empirically supported by Martens (1998) and others.

Massimb and Phelps (1994) discuss the trade-off between efficiency and liquidity for open outcry and electronic trading systems. They suggest greater efficiency but lower levels of liquidity under screen trading owing to less activity by locals. Also, open outcry is viewed as better suited to handle fast markets. Under electronic trading, higher trading costs in the form of wider bid–ask spreads are possibly to be expected owing to the increased uncertainty arising from the anonymity of trading. In contrast, Naidu and Rozeff (1994) present arguments supporting the view that volume and liquidity are higher under electronic trading owing to its stimulation of increased activity by liquidity traders, noise traders and information traders. Theoretical models suggest that if screen-based trading is less transparent than floor trading, there will be a disproportionate concentration of informed trading, thus increasing the adverse selection component of the bid–ask spread. However, in some liquid markets (e.g. foreign exchange) where market-makers play a less important role, the anonymity of screen trading has been viewed by some as advantageous (see Henker, 1999).

Particularly since the publication of findings of alleged collusion on NASDAQ by Christie and Schultz (1994) and Christie, Harris and Schultz (1994), regulators and policy-makers have placed increasing emphasis on questions of market transparency and the possibilities for collusive behaviour by market participants under different trading systems. Henker (1999) suggests that there is little potential for collusion among market-makers on an electronic trading system with anonymously posted prices because it is difficult to identify any agent who cheats on the colluding group. In contrast, under floor trading, the long-standing professional and personal relationships that evolve on a trading floor could induce co-operation among traders. Game theory shows that co-operation is a dominant strategy in a repeated game. There is ample opportunity for reciprocity among colluding traders and punishment for defecting ones.

Overall, there is a lack of agreement in the analytical literature relating to floor versus screen trading and the relationship between trading technology and market performance. However, in practice there has been a clear and increasing trend towards market participants favouring electronic trading, with a number of exchanges (e.g. LIFFE in 1998–2000, MATIF in June 1998, SFE in 1999, and Toronto Stock Exchange, TSE in 1997) having recently moved from trading floors to electronic systems. MATIF decided to go all electronic after a brief period of parallel floor and screen systems, during which the latter rapidly dominated trading volume.[3] Most such moves to electronic trading have followed long periods of controversy while the proponents of floor and screen trading have each argued that their preferred method offers better liquidity for investors. The next sub-section considers the empirical evidence on this issue.

5.1.4   Empirical comparisons of floor and screen trading

As suggested by Fremault and Sandmann (1995), owing to the lack of conclusive theoretical arguments, it is especially important to consider the empirical evidence on the performance of screen- versus floor-based trading systems. However, the existing evidence is found to be largely inconclusive. Comparisons between floor-and screen-based systems have typically been conducted in one of the following ways, dependent on the market setting:

1   *Comparison of screen-based trading of a given instrument on one trading system with floor trading on another*
    A heavily researched example is bund futures which were traded in both London and Frankfurt (e.g. Breedon, 1996; Breedon and Holland, 1997; Franke and Hess, 1996; Franses *et al.*, 1994; Frino, Mc Inish and Toner, 1998; Kofman and Moser, 1997; Kofman, Bouwman and Moser, 1994; Martens, 1998; Pirrong, 1996; Shyy and Lee, 1995). Detailed consideration of this literature appears in section 5.3.1 of this chapter

2   *Comparison of a financial instrument traded on the same exchange before and after a migration to electronic trading*
    Studies in this vein include Blennerhassett and Bowman (1998), Ferris, McInish and Wood (1997), Griffiths *et al.* (1998) and Naidu and Rozeff (1994). If automation reduces transaction costs, one would expect an increase in trading volume because informed traders can then profitably trade on less significant items of information (e.g. O'Hara, 1995). They are thus trading on information that has a smaller impact on price, which implies greater market efficiency. Further, a profit maximising exchange would move from floor to screen trading only if it expected to recoup the costs of implementing the new system through cutting costs on existing volume, by increasing volume, or both. The following evidence generally supports these propositions. Blennerhassett and Bowman (1998) investigate the impact of the switch from open outcry to electronic trading at the New Zealand Stock Exchange in 1991, and conclude that transaction costs declined as a result. There was an increase in the supply of liquidity as measured by the increased availability of bid and ask quotes. They also find that the proportion of trading volume transacted on-market increased significantly, and that trading shifted from Australia to the electronic

New Zealand exchange for three dual-listed stocks. Naidu and Rozeff (1994) examine the automation of the Singapore Stock Exchange in 1989, and find that this resulted in a substantial increase in trading volume for individual stocks but that bid–ask spreads and their variability increased slightly.

In contrast, Griffiths *et al.* (1998) examine data from the TSE which closed its trading floor in April 1997. They find that effective bid–ask spreads, trading volume and average trade size are generally unchanged following the introduction of electronic trading. Ferris, McInish and Wood (1997) examine the automation of trading on the Vancouver Stock Exchange and find that liquidity was not reduced relative to a comparable set of firms listed on US exchanges. Mean daily traded volume rose slightly in the post-automation period.

3 *Comparison of floor trading with (usually) after-hours screen trading of an identical instrument*

For various futures contracts traded at LIFFE, ap Gwilym (1999), ap Gwilym and Thomas (1998) and Henker (1998), report wider bid–ask spreads under after-hours APT trading than under floor trading. Chow, Lee and Shyy (1996) examine the differing trading preferences between floor and screen based systems at MATIF. Trading volume is higher on the floor, which they attribute to several factors: trade immediacy versus transaction costs, liquidity trading by locals, inertia to trade under a new mechanism, and transparency versus anonymity. They also find wider quoted and effective spreads on the screen based system.

Wang (1999) considers bid–ask spreads and market depth for the futures contracts traded on the SFE under open outcry during normal trading hours, followed by an after-hours screen trading session. During the period studied (the 1994 calendar year), the open outcry system opened at 08:30 and closed at 16:30 and was followed by the screen-based system between 16:40 and 06:00 on the following day. While controlling for news and information arrival, the paper finds that the bid–ask spread on the open outcry system was less sensitive to changes in volatilities. The results show that increased volatility caused an increase in spreads on the screen-based system that was about twice the magnitude of the corresponding change experienced in the open outcry system. Further, the condition of fast markets appeared to affect the two systems differently, and when the order arrival frequency increases spreads on the trading floor appeared to narrow, those on the screen based platform widened. The importance of adverse selection varied across the systems, with the screen-based system producing a larger adverse selection component than floor trading. This is consistent with the theoretical prediction of a disproportionate concentration of informed trading under screen systems.

Lehmann and Modest (1994) compare floor and screen traded stocks on the Tokyo Stock Exchange and find that the average trade size is larger for those traded on the screen-based system. Others have found the opposite result in different settings (e.g. Breedon and Holland, 1997 for the bund contract).

There have also been studies comparing screen trading of the same type of instrument on different exchanges (e.g. Kappi and Siivonen, 2000; Schmidt and Iversen, 1992). The objective of Kappi and Siivonen (2000) is to investigate the importance of differences in transparencies between the APT trading system at LIFFE and the automated DTB system. The results show that such differences have an impact on both bid–ask spreads and market depth, but the impact depends very much on the intensity of the information arriving in the market. In fact, the APT system is seen as the appropriate trading platform when a large amount of information arrives on the market, whereas the DTB seemed to be preferable when information arrival is relatively sparse. These results show that neither system had any *a priori* superiority with regard to liquidity, but such superiority was time-varying and dependent on market conditions. Schmidt and Iversen (1992) find that spreads vary on three competing automated systems for German stocks.

Researchers have investigated the impact of screen versus floor trading from a range of perspectives, including:[4]

- *Level of market liquidity and/or bid–ask spreads* (e.g. ap Gwilym, 1999; ap Gwilym and Thomas, 1998; Breedon and Holland, 1997; Fremault and Sandmann, 1995; Kofman and Moser, 1997; Pirrong, 1996; Shyy and Lee, 1995). As discussed in more detail below, these studies produced conflicting evidence.
- *Speed of information transmission* (e.g. ap Gwilym and Buckle, 1997; Breedon and Holland, 1997; Grunbichler, Longstaff and Schwartz 1994; Kofman and Moser, 1997; Sandmann and Fremault, 1996). There is further conflicting evidence here (discussed below).
- *Degree of market integration.* Kempf and Korn (1998) investigate the integration between the German Deutsches Aktien index (DAX) stock index and DAX futures. This market setting enables analysis of the integration between spot and futures markets for different spot market trading systems. Their main finding is that the markets are

more closely integrated when both spot and futures are screen traded. They conclude that, in order to achieve a high degree of integration between spot and futures markets, it appears preferable to trade both instruments on a screen-based system, rather than to have one floor traded and one screen traded.

- *Imitation trading* (Griffiths *et al.*, 1998). Biais, Hilton and Spatt (1995) report strong evidence from the Paris Bourse that a given type of event (trade or quote change) occurs with greater probability following an event of the same type than it does unconditionally (termed the 'diagonal effect'). They suggest three hypotheses to explain this, namely strategic order splitting, imitation trading and similar but successive reactions to the same events. Griffiths *et al.* (1998) test these hypotheses based upon TSE data. They are also able to investigate floor versus screen trading in this context by comparing securities that migrate from floor trading to screen trading with a matched set of securities that are screen traded throughout the sample period. They find stronger evidence of the 'diagonal effect' when securities are floor traded, and suggest that this is supportive of imitation trading. Because informed traders are more easily identified under floor trading, there is a greater likelihood of imitation trading.

- *Price clustering.* The importance of this issue arises from the fact that lower levels of price clustering are often associated with decreased trading costs, particularly in the form of the bid–ask spread (see Christie and Schultz, 1994; Christie, Harris and Schultz, 1994). ap Gwilym and Bennell (2000) find differing patterns of price clustering when comparing floor versus after-hours screen trading of Short Sterling interest rate futures at LIFFE. Intuitively, decreased levels of price clustering may arise on a screen-based system for several possible reasons. First, it is possible that the price and time priority rules in matching trades can offer an incentive for traders to make greater use of the full range of prices to enable submission of an order at a slightly better price, and thus jump the time priority queue in the order book. Secondly, there may be increased price competitiveness among traders, if an electronic system reduces costs. Thirdly, it could be that the electronic trading platform allows traders to refine their price resolution, i.e. the market can more easily achieve a finer price resolution owing to the greater ease of using a full range of prices on an electronic trading system compared to some floor-based systems, which are often reliant on hand signals.

- *Trader and customer surplus* (Domowitz, 1990). This paper concludes that an automated trading system performs better than floor trading with regard to price discovery, quantity determination and consumer surplus.

Here, we expand further on the first two of the above issues:

1 *Bid–ask spreads and market liquidity.* Studies of the relative bid–ask spreads on the German bund futures contract traded on the floor at LIFFE and electronically at the DTB have been inconclusive.[5] Kofman and Moser (1997) report that spreads are equal on both markets, while Pirrong (1996) reports narrower spreads on the DTB and Shyy and Lee (1995) report narrower spreads at LIFFE. This mixed evidence is partly a result of differing methodologies and sample periods (see the discussion of cross-listed securities later in section 5.3 of this chapter).

   The Nikkei Stock Average futures contract was traded on the Singapore International Monetary Exchange (SIMEX) under an open outcry system and at the Osaka Securities Exchange (OSE) under a screen-based system. Fremault and Sandmann (1995) use this setting to compare liquidity, mainly spreads and spread formation, in a floor system versus an automated system. They find that the automated trading system attracts less frequent but larger orders than the open outcry system. It is expected that depth in size in an automated system would be lower than in an open outcry system. They also find that bid–ask spreads are wider on the automated trading system compared to the open outcry system. Volatility, over short intervals of time, is found to be higher on the automated trading system and, contrary to the findings of Martens (1998) and Kappi and Siivonen (2000) for German bund futures, trading volume migrates to the automated system in times of high price volatility. Breedon and Holland (1997) suggest that in periods of market stress, orders flow to the trading system with the larger share of the market, regardless of trading platform.

2 *Information transmission.* One important context in which the empirical literature has investigated whether the type of trading system has an impact on information transmission is in analysing lead–lag relationships between cash and futures markets. In the absence of market frictions, the prices of securities and their derivatives must simultaneously reflect new information, otherwise arbitrage profits would be available. However, there are numerous market frictions which can cause prices in one market to lead or lag the other market, and one of these is the use of differing trading systems.

Differing trading systems in the cash and derivatives markets may influence any lead/lag relationship found between the two markets. If trading costs are lower in the electronic market, informed traders may trade on less significant pieces of information thus improving the price discovery process in that market and causing it to lead the floor traded market. Screen traded markets also reduce the time to process an order, route it to market and execute the trade, which could also cause an electronic traded market to lead a floor traded market. Another feature of screen traded markets which may contribute to a lead is that price information is captured and disseminated more quickly – this is particularly likely in heavy trading where observers of floor trading who report the price may fall behind the current market. In addition, traders may not know with whom they are dealing in screen traded markets and, since it has been argued (e.g. Admati and Pfleiderer, 1991; Forster and George, 1992) that informed traders prefer to trade in markets that are more opaque, this may also contribute to a lead in the electronic market.

US studies of the S&P500 index and its futures contract (Fleming, Ostoiek and Whaley, 1996; Stoll and Whaley, 1990) where both markets are floor traded find that futures lead the cash market by about 15–20 minutes. Stoll and Whaley (1990) also find a cash lead of 5 minutes. Grunbichler, Longstaff and Schwartz (1994) estimate the lead–lag relationship for the German DAX index where the stocks are floor traded and the futures trade by electronic order matching. They claim that the futures market exhibits a longer lead over the cash market compared to the US results. In contrast to Stoll and Whaley (1990), they do not find a 5-minute cash lead. However, since the later study by Fleming, Ostoiek and Whaley (1996) in a floor–floor setting reports similar results to Grunbichler, Longstaff and Schwartz's (1994) floor–screen setting, the results are inconclusive regarding the influence of the trading systems.

Shyy, Vijayraghavan and Scott-Quinn (1996) examine the lead–lag relationship of the French Compagnie des Agents de Change (CAC) index, where the cash market trades by electronic order matching whereas the futures market uses open outcry. The trading system hypothesis would thus imply a shorter futures lead or possibly a cash lead. Shyy, Vijayraghavan and Scott-Quinn (1996) find that the cash leads the futures by up to 5 minutes,[6] thus supporting the hypothesis. The paper uses quotes rather than transaction prices to remove infrequent trading effects, which is not consistent with other studies and thus the results should be viewed with caution.[7] ap Gwilym and Buckle (1997) investigate the lead–lag relationship between the Australian stock index and index futures. The ASX uses an electronic order matching system while the SFE had an open outcry trading system during the period studied.[8] The floor traded futures market was found to lead the electronic traded cash market by up to 20 minutes, in line with the above studies of the US and German markets. However the cash market is also found to lead the futures market by 5 minutes at times, thus providing weak support for the trading system hypothesis. Alternatively, the occasional spot lead could be due to traders who are informed about a particular share, rather than the index, choosing to exploit this firm-specific information directly in the spot market, rather than indirectly in the index futures market.

5.1.5 Conclusion

The academic literature recognises that market structure influences price formation. However, it does not provide unequivocal evidence for the superiority of any particular trading mechanism and thus does not justify any prescriptive regulatory influence in this regard. Further, the diversity of existing trading mechanisms are largely a product of historical developments rather than a result of different trading practices being more suited for particular products or commodities. There is no clear theoretical demonstration that certain trading mechanisms are more suitable than others for different products or trade types. The trading mechanism which is adopted when a trading system is established clearly has a first mover advantage. Exchanges with a monopoly or hegemony in a given instrument are likely to take a long time to convert to electronic trading. It is probably true that it would be advisable from a cost perspective for any new trading systems to operate screen-based order-driven trading systems, and most start-up trading systems of the past decade have been fully electronic. However, the mixed evidence presented in this chapter implies that there is no compelling motivation for every existing trading system to convert to screen trading.

5.2 Spreads

This section focuses on the behaviour of bid–ask spreads under different market structures. There is a body of empirical evidence which highlights that market structure has an important impact on bid–ask spread behaviour, e.g. in comparisons between auction and dealer systems, or between monopolistic specialist and competing market-maker structures. There is also evidence that the trading platform can influence bid–ask spread behaviour, which has been documented in the literature comparing floor versus electronic trading systems (this issue was discussed in section 5.1.2 of this chapter). This section is structured as follows: Section 5.2.1 analyses relevant theoretical models of the bid–ask spread, section 5.2.2 reviews the influence of preferencing, internalisation and collusion, section 5.2.3 discusses empirical evidence on bid–ask spread behaviour, and finally section 5.2.4 focuses on the intraday behaviour of bid–ask spreads.

5.2.1 Theoretical models of the bid–ask spread

Different trading mechanisms are likely to impact on the behaviour of the suppliers of liquidity, whether these are market-makers in a dealer market or limit order traders in an auction market (see section 5.1.1 of this chapter for further discussion of the relative merits of auction and dealer systems). The differing behaviour of liquidity suppliers is likely to impact the bidding strategy under different trading systems, which in turn is expected to generate different impacts on the components of the bid–ask spread (see below). In terms of total operational costs, auction markets are perceived to be more cost-effective than dealer markets. The former allow investors (both the public and market members) the freedom to trade against each other without the presence of an intermediary and this practice should reduce execution costs by matching market orders (orders that consume liquidity) with limit orders (orders that provide liquidity).

The theoretical literature has identified order processing costs, inventory costs and information asymmetries as the three key components which influence the size of the bid–ask spread. Order processing costs include rent, salaries and equipment. Inventory costs consist of two elements, namely price risk and the costs of financing the inventory. Price risk is the risk of movements in the security price while the securities are owned by the market-maker. The financing costs represent the opportunity cost of the funds tied up in financing the inventory, less any returns on the inventory (e.g. dividends, capital gains). As the expected holding period of the inventory lengthens, the price risk and financing costs increase; although the revenue from the inventory also increases with the holding period. The expected length of the inventory holding period decreases as the volume of trading increases and increases as the number of market-makers increases.

Amihud and Mendelson (1980) developed a model for specialists whereby spreads are widened as inventory imbalances accumulate. Ho and Macris (1985) use the collective ability of dealers to adjust inventory levels to argue that market depth is increasing in the number of dealers present on the market. This benefit, however, is achieved at a cost that is represented by wider bid–ask spreads. A multiple dealer market enhances the collective ability to absorb imbalances in inventory levels. Meanwhile, the competition provided by other dealers present on the market, who might have to manage smaller inventory levels, limits the individual power of each dealer to change the market's best bid and ask prices. In this situation, the fulfilment of large orders is facilitated, but the community of dealers will pay higher costs for carrying more inventory. Ho and Macris also argue that dealers' fixed costs (such as the opportunity costs of dealers' time) increase proportionately with the number of dealers on the market. These higher fixed and inventory costs are expected to translate into wider bid–ask spreads in dealer markets.

The final component influencing the size of the bid–ask spread consists of information asymmetries. To compensate for the risk of trading with a better informed counterparty (the adverse selection problem), a market-maker will increase the bid–ask spread (Copeland and Galai, 1983; Glosten and Milgrom, 1985). Market-makers are aware that some investors could be trading on superior information and thus increase the spread in order to offset the losses incurred from trading with these informed traders. In other words, the adverse selection component is the reward to market-makers for providing liquidity services under the possible risk of asymmetric information. Glosten (1989) argues that adverse selection can lead to cross-subsidisation between different types of trades. The market-maker is expected to make losses from trading with informed traders (who typically submit medium-sized or large trades) and tries to recover this lost revenue from small, liquidity traders.

The question arising in the current context relates to what type of market structure is most effective in protecting traders against the adverse selection problem. A possible approach to address this is to classify markets based upon whether they are auction or dealer markets, on the criteria of whether orders submitted to the market are all channelled to a single system or are submitted to individual dealers who do not necessarily share the information with others. The underlying difference between these two situations is the market participants' ability to view the order flow and the price discovery process and how they use such information to form trading strategies.

The information set of limit orders in an auction system is expected to be richer than the corresponding information sets of market-makers in dealer markets. The richer information present in an auction market is expected to deal more effectively with private information held by some traders and this should lead to reduction in the adverse selection component of the bid–ask spread. From an alternative perspective, informed traders will often prefer to trade in more opaque conditions (Admati and Pfleiderer, 1991; Forster and George, 1992).

Rock (1991) provides a further extension of this argument by using the specialist structure of the NYSE to show that the specialist has two alternatives for trading–either to take up the order himself or let it trade against the limit orders submitted to the market. This flexibility is expected to limit the specialist's losses due to adverse selection. Further, Benveniste, Marcus and Wilhelm, (1992) show how the specialist has sufficient power to provide discipline for informed traders, and this should reduce the losses suffered by specialists due to adverse selection.

It is difficult to precisely determine the impact and direction of the various types of behaviour, interactions between market participants and incentives in different market structures from a purely theoretical viewpoint. However, Biais (1993), by comparing models of a market similar to a Dutch auction (sealed bid) and a centralised auction market in the vein of Ho and Stoll (1983), shows that both have the same expected bid–ask spread, thus implying irrelevance in choice of market structure. However, the auction structure is expected to generate greater spread volatility. Viswanathan and Wang (1998) show that a risk-neutral customer would choose an auction system when the number of market makers is small and the variability of the trade size is low. The dealer system would be chosen when the number of market-makers is large and the variability of the trade size is high. Finally, these authors show that a hybrid limit-order/dealer structure, where trades whose size is lower than some exogenously fixed level are channelled to the limit order book while bigger sizes are transacted in a dealer mechanism, dominates the pure dealer system.

5.2.2 Preferencing, internalisation and collusion

A useful extension to the above arguments is provided by considering the trading practices that exist in different market structures. The practices of preferencing and internalisation have been suggested to support collusion, lead to inferior execution, and result in wider bid–ask spreads in dealer markets, relative to auction markets. Preferencing occurs where an order is directed to a market-maker who is not posting the best bid and ask prices but, because of best execution arrangements, provides an assurance that the order will be executed at the best quoted price. Under this practice, trades may be directed according to non-price considerations such as established business relationships and prearranged payments for order flow (Godek, 1996). Internalisation is an extreme case of preferencing and refers to the practice whereby a broker directs order flow to the in-house market maker. Some dealer markets allow preferencing and best execution of the order flow, and 'soft dollar' arrangements (which provide an incentive for internalisation) are not illegal.[9] In contrast, such arrangements are much less likely to materialise in auction markets unless the market is fragmented (see also Chapter 4).

These arrangements are expected to have a material impact on how market-makers deal with the adverse selection problem. Preferencing and internalisation imply that a long-term business relationship is built between traders (especially institutional investors) and the market-maker in a way that the latter should 'know their order flow' (in Huang and Stoll's, 1996 terminology). The implication is that market-makers are sufficiently familiar with their clients to be able to infer information from the order flow submitted, and hence effectively protect themselves from adverse selection.

According to Dutta and Madhavan (1997), Kandel and Marx (1997) and others, preferencing and similar arrangements are contrary to competitive behaviour since they make the order flow insensitive to quote changes. Under these circumstances, there is little incentive to engage in aggressive quote revisions since posting better quotes will not necessarily increase the order flow to the market-maker posting the best quotes. The outcomes suggested by the above authors are wider bid–ask spreads, inferior execution quality and higher market-maker profits.

Another issue for consideration is the 'free option hypothesis'. Copeland and Galai (1983) show that by posting quotes, dealers are effectively writing free options to the market. This hypothesis is assumed to be at work on dealer markets in two contrasting ways. First, if a market-maker decides against writing these free options, the operational savings could be shared by guaranteeing at least best execution and possibly improving on the best quotes, leading to better execution for preferenced order flow. Secondly, viewing the issue from a market-wide perspective, the unwillingness of dealers to make quote revisions to avoid giving free options and attracting possible negative repercussions from other market-makers, leads to less competition in quote revisions, leading to wider bid–ask spreads.

In addition, preferenced order flow can lead to better execution only if the trade occurs within the best quotes, which is normally the case when negotiation takes place. In turn, it is likely that negotiation occurs for larger orders (typically submitted by institutional investors) rather than for small orders submitted by retail investors. In line with Harris

(1993) and Grossman *et al.* (1997), this feature of dealer markets can account for the differential treatment of small and large orders. However, negotiation of prices within the spread normally incurs costs in searching for a dealer who is able to provide the best execution terms. A trader who seeks immediacy may decide in favour of preferencing his order flow (thus avoiding search costs), but the quality of execution is expected to be worse than that obtained by a patient trader willing to search for the best quote. Rhodes-Kropf (1997) shows that if price negotiation is commonplace, this will result in wide quoted spreads since dealers will expect a negotiation and subsequent price improvements from the wide spreads. This model shows that traders who cannot negotiate will be faced with wider spreads, thus leading to differential treatment of different orders on the same market.

Hansch, Naik and Viswanathan (1999) provide empirical evidence from SEAQ on preferencing and internalisation, and their impact on the quality of trade execution. They find that preferenced trades face inferior execution terms (wider spreads), but the market-makers executing the preferenced order flow do not realise larger profits. In contrast, internalised trades face narrower spreads. Importantly, they find no relationship between the extent of preferencing or internalisation and bid–ask spreads. The findings are consistent with the arguments relating to search costs and trading relationships discussed above, and do not imply any support for suggestions of collusive behaviour. Consistent with these findings, Booth *et al.* (2000) present evidence from the Helsinki Stock Exchange showing that internalised trades are subject to similar pricing practices to those for external trades, even though internalisation is perceived to be prone to manipulation and collusion.

Christie and Schultz (1994) present evidence of extreme price clustering in certain NASDAQ stocks in that odd-eighth quotes were virtually non-existent for 70 of 100 actively traded stocks. They suggest that this is not explained by Harris' (1991) negotiation hypothesis, trading activity, or other factors affecting bid–ask spreads, and raise the possibility that NASDAQ dealers implicitly colluded to maintain wide spreads. On 26 and 27 May, 1994, several US newspapers reported Christie and Schultz's (1994) results. On 27 May, dealers in several NASDAQ stocks sharply increased their use of odd-eighth quotes, and mean inside and effective spreads fell almost 50 per cent. Christie, Harris and Schultz (1994) document this abrupt change and report that virtually all dealers participated in this increased use of odd-eighth quotes.

Godek (1996) refutes the collusion hypothesis of Christie and Schultz (1994) and Christie, Harris and Schultz (1994), and argues that preference trading can explain their results. NASDAQ did not have time priority rules requiring the execution of orders with the agent who first posted the current best quote, and preferencing was allowed. Brokers and market-makers were not required to trade with the market-maker offering the best price, as long as they executed the trade at the best price. Preferencing can thus diminish the incentive to narrow the quoted spread. As the transaction occurs at the best price anyway, market-makers may routinely ignore a competitor offering an unusually good price.

Others have also challenged the collusion hypothesis. An economic explanation for the NASDAQ price clustering is proposed by Grossman *et al.* (1997) and Kleidon and Willig (1995) who suggest that market-makers will have a greater propensity to round quotations (i.e. the degree of clustering will be greater) when the economic costs of market making are higher. Grossman *et al.* (1997) suggest that the degree of clustering will depend on the balance between the costs and benefits of a finer price grid. Further discussion relevant to this issue appears in the next sub-section in relation to comparisons of spreads at NASDAQ and the NYSE.

5.2.3   Empirical evidence on bid–ask spreads

Empirical research has provided valuable insights through disentangling the various behavioural traits and incentives in different trading architectures to produce a number of specific results. Several such studies compare bid–ask spreads formed on different market structures, with a significant set of evidence based on comparisons of NASDAQ and the NYSE.

Huang and Stoll (1996) examine 175 paired securities on NASDAQ and NYSE and find that quoted spreads, effective half spreads and perfect foresight spreads are wider on NASDAQ. One possible explanation for such a result could be that NASDAQ does not protect effectively against the presence of adverse selection, in which case a wider spread must be posted by dealers. However, when Huang and Stoll computed the realised half spread (effective half spread less the price impact) they found that realised half spreads are still higher on NASDAQ compared to NYSE, and the adverse selection component of the effective half spread is larger on NYSE than on NASDAQ. These results imply that adverse selection is not the reason for wider bid–ask spreads on NAS-DAQ. The authors conclude that preferencing and internalisation are important factors that limit dealers' incentives to narrow spreads on NASDAQ. Bessembinder (1997) confirms the above findings, and also finds that price-rounding practices are associated with higher trade execution costs on NASDAQ but not on the NYSE.

There is also evidence that bid–ask spreads decreased for stocks which were traded on NASDAQ and then moved to the NYSE or AMEX. Christie and Huang (1994) report a narrowing of quoted and effective spreads for stocks making this switch. Barclay (1997) analyses 472 stocks that switched from NASDAQ between 1983 and 1992. There is a specific interest in differences in the effects on the bid–ask spread for stocks for which NASDAQ market-makers avoided odd-eighth quotes versus those for which these market-makers used both odd and even eighths. The reduction in spreads following a switch in listing is found to be substantial for the former group but smaller for the latter group.

The reforms which were implemented at NASDAQ in January 1997 were mainly aimed at enforcing mandatory display of customer limit orders and this was expected to offer investors transacting on NASDAQ more competitive quotes. According to the new rules issued by the SEC, a NASDAQ dealer receiving a customer limit order has four alternative ways to transact the order: (a) use inventory to accommodate the order; (b) send the order to another dealer for execution; (c) push the order through a proprietary trading system; or (d) post the order through the system by specifying the quote price and the quote size.

These rule changes have attracted substantial interest. Barclay *et al.* (1999) found that the rule change, allowing more scope for limit orders to be submitted to the market, produced a narrowing of the quoted and effective spreads by some 30 per cent compared with the pre-reform trading. The biggest drops in transaction costs were observed for stocks which had the widest spreads posted before the rule change. An important result is that the narrowing of the bid–ask spread does not take place at the cost of lower liquidity, since market depth was not materially affected after the rule change.

Under a situation of competing market-makers, each would be expected to adjust their quoted spread according to the current market and their own circumstances. For example, Snell and Tonks (1995, 1998) and Hansch, Naik and Viswanathan (1998) report that London Stock Exchange market-makers revise quotes according to their inventory position. Snell and Tonks (1995) also note that there is little evidence from their sample that market-makers exploit liquidity traders.

Reiss and Werner (1996) analysed spreads at the London Stock Exchange, taking into consideration differences in type of trade, trade volume and security. Their estimates reveal that medium to large trades typically receive discounts from the touch spread. The wider the touch, the larger are these discounts. Small and very large trades pay the touch and sometimes more. Reiss and Werner's results are important since they provide an insight into the behaviour of market-makers in dealer markets and how the interaction among market-makers can considerably complicate the relationship between spreads and trade characteristics. The authors provide a simple explanation for the discounts given by market-makers to larger traders. Reiss and Werner argue that 'by widening spreads, market makers can protect themselves against inventory imbalances and informed traders while simultaneously retaining an option to offer execution within the guaranteed quotes'.

Board and Sutcliffe (1995a and b) analysed inventory management on the London Stock Exchange, with particular interest in the pre-positioning and post-positioning of market-makers. They found that substantial adjustments in inventories are carried out by market-makers before and after the execution of a large trade. The implication from such results is that dealer markets are flexible in terms of accommodating different types of trades by using inventory levels to accommodate the order flow. Applying the Ho and Macris (1985) argument to these findings, one could conclude that keeping an optimal inventory level generates a cost that would have to be covered by a wider bid–ask spread paid by traders.

Booth *et al.* (1995) compared the bid–ask spreads of a German sample of stocks with those of a matched NASDAQ sample. Their results show that the IBIS system, predecessor of the XETRA system used by the German Börse, produced lower spreads than NASDAQ. The unrestricted access of competing potential counterparties generated greater competitive pressure on market spreads than in a dealer market.

A similar result is reported by Ellul (2000a) who compared the spreads of a matched sample of securities trading on SEAQ, the Paris Bourse and the German Börse. This set-up compares spreads on dealer (SEAQ), auction (CAC in Paris) and hybrid (IBIS) systems. The results show that quoted and effective spreads are much wider on SEAQ than those posted by CAC and IBIS dealers. In addition, both the quoted spreads and the effective spreads on IBIS, for most trade locations, are lower than those on CAC, implying that a hybrid system produces spreads that are narrower than both a dealer system and an auction system. The paper also finds that the adverse selection component of the spread is highest for CAC-traded securities and lowest for SEAQ-traded securities. This confirms that certain trading practices, such as preferencing, which are possible on dealer systems but quite difficult to implement on auction systems allow market-makers on dealer systems to get 'to know the order flow' and hence better protect themselves against adverse selection.

A closer analysis of trading on CAC and IBIS shows that competition, both in terms of the system's position in trade execution *vis-à-vis* other national systems on which the order flow can be directed and in terms of market share held by dealers operating in these systems, is higher on IBIS compared to CAC. The results show that the hybrid system has consistently generated lower spreads compared to the continuous auction system. In view of this, institutional and structural differences between the two systems, such as cost of access, the market position and the market concentration in the two systems were analysed to search for possible explanations.

One major factor that could provide an explanation for the spread differential is the level of market concentration on the two markets both in terms of the number of registered dealers trading on the two systems and the market share of the biggest dealers. The number of Société de Bourse members trading on CAC was over 60 as of January 1996 whereas there were 118 dealers trading on IBIS in the period January–November 1996. The data for IBIS dealers shows that out of these 118 dealers, some 92 dealers had a market share of less than 1 per cent in the period January–November 1996. These figures show that IBIS has managed to attract a higher number of dealers, possibly because the cost of access, in this case the fixed costs components, are lower on IBIS compared to those for CAC. This evidence provides a further example of market structure influencing the level of spreads.

5.2.4 Intraday bid–ask spreads

In most settings, market-making is a real time activity, where the market-maker is constantly responding to the information flowing from trades (the number of trades, the net order flow, trade size, the identities of traders, etc.), the quotes of rival market-makers, limit orders and the depth of the market, inventory levels, etc. Since there is the likelihood that trading costs will vary across the day, it is important to consider the evidence on intraday bid–ask spread behaviour under different market structures.

The theoretical and empirical literature shows that market structure can have an important influence on the intraday behaviour of bid–ask spreads. A clear distinction exists between the intraday behaviour of bid–ask spreads in markets occupied by a monopolistic specialist versus those with competing market-makers. In Brock and Kleidon's (1992) model, a single specialist has monopolistic power and is faced with a fairly inelastic transactions demand at the open and close of trading owing to the overnight accumulation of information prior to opening and the non-trading period after the close. The specialist can price discriminate during these periods, and this implies that a specialist market will have wide spreads near the open and close of trading (a U-shaped intraday pattern).

The theoretical literature also suggests a role for inventory control and information asymmetries in explaining the intraday behaviour of bid–ask spreads. Lee, Mucklow and Ready (1993) find evidence linking spreads to inventory control costs; in particular, higher trading volume is associated with wide spreads. Hence, for a specialist market, a U-shaped intraday pattern of spreads is also predicted from an inventory perspective, as a single market-maker may be forced to accumulate unwanted inventories during peak trading volumes, whereas competing market-makers will be (individually) less likely to accumulate such positions. Further, Chan, Chung and Johnson (1995) suggest that specialists and competing market-makers may differ in their ability to manage imbalances by using their bid and ask quotes. In maintaining a fair and orderly market, specialists cannot execute orders on only one side of the spread. In contrast, competing market-makers can set quotes to attract trades on only one side of the spread (and thus enhance their ability to avoid unwanted inventories). From the information asymmetry perspective, Admati and Pfleiderer (1988) predict narrow spreads during intraday periods when volume is high and prices are volatile, while Foster and Viswanathan (1990) predict narrow spreads when volume is high and prices are less volatile.

Recent research has examined the role of limit-order traders in determining the intraday pattern of spreads. Chung, Van Ness and Van Ness (1999) examine the effect of limit-orders interacting with specialists on NYSE spreads and find that the majority of bid–ask quotes reflect the interest of limit-order traders, and that specialists tend to quote more actively for low-volume stocks and during the early hours of trading when fewer limit-orders are submitted. Spreads are wide when both the bid and ask prices are only quoted by specialists, and narrow when both prices are quoted from the limit-order book. Specialist spreads are widest at the open, narrow until late morning and then level off for the rest of the day. Hence, it is argued that the empirically observed U-shaped intraday pattern of spreads largely reflects the intraday behaviour of spreads established by limit-order traders, and indeed is significantly associated with the intraday variation in competition among limit-order trades. Kavajecz (1999) also compares the limit-order book spread with that quoted by specialists and finds that the latter play an important role in narrowing spreads, especially for smaller and less frequently traded stocks.

Barclay *et al.* (1999) show how SEC rule changes affecting NASDAQ dealers, including one concerning limit-order trades, led to a change in the intraday bid–ask spread pattern towards that of the NYSE, suggesting that the wide spreads at the open reflect inherent price uncertainty after a period of market closure rather than market power. Spreads narrow during the day as the order book becomes deeper and price discovery improves, before falling sharply over the final 30 minutes as dealers do not wish to hold inventory overnight.

In support of Brock and Kleidon's (1992) model, Foster and Viswanathan (1993), Lee, Mucklow and Ready (1993) and McInish and Wood (1992) show that NYSE spreads follow a U-shaped pattern across the trading day. Others have reported U-shaped intraday spread patterns in different settings (e.g. Ma, Peterson and Sears, 1992 and Wang *et al.*, 1994 for CME futures). In contrast, in markets with competing market-makers, a different pattern has been frequently reported. Spreads on NASDAQ, London Stock Exchange and the CBOE are found to be wide at the open but narrow at the close by Chan, Christie and Schultz (1995), Kleidon and Werner (1993) and Chan, Chung and Johnson (1995), respectively. The suggested explanation is that dealers in a competitive environment will narrow spreads near the close as a means of inventory control, while specialists will exercise their monopoly power in widening spreads at a time of high and inelastic demand.

The distinction between specialist and multiple market maker institutional structures has proved useful in discriminating between competing theories of the intraday behaviour of bid–ask spreads. Chan, Chung and Johnson (1995) compare the intraday behaviour of spreads for a sample of NYSE stocks and their associated options traded on the CBOE. The former is a specialist market, while the latter involves multiple market-makers, and hence the authors can attempt to distinguish between the influence of market structure, adverse selection and inventory control for the intraday patterns. They conclude that higher uncertainty at the opening of both markets can explain the wide spreads observed, but that information cannot then explain wide stock spreads and narrow option spreads at the close. The narrow option spreads are therefore likely to arise from a differing market structure.

There is a body of empirical evidence from the UK on this issue. There are some conflicting results, which are probably a by-product of differing methodologies for spread calculation, differing samples of securities and differing time periods. Abhyankar *et al.* (1997) find a U-shaped pattern in intraday bid–ask spreads for UK equities. Kleidon and Werner (1993) find wide bid–ask spreads at the market open and narrow spreads at the close. Levin and Wright (1999) examine a sample of 100 UK stocks and find a U-shaped pattern in the touch, while the average bid–ask spread for individual market makers is largely flat across the day.

Under the open outcry system, the LIFFE futures markets consisted of competing market-makers, and this structure therefore implies that bid–ask spread behaviour might be expected to resemble the above evidence on the CBOE. Evidence to support this conjecture, using a range of different spread calculation methods, appears in ap Gwilym and Thomas (1998, 2002). For FTSE 100 stock index futures and several government bond futures, they consistently observe spreads which are relatively wide at the open, stable across the day, and narrower at the close. Further, there is evidence that spreads are not always wide at the open but are consistently narrow at the close of floor trading. High spread volatility at the open may reflect a tendency for traders to set wide spreads on mornings following eventful overnight periods and 'normal' spreads otherwise. A further notable observation is an increase in spreads at times of information arrival, e.g. New York opening time.

Similar evidence is found in ap Gwilym, Buckle and Thomas (1997) for FTSE 100 index options and Abhyankar, Copeland and Wong (1999) for FTSE 100 index futures. Contrasting evidence is reported for FTSE 100 index futures in other studies by Henker (1998) who reports flat spreads across the day, and Tse (1999) who reports an inverted U-shape. Also, Franses *et al.* (1994) report flat spreads across the day for Bund futures at LIFFE. The primary difference in these latter studies is the absence of wide spreads at the market open, which is potentially a symptom of differing spread calculation and intraday data selection.

5.3   Cross-listing

The globalisation and automation of financial markets has led to an increase in competition among exchanges through the cross-listing of identical assets, and in some cases this has led to battles for dominance of the trading. Cross-listing can arise either from such competing list-ings at different exchanges (e.g. German Bund futures contracts at LIFFE and DTB), or as a result of explicit co-operation between exchanges, e.g. Eurodollar futures contracts at SIMEX and CME since 1984 (see Williamson, 1999). In either case, common motivations for companies seeking a cross-listing of their shares include extension of trading hours beyond those offered by existing listings (particularly in the case of international cross-listings) and enhancement of the price discovery process. For example, overnight suspension of trading can often result in significant pricing errors at the subsequent market opening.[10] From an alternative perspective, many firms issuing shares have sought multiple listings as a means of increasing the liquidity of their stock with the ultimate aim of decreasing the cost of capital. Such an outcome is supported by several theoretical models of international asset pricing.

Securities involved in multiple listings may not be perfect substitutes because they are traded in different currencies or time zones, and so the introduction of multiple listing may generate additional trading volume.[11] However, it is also possible that multiple listing splits an unchanged total volume between the exchanges, leading to lower liquidity than would be the case for a single listing. Given the importance of liquidity to traders, this can lead to the migration of trading to a single exchange. While overall volume for a security may increase following a cross-listing, the relative costs of trading on an exchange are likely to determine where the bulk of trading volume ultimately resides. Clearly, a key determinant of an exchange's ability to maintain a security's listing will be its ability to attract order flow.

Madhavan (2000) presents a simple theoretical model of an identical security trading on two exchanges, which indicates that if order processing costs are a decreasing function of trading volume, in the long run there will be consolidation into the exchange with lowest costs. Rational informed traders would initially split their orders between the two markets to maximise their advantage from the information asymmetry. There will be no incentive for liquidity traders to split their orders and they will consolidate their trading geographically (e.g. Garbade and Silber, 1979; Mendelson, 1987) or inter-temporally (e.g. Admati and Pfleiderer, 1988). Under this model, pooling orders will provide greater informational efficiency in prices than decentralised trading across fragmented markets.

However, Kofman and Moser (1997) note an exception to this which could lead to sustained market segmentation despite the existence of cost frictions, whereby a difference in trading transparency between competing exchanges can offset a cost differential. An example of such a situation could occur when a cross-listing involves one listing on a floor traded exchange and the other listing on an automated exchange (see section 5.1.2 of this chapter for further discussion of this issue). Further, if different market segments are catering for different trading clienteles, this would also imply a continuance of multiple listing.

The empirical evidence provides both supportive and contradictory examples for the simple model described in Madhavan (2000). The obvious example of two exchanges with differing costs is the case where one is floor based and the other is screen based. As discussed in section 5.1.2 of this chapter, screen-based trading systems provide important cost savings over floor-based systems, which can be passed on to users. Thus, according to the above model, if a situation existed where an identical security traded on two such exchanges, one would hypothesise that trading would eventually be consolidated onto the screen-based exchange. This hypothesis is strongly supported by the observed migration of trading in the German Bund futures contract from LIFFE to the DTB in the late 1990s (see section 5.3.1). It should be emphasised that the migration of trading in this contract to Germany was primarily driven by large cost differences between trading systems. Additionally, there is much contradictory evidence where many markets are fragmented and remain so for long periods of time.

5.3.1   Cross-listing of German bund futures contracts

It is historically rare for similar competing futures contracts to continue to trade simultaneously on different exchanges. Perhaps the most notable example is that of the German long-term government bond (bund) futures contracts, while other cases are highlighted in the next section. During the 1990s, similar bund contracts traded on both the DTB[12] and LIFFE. Trading of such contracts at LIFFE commenced in September 1988, with the DTB following in November 1990. Initially, LIFFE dominated the market, and then consistently held around 70 per cent of market share from 1992 to 1996. This declined to around 55 per cent during 1997, and then fell during 1998 to below 10 per cent. The contract was then delisted by LIFFE.[13]

This scenario provided an ideal opportunity for the analysis of the price, volatility and trading dynamics that take place in a cross-traded scenario, and was investigated by a number of researchers. Moreover, this trading in bund futures provided an important comparison of whether different market microstructures matter, because at the time LIFFE operated an open outcry trading system together with after-hours Automated Pit Trading (APT), whereas trading on the DTB was fully automated through an order book. The latter aspect is considered in detail in section 1 of this chapter. The following studies are discussed in the chronological order of the sample periods examined. It is important to note that these studies found a very close contemporaneous link between the two exchanges, and the differences discussed below are relatively small. (see Table 5.2)

Franke and Hess (1996) were among the first to analyse the impact of the introduction of the Bund futures contract on the DTB. Their sample

Table 5.2 Summary of the evidence from empirical results obtained for bund futures contracts traded on LIFFE (open outcry/APT) and the DTB (automated)

Study	Bid–ask spreads	High and low volatility periods
Franke and Hess (1996)		Greater volume on LIFFE under high volatility.
Kofman and Moser (1997)	Little difference in spreads across systems, larger adverse selection component on the DTB	
Pirrong (1996)	Narrower spreads on the DTB	
Shyy and Lee (1995)	Wider spreads on the DTB	
Breedon and Holland (1997)	Similar spreads	Tendency for trading to move to LIFFE during volatile periods
Martens (1998)		Greater liquidity and price discovery on LIFFE under high volatility; it shifts to the DTB under low volatility.
Frino, McInish and Toner (1998)	Narrower spreads on the DTB.	Greater widening of spreads on the DTB under high volatility
Kappi and Siivonen (2000)	Wider spreads on the DTB but the DTB slightly deeper	

period is from January 1991 to December 1993 and hence covers the initial period of cross-listing. This paper analyses (a) whether the different transparency regimes on the two exchanges, especially information about the order flow away from the best bid and ask quotes, had any impact on the provision of liquidity; (b) whether such differences mattered when there was a shortage of fundamental information or news in the market; and (c) what was the impact of high volatility upon liquidity.

They find that a greater degree of trade transparency, in this case more detailed information on quotes and relevant volumes set away from the best quotes in the market, made a significant contribution to the provision of liquidity to the market. This contribution appears to be more important in periods characterised by low trading volumes. The authors argue that such information becomes relatively more important when there is a shortage of more fundamental information in the market.

The authors argue that volatility can be considered as a proxy for the intensity with which trade information is arriving. The paper finds that the DTB was less liquid in periods when the level of volatility was high.

They argue that when information intensity was low, the information contained in the DTB order book was of relatively higher value than that provided by LIFFE and, consequently, the DTB attracted traders, making it more liquid in such periods. Alternatively, when the level of information intensity was high, this information was of little incremental value and liquidity was greater on LIFFE. This evidence indicates that both exchanges made contributions to the price discovery process, with the relative importance of each exchange dependent on trading circumstances. Although this appears to be a plausible inference, there must have been other factors which outweighed its importance, since almost all trading subsequently migrated to the DTB.

Kofman and Moser (1997) set out two major objectives of their research: (a) to analyse whether market-makers acting on the two systems were setting their quotes conditional on the level of transparency allowed by the two systems; and (b) whether, after controlling for transparency differences, equality of trading costs across the two systems led to a situation where neither exchange could claim leadership, resulting in a bi-directional flow of information where both exchanges made contributions to the price discovery process.[14]

Kofman and Moser (1997) consider spreads and spread components together with lead–lag relationships for the bund futures using a 30-trading day sample during March and April 1992. During this sample period, LIFFE had around 60 per cent of market share in this contract. Despite the fact that the commissions charged at LIFFE were somewhat higher than those charged at the DTB, it was obviously able to attract sufficient order flow at that time. The results show that trading costs were equal across the two systems but the components of the spread varied across the systems, with a larger adverse selection component at the DTB. This indicates that lack of knowledge of the identities of traders submitting orders on such a system leads to more adverse selection possibilities.

Moreover, fundamental variances[15] were also equal across the two systems and this shows that information flowed in both directions, with instantaneous feedback from one trading platform to the other. Documented instances of differences in the observed variances can be ascribed to conditions arising in one system which were unrelated to the price discovery process. The conclusion was that neither exchange seemed to be leading the other. Kofman and Moser (1997) conclude that 'the marginal uninformed trader on the DTB and LIFFE seems to be indifferent to the trading system. Whereas informed traders will typically prefer the automated system for anonymity, the uninformed trader will simply look for lowest cost. Information asymmetry and time-varying expected returns costs add up on order processing costs bringing trading costs to break-even level across exchanges.'

Pirrong (1996) uses trade data from July 1992 to June 1993 and finds that bid–ask spreads at the DTB are no higher and sometimes lower than those at LIFFE. He concludes that automated systems can be more liquid and deeper than open outcry systems. In contrast, Shyy and Lee (1995) find wider bid–ask spreads at the DTB, but the DTB leads LIFFE in price discovery. These results should be viewed with caution since only six days of quote data from November 1993 were used in the study.

Breedon and Holland (1997) seek to reconcile the conflicting results of the earlier studies of bund cross-listing, and suggest that the conflict largely arises from whether quote or trade data had been used. Their sample consists of a full record of trade and quote data for the June 1995 contract between 10 April and 2 June 1995. They find that variable transaction costs and the contribution to price formation of each exchange is similar. They identify the main differences between the exchanges as larger trade sizes at LIFFE and a tendency for trading to move to LIFFE during volatile periods.

Martens (1998) uses data from September to December 1995 to investigate the contribution that each exchange made to the price discovery process for the bund contract. In this case, price discovery is defined as the innovations in the true price of the asset discovered through trading in the two systems. The information share that each exchange made to the price discovery process is the proportion of the efficient price (true price) innovation variance that arose from the trading on that exchange. Another question asked is whether there was any identifiable price leadership by either exchange.

It is argued that open outcry systems are more efficient in fast moving markets, mostly owing to the way quotes are disseminated and prices released. Under its open outcry system, competing market-makers at LIFFE could change their quotes through a simple hand signal. This was not so for the order book at the DTB, where quotes were disseminated electronically and old quotes had to be withdrawn before new ones could be introduced. This lack of speed in handling quotes also inhibited traders from entering quotes in the limit order book if they were afraid of losing out owing to fast-moving prices. However, since the electronic order book provides more information, it becomes more important in periods of little trading, when trade information is scarce. The outstanding orders then provide insight into the nature and dynamics of the order flow, whereas under open outcry the only information arises from trading, which is thus obviously limited in quiet trading periods.

The empirical results confirm the hypothesis tested by the paper. Both exchanges are found to have contributed to the price discovery process. In high volatility periods, LIFFE made the largest contribution to the price discovery process, whereas in low volatility periods, the DTB had the largest share of the price discovery. Therefore both exchanges fulfilled an important role in the efficiency of the asset's prices, although their contribution was time-varying.

Frino, McInish and Toner (1998) build on the findings of a number of the above prior studies in their investigation of the bid–ask spread on the bund contract at LIFFE and the DTB. A key difference arises in that whereas previous work considered periods during which LIFFE had a higher proportion of the traded volume of the bund futures, this paper considers a later period (October–November 1997) when parity in the traded volume between the two systems was observed. Contrary to some previous findings, Frino, McInish and Toner (1998) report that spreads on the screen trading system at the DTB were narrower than those at LIFFE, even after controlling for the differences in the determinants of the bid–ask spread. However, spreads on the DTB were found to increase more rapidly in periods of high volatility. They conclude that automated exchanges can provide greater liquidity, but their relative performance deteriorates under high volatility.

Kappi and Siivonen (2000) take a different perspective on the cross listing of Bund futures by analysing liquidity on the after-hours APT system on LIFFE and the screen trading system used by the DTB. The sample period considered is from August 1997 to February 1998. There were similarities between these two screen-based systems in that both were computerised platforms incorporating a consolidated limit order book, but there were some important differences. The first arises from the fact that APT was based upon pit trading and therefore incorporated trader identities through using mnemonics (therefore there was no anonymity in trading). A second difference was that pre-trade transparency differed across the two systems, whereby the DTB showed the *10* best bid and ask quotes together with the corresponding volumes, while the APT showed only the single best ask and best bid quotes with the corresponding volumes. Clearly there was more information on market depth and liquidity on the DTB system compared with APT. A third difference is that the DTB used price and then time precedence rules while APT allocated market orders across limit orders at the same price on a pro-rata basis.

The objective of Kappi and Siivonen (2000) is to investigate whether these differences in transparencies mattered. The results show that such differences have an impact on both bid–ask spreads and market depth, but the impact depends very much on the intensity of the information arriving in the market. In fact, the APT system is seen as the appropriate trading platform when a large amount of information arrived on the market, whereas the DTB seemed to be preferable when information arrival was relatively sparse. These results (Table 5.2) show that neither system had any *a priori* superiority with regard to liquidity, but such superiority was time-varying and dependent on market conditions.

Breedon and Holland (1997) note that further important aspects of price formation to consider in the context of cross-listing are the location of price discovery and the speed with which one exchange reacts to price discovery in the other. For the bund contract at LIFFE and the DTB, the evidence is again mixed. Shyy and Lee (1995) find one-way causality from the DTB to LIFFE using quote data only, while Kofman and Moser (1997) report bi-directional causality using quote and trade data. The latter has the disadvantage of a more serious non-synchronous data problem, thus biasing causality toward the higher turnover exchange (LIFFE at that time). However, after addressing such methodological problems, Breedon and Holland (1997) still find bi-directional causality between the exchanges.

A final issue to raise on the cross-listing of the bund futures is the observation of small (about 1.5 basis points) but persistent price differences across the exchanges, with LIFFE being the more expensive. Breedon (1996) investigates a number of possible explanations for this phenomenon but finds that none is important enough to explain the observed difference. This raises questions regarding the links between dually traded futures contracts and the underlying asset in cases where physical delivery is rare.

5.3.2 Cross-listing of other futures contracts

There are several stock index futures contracts which have been traded on more than one exchange, e.g. Nikkei Stock Average futures traded at SIMEX from September 1986, at OSE from September 1988, and at CME from September 1990. In terms of interest rate contracts, the examples include JGB futures traded on both SIMEX and the Tokyo Stock Exchange, and Euro-yen futures traded at both SIMEX and the Tokyo International Financial Futures Exchange.

The Nikkei Stock Average futures contract was traded on SIMEX under an open outcry system, while OSE employs a screen-based system. The

SIMEX futures contract has a number of advantages over that trading at Osaka, including lower transaction costs, no exchange tax, no suspension of trading for a lunch break, open for 15 minutes longer, and the ability to trade other futures quoted on the same exchange (see Semkow, 1989).

Fremault and Sandmann (1995) use this setting to compare liquidity, mainly spreads and spread formation, in a floor system versus an automated system. Volatility, over short intervals of time, is found to be higher on the automated trading system and, contrary to the findings of Martens (1998) and others for German bund futures (see section 5.3.1), trading volume migrates to the automated system in times of high price volatility. Breedon and Holland (1997) suggest that in periods of market stress, orders flow to the exchange with the larger share of the market, regardless of trading platform. Fremault and Sandmann (1995) conclude that 'a viable dual market equilibrium has developed over time that seems to be driven more by transaction costs and other exogenous trading restrictions than by inherent inefficiencies of one of the competing trading technologies'.

Bacha and Vila (1994) use data from 1985–91 to investigate the impact on market volatility of the introduction of new listings of Nikkei stock index futures at the OSE and CME. They report important findings that the introduction of the OSE listing significantly reduced market volatility while increasing volume in the existing listed SIMEX contract. Subsequently, when the CME listed its similar contract, volatility once again declined for the existing listed contracts at the two other exchanges. Clearly this can be viewed as evidence that multiple listing can have a stabilising effect. Additionally, they find that interday volatility was not significantly different between the SIMEX and the OSE, but intraday volatility was lower at the OSE. There is only weak evidence that the latter may have been a result of the OSE's higher margins and tighter price limits.

Board and Sutcliffe (1996a) studied the cross-listing of futures contracts on the Nikkei Stock Average in Osaka and SIMEX, both of which were traded in Japanese yen and had the same final settlement value of the index. Using daily opening and closing prices from 1988 to 1993, the mispricings from a spread between the Osaka and SIMEX futures were small and reduced over time. They did not decrease in size as delivery approached, presumably because there was no reduction in dividend and interest rate risk, since these risks are irrelevant to such spread arbitrage. The mispricings were symmetrical, indicating no systematic underpricing or overpricing, which may be because selling futures is as easy as establishing long positions. The daily mispricings were not autocorrelated, and there was little evidence that mispricings for a given contract tended to change sign. This may be because, since no shares are traded, transaction costs are similarly very low for both establishing a new arbitrage position and for an early unwinding.

Board and Sutcliffe (1996a) also studied the cross-listing of futures contracts on the Nikkei Stock Average in Osaka and the CME using daily opening and closing prices from 1990 to 1993. Although both contracts are based on the same final settlement value of the index, the Osaka contract is denominated in Japanese yen, while the CME contract is in US dollars. Riskless arbitrage is not possible for two reasons: the Osaka and CME exchanges are never open synchronously, and a forecast of the exchange rate at delivery is required in setting the spread ratio. Board and Sutcliffe (1996a) found that the mispricings were small, symmetrical, and unaffected by contract maturity. There was modest positive autocorrelation in the daily mispricings, and this was partly due to persistence in the errors in forecasting the final exchange rate. Finally, there was little persistence in the sign of the mispricing for a given contract.

Spread arbitrage provides another way in which identical securities traded on different exchanges are linked, and the above results for the futures contracts on the Nikkei Stock Average traded in Osaka, SIMEX and the CME indicate that international futures exchanges are highly integrated, despite the time gaps and currency risk between Osaka and the CME. Indeed, since the transaction costs for spread arbitrage are very low, the price linkage is even tighter than between the spot and futures markets.

Spread arbitrage between Nikkei Stock Average futures on Osaka and SIMEX was supposedly conducted by Barings Futures (Singapore) and their employee Nick Leeson. Two reasons were given to explain the possibility of temporary but highly profitable differences in price between Osaka and SIMEX which this arbitrage was designed to exploit (BoBS, 1995, sections 3.28 and 3.29). First, the Osaka exchange tends to attract Japanese business while SIMEX tends to attract offshore business, leading to differing demand and supply factors and thus temporary price differences. Secondly, the Osaka exchange is screen-based while SIMEX was floor-based, leading to differing speed of information transmission. In fact, Leeson was not engaged in such spread arbitrage, and his positions were speculative. The reality of an absence of consistently profitable arbitrage opportunities is consistent with the Board and Sutcliffe (1996a) findings discussed above.

Further studies have investigated cross-listing of commodity futures. Branch *et al.* (1984) studied silver futures traded on both Comex and the CBOT, finding that futures prices on the two exchanges were almost identical. A similar conclusion was reached by Silber (1981) in a study of gold futures traded on both Comex and the CME. This suggests that the prices on the two exchanges are linked together such that they effectively become one market. In this case, liquidity may not be reduced by cross-listing, except to the extent that there are transaction costs in switching business between the two exchanges. Indeed, arbitrage transactions exploiting any price discrepancies between the two exchanges will increase volume and liquidity at both exchanges.

5.3.3 Cross-listing of equities

There have been many empirical studies focussing on equities simultaneously trading at more than one exchange. Foerster and Karolyi (1998) find reduced trading costs for Toronto Stock Exchange stocks which introduce further listings on US exchanges, and attribute this to the impact of the competition between the exchanges for order flow. Hasbrouck (1995) examines US stocks simultaneously traded at the NYSE and other North American exchanges, while Harris *et al.* (1995) study IBM stock traded on several US exchanges. The results of these two studies indicate that the dominant role of the NYSE in price discovery is attributable to its also having a major part of the volume traded in these stocks.

Werner and Kleidon (1996) investigate the intraday dynamics of UK stocks cross-listed in the UK and USA. They find that the intraday behaviour closely resembles that for similar stocks which have a single listing. Cross-border competition for order flow is found to reduce bid–ask spreads. De Jong, Nijman and Röell (1995) compare French stocks under continuous auction (at the Paris Bourse) and dealer (SEAQ International) systems. They find that the quoted spread in Paris is lower than in London for small transactions, up to roughly the normal market size. However, the Paris exchange is not as deep, so the spread rises for large transactions (Röell, 1992).

Ellul (2000b) investigates (a) which type of liquidity provision set-up generates lower volatilities, taking into consideration market depth and breadth; (b) the strategic interactions between the limit order book and the market-makers; and (c) how the order flow behaves at times of price uncertainty. To investigate these issues, data is used from FTSE 100 index securities listed on the London Stock Exchange, which are now traded on two parallel systems – an order-driven system (SETS) and a dealership system. This environment provides an ideal place for the analysis of price volatility and trading behaviour on the two systems and the strategic interaction between them.

This study finds that prices on the dealership system track the security's true price more efficiently. The analysis is undertaken by extracting the price volatility, measured as the deviation of the trading price on both the auction and the dealership system from the true 'system-wide' price, which is calculated using a state–space model that extracts the information content in the order flow. The dealership system is found to be more robust than the auction system, in that it can transact higher volumes with lower price volatility. This evidence suggests that market-makers provide price stabilisation, even if they have no binding obligation to do so, thus improving the market's quality. However, the order book appears to be contributing to the price discovery process, in that limit order imbalances are found to contain useful trade information. In terms of trading behaviour, the paper finds that in an exchange that provides trading choices for different traders, as price uncertainty increases, traders are not encouraged to provide liquidity on the order book through limit orders. Instead orders migrate to the dealership system for execution there.

5.3.4 Conclusion

The voluminous empirical evidence on the Bund futures contract clearly suggests there should be no reason for regulatory concern regarding multiple listing of a given security. This research typically found that both exchanges which listed this contract fulfilled an important role in the efficiency of the price discovery process, and each made important contributions which were time-varying owing to their particular advantages under differing market conditions, e.g. high or low trading activity and volatility. The migration of trading in this contract to Germany was primarily driven by large cost differences between trading systems (see section 5.3.1 of this chapter), rather than any inherent weakness in cross-listing. Evidence from other market settings offers further support to the conjecture that the various potential benefits (e.g. increased trading volumes, lower trading costs due to competition among exchanges, and a reduced cost of capital for issuing firms) from multiple listings typically outweigh any risks of reduced liquidity.

Notes

1 It should be noted that each electronic system has its own specific characteristics (see Domowitz, 1993).
2 Bollerslev, Domowitz and Wang (1997) test a model of the operation of an electronic order book and are able to produce good out-of-sample predictions.

3 Henker (1999) cites this as evidence that potential knowledge of the trading source (under a floor system) does not necessarily reduce transaction costs nor determine the success or failure of a trading system.

4 Some studies should be viewed with caution owing to short sample periods (e.g. 15 days in Chow, Lee and Shyy, 1996; 6 days in Shyy and Lee, 1995). Also, valid comparisons can be difficult when different researchers have used trade versus quote data.

5 The DTB has subsequently merged with the Swiss exchange SOFFEX to form Eurex.

6 They use minute-by-minute data and have only five lags in the estimation thus they do not test for leads/lags for periods longer than 5 minutes.

7 Also, the sample period used in the study is one month and such a short sample period may give an untypical result.

8 The SFE announced in October 1997 that it was to move to electronic trading by the first quarter of 1999. This change was completed by December 1999.

9 Board, Sutcliffe and Vila (2000) note that internalised order flow is pervasive at the London Stock Exchange. They also report detailed evidence of fair weather market-making, a related but distinct form of trading practice, which involves a market-making firm not being as committed to its function as implied by their obligations to the market.

10 Yamori (1998) presents empirical evidence that international cross-listing of Japanese stocks benefits the price discovery process at the opening of the Tokyo Stock Exchange.

11 Yagil and Forshner (1991) present a theoretical model showing that the expected return on a cross-listed security will be higher, while its variance will be lower compared with an otherwise identical single-listed security.

12 This exchange has since merged with the Swiss exchange SOFFEX to form Eurex.

13 A euro-denominated German bund futures contract is currently trading at LIFFE.

14 Kofman, Bouwman and Moser (1994) and Franses *et al.* (1994) use the same dataset for further modelling of price dynamics between the exchanges.

15 Removing time-varying components from the variance process results in standardised residuals, from which Kofman and Moser (1997) estimate the standardised variance. They measure observed variance by unconditional variance and fundamental variance by this standardized variance. The latter measure relates only to asset-specific conditions and is free from market-specific conditions.

6
Policy Responses to Fragmentation

This chapter examines the regulatory implications of market fragmentation and consolidation. It begins with a brief summary of the arguments advanced at greater length in Chapter 4. This is followed by a longer analysis of regulatory effects, together with a description of suggested responses.

6.1 Recapitulation

6.1.1 Fragmentation of markets

Recent advances in technology have made it relatively cheap to enter the business of operating trading systems, and the use of telecommunications equipment means that there are no longer any geographical limitations to the reach of such systems. This has led to competition among incumbents, mergers and the emergence of new entrants. Among the new entrants, the ATSs have attracted the most attention. They are electronic systems that, in many ways, are like exchanges. Certainly they perform many of the trading system functions of traditional exchanges but offer alternative trading venues that are often subject to different regulatory requirements.

Thus the market for trading services has become contestable, and trading is fragmenting across a number of trading venues. In turn traditional exchanges have adopted governance structures and business plans that are more appropriate to a competitive market. As exchanges become more like normal commercial businesses, so the analysis of the industry becomes susceptible to the normal concepts of industrial economics – competition, barriers to entry and so forth.

We consider 'the market' to be all trading in a single security (or its very close substitutes). A fragmented market is one in which there are two or more separate and distinct trading systems, such that the price on one trading system could differ significantly from that on another. Multiple trading systems need not lead to market fragmentation if there are links between these trading systems such that arbitrageurs can operate to equalise price differences. These links need not be physical links. Common access to the multiple, competing trading systems and to information about trading on those systems ensures that price fragmentation does not occur, although there are distributional consequences (profits for arbitrageurs at the expense of other users).

6.1.2 Consolidation of markets

While fragmentation is increasingly likely, there is also a movement towards market consolidation. This is demonstrated by the attempts of exchanges to forge alliances, and the concerns of smaller exchanges that they will lose out to larger exchanges. There are two strong economic forces for the consolidation of trading venues – economies of scale and network effects.

Economies of scale reflect the fact that setting up trading systems is largely a high fixed cost/low marginal cost business. Trading systems, once set up, can accept additional orders at close to zero additional cost. This provides an incentive for trading systems to seek additional business since it reduces their average cost, and gives an advantage to the most successful trading systems, in that they will have the lowest average cost. Network effects reflect the fact that the more potential counterparties there are on a system the higher is the probability of finding a matching counterparty – or liquidity attracts liquidity. Network effects offer a strong first mover advantage, and so tend to buttress the position of incumbents. This is especially true if the position of the incumbent trading system is supplemented by restrictions on the trading of listed stocks on other trading systems. However, technology means that networks can be linked together to stretch across several trading systems, either through formal links, informal links or the actions of adapters (entities that offer a single point of access to multiple trading systems).

Both economies of scale and network effects are powerful drivers for consolidation to an extent that is limited only by technology and market segmentation. If technology can offer global reach then the natural market for a trading system is also global. However, global reach is valuable only if there is global interest. If investors in one country are not interested in the securities of another then there is no network effect from offering access to a trading system in both countries (though there may still be economies of scale if the trading is sufficiently similar in both countries). Institutional factors may also weigh against consolidation – differences in trading structure (such as transparency), regulatory conflicts and differences in settlement have all been cited as reasons preventing consolidation.

6.1.3 Economic effects of fragmentation

This section summarises the main economic effects of fragmentation that could be viewed as harmful. It focusses on policy responses aimed at limiting any possible detrimental effects and encouraging the benefits. There are a large number of possible effects, and we have included some that have been claimed, but which we see as implausible.

To simplify the discussion, the effects have been grouped under three main headings – price quality, commercial pressures and regulatory issues.

A Price quality. Fragmentation may lead to more internalisation of order flow within broking firms and result in more price matching, that is, transacting business away from the main market at prices determined in the main market. Such internalisation and price matching lessens the reward to liquidity providers since their competitive quotes will be used as benchmarks, but their orders may not get filled.

Fragmented markets will very likely result in differing levels of transparency for different trading systems. If this reduces the overall level of transparency, price formation may be less efficient.

Access to some parts of the market may be restricted, and so prices may not reflect all the order flow. In addition, some types of user may be denied access to the best prices. However, if the access restrictions reflect real factors (such as ability to settle) then the restrictions are justified (and it is hard to see commercial ventures excluding users for non-commercial reasons).

In a fragmented market, liquidity may be spread more thinly across multiple venues. However, it is unlikely that marginal trading systems would seek to enter markets where liquidity was so limited. Linkages, formal or informal, lessen the effect on market users. Additionally, lower costs and more flexible trading opportunities may increase trading volume, and hence total liquidity. Arbitrage trading between systems will also increase the volume of trading.

Formal support for liquidity, which usually involves special privileges for liquidity providers and some form of cross-subsidy (e.g. NYSE specialists), will be hard to maintain where no single trading system has the monopoly position necessary to support such privileges.

B *Commercial pressures.* Competition is likely to lead to innovation and lower costs. Direct costs may increase initially because of duplication, but experience suggests that competitive pressures will eventually drive down costs. Implicit trading costs (price impact and opportunity cost) could rise if trading systems were strictly segmented and liquidity was split, but this is unlikely. The overall effect will most probably be an increase in liquidity, together with greater ability to execute orders in the most appropriate way, given the circumstances of the order.

Cross-subsidies between different types of user or order are not sustainable in a competitive situation. This will increase the relative costs to certain types of trader, the most likely losers being informed traders. It is not yet clear whether retail traders will gain or lose, as their orders are uninformed, but subject to fixed processing costs.

Fragmentation affects the value of price data, which is a valuable revenue source for exchanges. Competition may depress the price of such data, but it may allow some systems to charge more if their data is judged to be of a higher quality. Incumbent exchanges may also use their ownership of information to restrict the ability of 'parasitic' newcomers to attract business.

C *Regulatory issues.* Best execution becomes more complex to judge and regulate when there is a range of trading possibilities. The increase in trading venues is also likely to bring a wider range of ways of handling an order, further complicating best execution.

Fragmentation might lead to regulatory arbitrage and a race for the bottom, resulting in a general lowering of standards. However, at the same time, competition will impose discipline on trading system providers and weed out those systems that have regulatory features that do not meet market needs.

Diversity means that monitoring and enforcement activities must operate across trading systems. This is because wrongdoers may try to mask their manipulatory or other activities by operating across trading systems.

The current distinction between RIEs and brokers means that some ATSs, that chose to operate as brokers, are required to report to an RIE that they may see as a competitor.

6.2 Policy responses to fragmentation

This section considers various possible policy responses to a fragmented market.

6.2.1 Links between trading systems

If a market is fragmented between a number of trading systems, the resulting loss of network benefits can be reduced by linking trading on the various trading systems together into an integrated system. Provided there is sufficient transparency for each investor to know what deals are currently on offer on each trading system, and any investor is able to have their order executed on any trading system, the aggregate network benefits will be preserved.[1] In essence it is one market (although some of the trading details may differ from trading system to trading system, e.g. anonymity, transparency, clearing, etc.) The big question concerns the form that these links between fragmented trading systems should take.

Type of linkage system

Three alternative answers to this question will now be considered: a mandatory central limit order book, the establishment of official information and interaction systems, and reliance on informal linkages.

1 *Mandatory CLOB.* At one extreme is a mandatory consolidated or central limit order book (CLOB) with a single price–time priority system, which essentially retains a single market, and has been advocated by Mendelson and Peake (1994), among others. A CLOB would ensure that the network benefits are not lost as the market fragments because all orders are exposed to each other in the CLOB. A CLOB provides a single price discovery mechanism. It also ensures there are no 'trade-throughs' (or 'over-reaching')[2] and no price matching, and it minimises the costs of providing free options by posting limit orders because price–time priority is enforced across all trades and trading systems. It also provides a high level of pre-trade transparency.

However a mandatory CLOB has been subject to a range of criticism:[3]

- Rerouteing orders into a CLOB increases costs, and delays execution.
- A CLOB provides a central point of failure, e.g. the system depends on a single set of hardware and software.
- A CLOB is resistant to change and prevents innovation.
- A CLOB has problems when it aggregates orders from a number of different trading systems which offer a different trading service, e.g.

different rules, clearing mechanisms, anonymity, transparency, etc. This is because price is not the only characteristic that is relevant to customers. Therefore, investors may prefer to hit quotes out of price–time priority, and a mandatory CLOB would prevent some investors trading on their preferred trading system. In the words of the NYSE (2000) 'investor choice is eliminated'.

- A CLOB with price–time priority does not offer sufficient reward to market-makers who provide liquidity and stability, e.g. NYSE specialists. It is essentially an order-driven system, and so has little place for dealers. The withdrawal of this service would, in the opinion of the NYSE, lead to wider spreads (James Buck of the NYSE, SEC, 2000b).
- Trading systems become mere entry portals for the CLOB.
- A mandatory CLOB can be bypassed by trading overseas, or by using related (e.g. derivative) markets.
- The NYSE view is that, rather than reducing fragmentation, a CLOB would increase fragmentation because it would be unable to handle large trades, which require the creation of a separate upstairs market (James Buck of the NYSE, SEC, 2000b). Alternatively, if the CLOB caters for large trades by allowing their true size to be hidden, this damages transparency because the true market depth is greater than stated (NYSE, 2000).
- A CLOB may be unsuitable for illiquid assets, and a dealer market may be more successful. The NYSE (2000) claim that a CLOB would lead to wider spreads for the less actively traded stocks, and more volatility for all stocks as the specialist would no longer be cushioning price movements.
- New trading mechanisms may emerge which are beyond the legal area covered by the mandatory CLOB, in which case the market is fragmented and price–time priority is no longer enforced.

2 *Information and interaction systems.* A different approach is to establish a system which provides consolidated trade and quote information for all trading systems, and allows traders on different trading systems to interact, i.e. it promotes transparency and access. The Americans have created the National Market System (NMS) for shares, which consists of three parts covering (a) pre-trade information on quotes and limit orders, (b) post-trade information on actual trades, and (c) trading.[4]

(a) *The Consolidated Quotations System* (CQS) allows traders on every trading system to see the best bid and ask quotes ('the top of the book' or the national best bid and offer, NBBO) available on the various trading systems linked to the system. However, it may not actually show the best available bid and ask quotes, as the NYSE does not always put its best prices on the system, and some exchanges may exclude quotes from customers, Mendelson and Peake (1994). Richard Levin (NexTrade) (SEC, 2000b) argued that the ATSs are being shut out of the NMSs by the unanimity requirement for changes to the NMS, and that this situation should be changed.

(b) *The Consolidate Tape System* (CTS) produces a record of the trades on all US exchanges. However, some after-hours trades on the NYSE and elsewhere are not reported, trades are often reported out of time sequence, and trade prices are rounded to the nearest one-eighth of a dollar (Mendelson and Peake, 1994).

(c) Americans also have the *Interexchange Trading System* (ITS) which allows traders on one exchange to hit quotes on another exchange. However, its main role in practice is to allow dealers to engage in price matching, which has a negative effect on liquidity and price discovery (see section 4.6.4) (Amihud and Mendelson, 1996). In his evidence to the SBC (2000) Richard Grasso (NYSE) proposed that the ITS be phased out, and reliance placed on informal links, while Robert Wood (University of Memphis, SEC, 2000b) stated that 'ITS has demonstrated its willingness to go to great lengths to hinder competition, as was demonstrated in their treatment of Optimark'.

The Canadian Securities Administrators (2000) are implementing a data consolidation system to display quotes and trades from Canadian exchanges and ATSs, and to transmit orders, i.e. to provide the same service as do the CQS, ITS and CTS in the USA. The Canadian data consolidation system will cover the equity, equity option and fixed income markets.

Systems such as the NMS do not overcome the problem of a lack of time priority. Indeed, no alternative system has been proposed which ensures time priority as between trading systems.

3 *Informal linkages.* The other extreme solution is for there to be no formal links between trading systems, and to rely on the informal links created by traders (and their agents) searching for the best deal (and meeting the requirement for best execution). Provided there is sufficient access and transparency by individual trading systems, traders (or brokers) can use computers to track the prices and depth offered on each trading system in real time, and submit orders electronically to the chosen trading system. If one or more of the trading systems has a dealer system, these dealers may wish to make sure

that their quotes are in line with prices elsewhere. If not, they may find themselves the victims of arbitrage trading.

The evidence is that the widespread use of computers has made the informal linking of trading systems a very powerful process for preserving network benefits. Thus, in the USA ATSs have developed which route orders to the exchange or ATS currently offering the best price, e.g. Archipelago. Fidessa, which is run by Royal Blue of Woking, Surrey, UK, acts as an information data aggregator or system adaptor,[5] and displays the best orders from the order books of a wide range of trading systems in the USA, Europe and Asia. For example Fidessa displays both the London Stock Exchange and Virt-x orders on the same screen, as does Reuters. Eight US ATSs are building a private network to link their order books together. Interactive Brokers and other US brokers have built automatic order routeing systems which collect the prices currently available on US trading systems and aim to execute each customer order against the best available price. In Europe, Pagano and Röell (1993) found that, while there are no formal links, prices on SEAQ-I and the Paris Bourse are very tightly linked by an arbitrage relationship.

Choice of linkage system

As mentioned above, there are a number of important problems with a CLOB. In the USA there is little enthusiasm for a CLOB, and some strong opponents. Despite a general acceptance that market-wide price–time priority is desirable, a CLOB is unlikely to be introduced.

If a mandatory CLOB is eliminated, this leaves the choice between formal and informal links. Since 1975 the USA has operated the NMS, which links together the recognised US stock exchanges, but this system has been subject to a range of detailed criticisms. Rapid improvements in information technology mean that the case for a single 'official' linkage system, such as the NMS, is much weakened. In evidence to the SEC (2000g), Robert Britz (NYSE) revealed that the NYSE had decided to withdraw from the official linkage system in the USA, and was comfortable with a situation of competing data distribution systems. Gerald Putnam (Archipelago) also supported the competitive distribution of data, with the comment that single veto distribution structures (as the USA currently has) are unworkable (SEC, 2000 g). Mark Minister (Bridge) supported the idea of competing data consolidators (SEC, 2000 g). In his evidence Rick Ketchum (NASD) said that 'we do believe passionately that a means of providing consolidated information is terribly important' (SEC, 2000g). Thus, the regulatory challenge is to design a competitive system that delivers consolidated data. Some ideas considered by the SEC were (a) a fully competitive system, (b) the existing US system, (c) the operation of a single consolidated system to be awarded to the best tender, (d) a single consolidated best bid and offer, but with competing data vendors free to supply any other information.

Cheap electronic communication, coupled with competition, has led to the development of informal systems, and US commentators are generally confident that informal systems are now sufficient to link trading systems together. Informal systems for quote and trade data do not have a central point of failure, are not resistant to change, and allow customers to hit quotes out of price–time priority on their preferred trading system. It is also impossible for a trading system to exclude others from access to the system in the way that the NYSE has excluded the ATSs from access to the NMS. In addition, while the official US systems must carry the specified information, some of this data is of very little use to investors,[6] and informal systems would be free to tailor the data they carry to suit the requirements of their customers.

However, informal systems do not ensure the availability of consolidated data and a market-wide best bid and offer (although data aggregators could provide such consolidated data), and may lead to high charges for quote and trade data, particularly for retail investors. Such informal systems may also create a barrier to entry for new trading systems, as entrants might find it difficult to distribute their price and trade data.

As the NMS reveals, there are three main functions that a linkage system can perform:

(a) *pre-trade transparency* – e.g. the consolidated best bid and offer prices, or 'the top of the book'
(b) *post-trade transparency* – e.g. details of the price and quantity of previous trades
(c) *trading system access* – the ability to hit quotes and limit orders on all trading systems.

The balance of advantage between formal and informal linkage systems may differ as between these three functions, and it may be sensible for different functions to be organised in different ways. Therefore each of the three functions performed by a linkage system will be considered separately.

Pre-trade transparency   If traders and their agents are to ensure best execution they need to be aware of all the available quotes, i.e. consolidated data. Since best execution may involve hitting an inferior price in order to get the preferred anonymity, settlement etc; just looking at the 'top of the book' (e.g. CQS) may not be sufficient, and traders can benefit from seeing the entire book.

This raises the question of the probability of a competitive market (i.e. an informal system) producing a situation where quote information (top of the book or the entire book) for all trading systems is supplied at an acceptable cost to traders. Data from trading systems with high volumes is more valuable than data from trading systems with low volumes because it is generated by a larger network, and so is more informative. Even if the revenues from selling market data are shared in proportion to trading volume (as in the USA), the trading system with the largest order flow (or network effect) has a clear incentive not to co-operate with smaller trading systems in the distribution of price data. This is evidenced by the uncooperative behaviour of the NYSE in the USA. A large trading system can create a barrier to entry by forcing new entrants to set up their own arrangements for the distribution of market data,[7] to which traders will attach much less value because of their small volume. Hence a consolidated pre-trade system may not emerge from competitive forces, and each trading system will sell their price information separately in competition with every other trading system. Of course some information aggregators may well produce data covering a number of trading systems, but such data will probably exclude some trading systems and be more expensive and not much more informative than data from the primary trading system.

Reliance on informal links to distribute price information means that there is no official national best bid–offer (or market-wide 'yellow strip' or 'top of the book' or NBBO) against which the quality of execution can be judged, e.g. as supplied by the NMS in the USA. Data vendors and information aggregators will construct their own best bid–offer prices, but these may differ between vendors and aggregators, leading to some ambiguity when judging the quality of the price obtained. In a competitive market, an aggregator may emerge to produce consolidated data from all trading systems, and therefore reveal the truly best bid–offer, as revealed in published quotes. However, this data may not be purchased by all market participants.

Some market participants may choose to buy data from only the primary trading system. In which case there is a danger that the market may fragment because not all traders will be aware of the prices on all trading systems, e.g. traders may buy London Stock Exchange information, but be unaware of Virt-x or Jiway prices. If few traders are aware of the prices offered by a trading system, that trading system will get little order flow. Therefore, every trading system has an incentive to make sure that those who route orders see their quotes. This produces some downward pressure on the prices at which trading systems sell their quote data, and may even lead to quote data being supplied free to large brokers and investors. But some investors may be unable to afford this data, e.g. retail customers.[8] Initially, a new trading system may choose to offer its quotes at below cost in order to gain customers and volume. Once it has built a strong network of customers, the trading system can then increase the fees for its quotes.[9] A requirement to obtain best execution (which is not defined in terms of the prices of the primary trading system) may counteract a move to ignore the prices on some small trading systems.

The alternative approach to the provision of quote information is that followed in the USA of an official information system. All trading systems could be required to collectively sell their price data to some central organisation, who would then sell consolidated data to information vendors, e.g. Reuters, Bloombergs, etc., for resale to market participants and others with an interest in such data. This has the advantage that consolidated data is provided, ensuring that everyone who buys this data acquires at least 'the top of the book' for the entire market. However, since the data is supplied by a cartel of trading systems, high prices may be charged, leading to some customers being effectively excluded, e.g. retail investors. Since the data is consolidated by some organisation before supply to the data vendors, there is a central point of failure.

Post-trade transparency   The arguments concerning the choice between competitive (informal) and consolidated (formal) supply of this information are similar to those for pre-trade transparency.

While traders do not need trade information to obtain best execution, to be sure they have obtained best execution they need to see a record of trades on all trading systems, i.e. consolidated post-trade data. If trade data from all trading systems is consolidated by some central organisation, all traders who buy any trade data will have access to the entire transaction record. Under a competitive system, the provision of consolidated trade data may not occur, for the same reasons as arise in the provision of consolidated quote data. The primary trading system will not wish to merge their data with that of small trading systems, hoping that the extra expense of buying trade data from the smaller trading systems will lead to traders buying data only from the primary trading system. There is also a danger that high prices will be charged to data vendors by a monopoly supplier.

Trading system access   A linkage system which allows traders to route orders to hit their chosen order or quotes on any trading system ensures access. Such order interaction is important in encouraging price competition, strengthening price priority and achieving best execution. Access does not mean that every retail trader can personally route their order to every trading system, as those with direct access to a trading system are able to act as agents for those without such access, e.g. retail orders can be routed to a specified trading system via a broker. Given the benefits from the increased network effects, trading systems are usually keen to allow access to their trading facilities. However, some brokers may not acquire access to all trading systems, because of the expense and effort involved. A formal linkage system, such as ITS, to which all brokers have access would ensure that each broker is able to ensure best execution.

Choosing between formal and informal linkage systems   In considering the choice between formal and informal linkage systems for pre- and post-trade transparency and access, some comments to the SBC and SEC have supported the NMS, while others have recommended informal systems. David Downey (Interactive Brokers) (SBC, 2000) supported a revised US national information system with price matching outlawed. In this system traders would have to post their best prices on the system to attract order flow. Harold Bradley *et al.* (American Century) (SEC, 2000b) advocated reliance on informal links, and opposed a CLOB. Similarly, James Buck (NYSE) (SEC, 2000b) supported the use of informal links, as did Sam Miller (Orrick, Herrington and Sutcliffe) (SEC, 2000b), Wayne Wagner (Plexus Group) (SEC, 2000b) and Robert Wood (University of Memphis) (SEC, 2000b). Reliance on brokers automatically searching out the best available prices for their clients was advocated by Thomas Peterffy *et al.* (Interactive Brokers) (SEC, 2000b). However, Jerry Putnam (Archipelago) cautioned the SBC (2000) that trading systems should be stopped from preventing other trading systems gaining access to such systems in the way that the NYSE had shut out Optimark and Archipelago from the ITS.

The SEC's view now tends towards using competitive informal systems to link trading systems. 'The Commission believes that wherever possible, market-based incentives, and not government imposed systems, should determine the connections between markets' (SEC, 2000e). 'Given fair access, the Commission questions whether mandating a particular form of automated electronic linkage across markets is the best means of ensuring access' (SEC, 2000e).

In making the choice between formal and informal systems, the three functions (pre- and post-trade transparency and access) will be considered separately.

(i) *Pre-trade transparency* plays a crucial role in preventing market fragmentation and ensuring best execution. For a number of reasons, a market-wide best bid–offer is very useful, and it is not certain that this will be generated by a competitive (informal) system. Since best execution encompasses other dimensions of a trade than price, brokers need access to the best bid and offer prices on each trading system. There is a case for some precautionary intervention to ensure that a consolidated best bid–offer is widely distributed. Hopefully, competitive informal systems will meet this need and an official data consolidator will prove unnecessary. However, there is still a regulatory need to ensure that any data consolidator does not unreasonably exclude new trading systems from their systems. There are also fears that some market participants will be priced out of buying quote data, and there is a clear case for the regulators to set upper limits on the prices at which quote data can be sold.

(ii) *Trade data* can be useful for those traders who wish to extract the information available in the order flow, but it need not be purchased by all traders. There appears to be only a weak case for regulators to require the provision of consolidated trade data. Traders should be able to check whether they have received best execution, and this provides an argument for setting upper limits on the price charged for trade data. However, the audit of best execution can be performed many hours after the trade, and so there could be price discrimination between current and stale trade (and quote) data, with much lower prices being charged for stale trade (and quote) data.

(iii) The ability to *hit quotes on any trading system* is important for brokers if they are to ensure best execution. But, if they are prepared to offer price matching, their customers may still get the best quoted price, even if their broker is unable to hit the best available quote because they lack access to the trading system concerned. However, if the non-price dimensions of the trade are important, price matching may not give best execution. The appropriate policy here may be reliance on the pressure created by the best execution rule for brokers to have access to all trading systems. The dominant trading system in any market has an incentive to try to prevent rival trading systems from benefiting from its network effects (e.g. price discovery and liquidity). Therefore regulators need to ensure that a dominant trading system does not try to exclude other trading systems from its network benefits by failing to allow access, and by being non-transparent to outsiders (as did the Inter-Dealer Broker (IDB) equity systems in London).

6.2.2 Pricing trading data

While there is competition between data vendors and aggregators, each trading system is ultimately a monopoly vendor of their own trade and quote data. Exchanges in the USA currently derive about 20 per cent of their revenues from the sale of quote and trade data (see Table 4.2), and so the pricing of trading data is an important issue. In the USA equity market data is supplied to data vendors and aggregators by four cartels (or networks) of the trading systems concerned, and the prices at which the data is sold must be approved by the SEC.

Robert Britz (NYSE), Carrie Dwyer (Charles Schwab), Gerald Putnam (Archipelago), Edward Knight (NASDAQ) and Stuart Bell (Bloomberg) (all CFS, 2001a) told the House of Representatives that the monopoly supply of trade and quote information in the USA by organisations such as SIAC and OPRA should be ended. The same suggestion was made by Hardy Callcott (Charles Schwab) and Cameron Smith (Island) (CFS, 2001b). If exchanges were allowed to sell their trade and quote data separately to data vendors, under the SEC's Vendor Display Rule these data vendors would have to supply consolidated data to their clients. Since each data vendor would have to buy the data from every exchange, this would allow exchanges to charge extortionate prices to data consolidators.

If trading systems and data consolidators are allowed to charge high prices for their data (and exclude those unwilling to pay these prices), this will compromise market transparency. In the words of Arthur Levitt (2001) 'allowing unfettered market forces to dictate the cost of pricing data is in direct tension with the mandate for market transparency'. To overcome the problem of data consolidators being required by the Vendor Display Rule to buy data from every exchange, Edward Knight (NASDAQ) proposed that reliance be placed on the SEC to prevent exchanges charging excessive prices (CFS, 2001a). Cameron Smith (Island) suggested a different way round this problem, which is the abolition of the Vendor Display Rule (CFS, 2001b).

The sale of trading data is a major source of revenue for trading systems ($410.6 million for US exchanges in 1998, SEC, 1999), and is becoming increasing important as they shed other activities. Therefore, trading systems need to be allowed to make a reasonable profit on this activity. The pricing problem for regulators is that trading data is a joint product (produced jointly with the trading process) and so has joint costs. In consequence, it is not possible to compute a 'correct' total cost for the production of trading data which might be used in assessing the reasonableness of the price charged for the data. The marginal cost of collecting and supplying the data can be computed, but this is likely to be very low, and give an unreasonably low price. The SEC (1999) is required to ensure that the prices set for the supply of data are 'fair and reasonable' and 'not unreasonably discriminatory'. It does this by reference to the costs of providing the data, although the SEC has some flexibility. The SEC policy has been to expect data fees to be negotiated between the trading systems and the data vendors after a public consultation process. The SEC accepts that allocating the common costs in producing market data is 'an extremely difficult task' and that 'no Commission choice among the various [fully distributed cost] methods could be justified solely on economic criteria'. However, it is the view of the SEC that a flexible cost-based approach can be used for judging the reasonableness of prices for market data, primarily by the SEC specifying the proportion of common trading system costs that can be counted as part of the costs of producing the data.

NASADQ has proposed that exchanges be rewarded for supplying additional data, above and beyond that required by the NMS system. Edward Knight (NASDAQ) proposed that, as well as selling basic data on quotes and trades, exchanges be allowed to sell 'enhanced data' (e.g. market depth) separately from the basic data (CFS, 2001a). Presumably, there would be no requirement for data vendors to supply consolidated enhanced data. Such a development gives exchanges an incentive to increase transparency, but raises issues concerning access to such data for all investors.

The UK is likely to become a fragmented market which relies on informal linkages, where trading systems sell their data separately, rather than as part of a cartel. In this case, trading systems have a strong incentive to make their trading data available because, if traders are unaware of the quote and trade information for a particular trading system, there will be little order flow to that trading system. However, competition between trading systems raises the possibility of restrictive practices by the dominant trading system in the market for trading data. Arthur Levitt (2001) stated that in the USA before 1975 'dominant markets held pricing data close to the vest and wielded it like a club in competition with other markets'. For example, they may insist that their data is not combined with that of smaller rivals (as has the NYSE). There is also the possibility of discriminatory pricing, e.g. low prices to shareholders in the trading system, or a pricing structure that consists of just a flat fee for access to all of the data to shut out small data vendors, etc.[10] Such policies would tend to limit competition and innovation.

Since the market in trading data is potentially open to restrictive practices, cartels and monopoly pricing, some sort of regulatory oversight is needed. As specified by the FSMA (2000, sections 159–164, 302–306), the appropriate regulatory authority for investigating any adverse effects on competition flowing from the behaviour of the FSA is the Office of Fair Trading (OFT). Hence, ensuring competition in the market for the supply of trading data is the responsibility of the OFT.

6.2.3   Access to price sensitive information

Equity market traders need timely access to price sensitive information. In the UK, until 30th April 2000 companies were listed by the London Stock Exchange, who also operate the Regulatory News Service (RNS). The RNS has a monopoly of the release of price sensitive information by listed companies (regulatory information). In a fragmented market, allowing one trading system to have a monopoly of the right to distribute vital trading information appears potentially anti-competitive.

There is also the problem that the London Stock Exchange does not make any separate charge for the services provided by the RNS, with company announcements being disseminated at no direct charge to the company concerned. Companies pay a fee for being listed, and part of this fee is to cover the cost of the regulatory announcements that companies must make to comply with the requirements for being listed. However, the listing fees are now received by the FSA, who make a payment of £1.5 million to the London Stock Exchange for the RNS. In consequence, the London Stock Exchange have little incentive to improve the service provided by the RNS, and a strong incentive to minimise its costs.

The FSA (2001a) has proposed the introduction of a competitive system for the distribution of price sensitive information. Listed companies will be able to pay one of a number of competing primary information providers (PIPs), e.g. the RNS, to disseminate the company's regulatory announcements to secondary information providers (SIPs), e.g. Reuters,

Bloomberg, Dow Jones. The SIPs are expected to aggregate the regulatory announcements from all the PIPs, and so offer the complete set of company announcements to their customers.

The advantages of the proposed structure include ending the monopoly supply of vital trading information, and linking the service provided to the fees charged. However, there are a number of dangers in this proposed structure. Some of these dangers are similar to those for the competitive distribution of trade and quote data by exchanges:

(a) Since companies are to be charged for making announcements, they may choose to make fewer announcements, so depriving the market of price sensitive information and impeding price discovery. This can be prevented by the FSA ensuring compliance by companies with the listing rules.

(b) Each PIP has a monopoly of the dissemination of regulatory announcements by the companies who are its clients. This might lead to high prices being charged to SIPs, although the FSA thinks this is unlikely.[11] The FSA intend leaving prices to market forces, and are not proposing any price cap on PIPs. The way in which market forces will counter high prices being charged by a PIP is not set out by the FSA. One possible constraint on the prices charged by PIPs is that each company will generally wish to see its regulatory announcements widely disseminated at low cost because this may increase its share price. In consequence, companies may switch their regulatory announcements to a PIP that charges fees which are acceptable to the SIPs.

(c) Because of the high prices charged by some PIPs, or for some other reason, one or more SIPs may not aggregate all company announcements. The FSA thinks this will not be the case, and that all SIPs will carry the complete set of company announcements on their systems. It is possible that some traders may be interested in only a sub-set of the market, e.g. small companies, and SIPs may offer such clients a customised supply of regulatory information covering a restricted set of companies.

(d) Owing to the high prices charged by PIPs, or for some other reason, SIPs may charge high prices for real time access to price sensitive announcements. The FSA have been assured by prospective SIPs that they do not plan to raise their prices. In addition, if each SIP is offering the full set of regulatory announcements, this will be a competitive market with rival suppliers offering similar services and this competition will tend to keep prices down. At present private investors have access to free or low-cost real time full text regulatory information via the internet, and the FSA anticipates that this situation will continue. However, it is not clear why, when they have to pay to acquire this information, SIPs should give it away to private investors.

6.2.4 SEC proposals for dealing with fragmentation

As part of a consultation exercise, the SEC (2000a) proposed two main ways of addressing the problems of a fragmented market. These involved the regular publication of aggregate information on the performance of trading systems and brokers, and preserving inter-trading system price–time priority. Both of these proposals were complementary to a good linkage system:

1 *Increased aggregate post-trade transparency*. The SEC could require each trading system to publicly disclose information on a regular basis concerning their performance, so that users and potential users of the trading system (chiefly brokers) can assess the nature of service they are likely to receive from the trading system. For example, each trading system may publish the following average statistics for each time period: the effective spreads for market orders, the percentage of market orders that receive price improvement, the fill rates for different types of limit order, the time-to-fill for different types of limit order, the nature of the order flow (market orders, limit orders, etc.) and the time delay in displaying public limit orders. In addition, trading systems could make available comprehensive data-bases of raw market information to permit independent analysis by brokers, the press, and academics.

     To help customers in selecting brokers, brokers could be required to publicly disclose the types of orders they routed to different trading systems, any agreements they have on routeing order flow (including the payments) and the quality of execution they have obtained for their clients.

     The NYSE already provides brokers with aggregate NYSE price improvement data quarterly, and order-by-order price improvement data under the 'NYSE PRIME super' system, NYSE (2000). Richard Levin (NexTrade) (SEC, 2000b) and Marshall Blume (University of Pennsylvania) (SEC, 2000b) supported the proposal that trading systems and brokers disclose information on their performance and payments for order flow. However, Meyer Frucher (Philadelphia Stock Exchange) (SEC, 2000b) questioned this SEC proposal on the grounds that brokers already have all the information they need from trading systems on execution quality, while customers would not understand such information. Junius Peake (University of Northern Colorado) (SEC, 2000b) is opposed to this suggestion, while Thomas Peterffy *et al.* (Interactive Brokers) (SEC, 2000b) think that the information will prove too complicated for an easy and comprehensive explanation by brokers to their customers, and so will have little effect. This SEC proposal increases post-trade transparency but, of itself, does not deal directly with linking fragmented markets.

2 *Preserve inter-trading system price–time priority.* The SEC has proposed a number of different ways of trying to ensure that market-makers cannot step in front of previously posted limit orders or dealer quotations by matching their price. Implementation of these proposals will encourage traders to post limit orders and aggressive quotes (see section 4.6.4). However, they do not deal directly with linking together fragmented markets:

A *Prevent price matching.* Internalisation and payment for order flow would be permitted only when the price at which the trade is executed is *better* than the best available quote; as proposed by the NYSE. This would promote price–time priority across all trading systems as market-makers and specialists would not be able to step ahead of earlier limit orders by price matching. It requires a national information system displaying the best bid and offer prices together with their times. Stoll (2001) supports this proposal because it would discourage preferencing and increase the incentive to post good quotes. However, this proposal has been opposed by Sam Miller (Orrick, Herrington & Sutcliffe, SEC, 2000b) as likely to lead to increased order flow for the NYSE at the expense of other trading systems; and a worse deal for customers due to higher overall transactions costs. It is opposed by Thomas Peterffy *et al.* (Interactive Brokers) (SEC, 2000b) because it leads to a lack of transparency, as dealers are encouraged to trade at undisclosed prices.

B *Expose market orders to price competition.* Before execution, trading systems would have to expose their orders to price competition. This might mean that an acceptable exposure regime led to price improvement for a specified percentage of orders, or that before acting as counterparty, a market-maker would have to expose the order to the market at a one-tick improvement on the best available price for a specified length of time to see if any price improvement is possible. To inform the entire market of such proposed trades would require a national information system. The NYSE view of this 'stop and expose' proposal is that a time exposure longer than 30 seconds would be required, and they are generally opposed to this proposal (James Buck of the NYSE, SEC, 2000b).

C *Preserve national price–time priority for customers.* Under this proposal market makers would not be allowed to trade ahead of previously submitted investor limit orders. This would prevent market-makers and specialists from stepping ahead of existing customer limit orders by matching their price. Since price–time priority is already enforced by individual trading systems, it would have an effect only on inter-trading system trades. It requires a national information system displaying all customer limit orders, and Thomas Peterffy *et al.* (Interactive Brokers) (SEC, 2000b) argue that this would be almost as difficult as building and maintaining a CLOB. They also suggest that, if there were regulatory advantages to being a customer, the definition of a 'customer' needs to be clear and precise.

D *Give inter-trading system time priority for price improvements.* The *first* limit order or dealer quotation to improve the national best bid and offer would receive inter-trading system time priority. Subsequent limit orders or quotations at this price would not receive time priority. This would provide an incentive to improve the present price, but no incentive to increase the depth at this price. This would require a national information system displaying the price-improving limit orders or quotations.

E *Establish price–time priority for all displayed trading interest.* Under this proposal all orders and dealer quotations would be given inter-trading system price–time priority. They would all be publicly displayed, and orders executed automatically. This is essentially a CLOB, and is strongly supported by Junius Peake (University of Northern Colorado, SEC, 2000b), while Thomas Peterffy *et al.* (Interactive Brokers) (SEC, 2000b) are opposed to a CLOB.

After considering the comments received on the above six proposals, the SEC (2000e) decided to take no action on their proposals A–E which were designed to preserve inter-trading system price–time priority. However, they did propose rules for increased aggregate post-trade transparency. The SEC argue that, as brokers' commissions have declined, the relative importance of execution costs has increased.

(a) *Market centres.* They proposed that each equity market centre[12] publish monthly electronic reports giving statistics on the execution quality for each security they trade.[13] To aid comparison between market centres, the quality measures will be computed in a uniform manner by every market centre. So that the performance of a market centre is not damaged by receiving a difficult order flow, the quality measures for each stock will be disaggregated by five types of order and four order sizes, i.e. 20 rows of output per stock traded. Reports with this level of detail can now be produced and distributed at little cost by market centres because of the use of computers and the internet. It is expected that these reports will be analysed by brokers, the financial press, consultants, academics and other market centres, who will produce summaries for investors.

(b) *Broker–dealers.* In addition, broker–dealers that route equity and options orders must publish each quarter a report which describes their order routeing practices, including any payment for order flow and internalisation arrangements. These reports are intended for investors and, in addition to these aggregate reports, individual investors will be able to request details of where their own orders were routed. For options, broker–dealers will have to tell their customers when they execute an order at a worse price than the best quote published on the options quote reporting system. This will encourage options brokers and trading systems to obtain execution for their customers at the best price. The SEC is considering proposing a similar rule on trade-through disclosure for equities, including the possibility of comparison with the best quote when the order was received, as well as executed, SEC (2000e). This raises the interesting idea of revealing poor execution owing to delays.

In addition to requiring the publication of data on execution quality and order routeing, the SEC (2000e) proposed some other actions. They wish to see ATS quotes included in the CQS. However, there is a problem over ATS access fees. ATSs in the US currently charge non-subscribers to the ATS an access fee of between ¼ cent and 1½ cents per share to trade with orders displayed on their systems (SEC, 2000e). Since ATSs do not act as a principal, they recoup their operating costs by explicitly charging access fees to non-subscribers, and subscription fees to subscribers. The consequence is that when non-subscribers evaluate the competitiveness of ATS quotes, they must allow for this access fee, which is not charged by NASDAQ or the listed markets, e.g. NYSE and the regional exchanges. Given the previous tick size of ¹⁄₁₆th (or 6.25 cents), a better price on an ATS would still be the best price after allowance for access fees. However, after decimalisation, this may not be the case.

The SEC proposals for the publication on data on order routeing and execution practices were welcomed by Michael Dorsey (Knight Trading

Group), Gary McFarland (individual investor) and William O'Brien (Brut) (all SEC, 2000f). Alan Shapiro and Howard Kohos (Transition Auditing Group) strongly supported the proposals, and made many detailed suggestions for refining them in the light of their experience of providing a similar service to their clients (SEC, 2000f). Thomas Peterffy and David Battan (Timer Hill Group) supported the proposals, and suggested they be extended to options (SEC, 2000f). Robert White (a professional investor) welcomed the proposed disclosure of payment for order flow, which he regards as a kick back that should be outlawed.

A number of other comments on the SEC proposals expressed general support for the idea of a high level of transparency for order routeing and execution, but criticised some of the details of what was proposed. Robert Gasser (J.P. Morgan) supported the proposals, but expressed worries about the costs of the disclosure regime and the possibility that the disclosure requirements would lead to law suits (SEC, 2000f). Richard Brueckner (Pershing Division of Donaldson, Lufkin and Jenrette Securities Corporation) was concerned that the data might confuse retail investors, and that those interpreting this data for the benefit of private investors would do so in a biased manner (SEC, 2000f). He was also concerned about creating class action lawsuits and the lack of proposals to audit the information released; and he questioned the need to disclose internalisation arrangements. Mark Sutton (Securities Industry Association) supported the proposals, but was concerned that execution quality will concentrate on price and speed, and neglect other aspects of best execution (e.g. transactions costs, transparency, anonymity, reliability) (SEC, 2000f). He was also worried that the average realised spread is an unsuitable comparator, that there may be a proliferation of law suits, and that some of the required information is useless (e.g. cancelled orders and the trading system to which an order was routed). Jeffrey Brown (Cincinnati Stock Exchange) commended the SEC for their proposals, but suggested that the SEC should simply require market centres to publish the entire processing history of each order,[14] which is already collected by trading systems (SEC, 2000f). He also criticised the use of the national best bid and offer (NBBO). Edward Nicoll (Datek Online Brokerage and the Island ATS) supported the proposals, but made a number of detailed suggestions for their improvement (SEC, 2000f). Wang (UBS Warburg's EMM Unit) enthusiastically supported the proposals, but suggested that simply requiring the publication of the raw order execution history may be a better approach (SEC, 2000f). Andrew Davis and William Surman (Rock Island Company) applauded the proposals, but suggested that the period for the computation of the average realised spread be reduced from 30 to 5 minutes, and that consolidated reports be produced (SEC, 2000f).

Some commentators were opposed to the SEC proposals, although none was opposed to greater transparency. Roger Blanc, on behalf of Ameritrade, DLJ Direct Inc, National Discount Brokers, T D Waterhouse Group and Wit Capital Corporation opposed the disclosure proposals as they go 'far beyond what is sensible or required' (SEC, 2000f). Blanc's objections include the cost of disclosure; the focus on features of order routeing and execution that can be quantified, at the expense of features such as service, likelihood of execution, reliability of the systems and speed of execution, which are harder to quantify; the incentive created for brokers and market-makers not to deal in hard-to-execute stocks and hard-to-execute trades, the blunting of market forces and the stifling of innovation and the increased likelihood of class-action litigation. Robin Rogers (Morgan Stanley Dean Witter) did not support the proposals (SEC, 2000f). He pointed out that the SEC proposals do not solve the problem of fragmentation, are overly technical and will not be understood by, or be of use to, investors, focus on the quantitative aspects of best execution, may facilitate lawsuits, will be costly and are not audited. Rogers concluded that any disclosure should be voluntary. Lanny Schwartz (Philadelphia Stock Exchange) had significant reservations about the proposals. In his view, investors may be misled by the data and should rely on the advice of their brokers, some aspects of the service cannot be quantified and so may be ignored, and the new systems will cost the Philadelphia Stock Exchange $500,000 to create. Deborah Lamb and Maria Clark (Association for Investment Management and Research) criticised the proposals on the grounds that they do not address fragmentation, the information is not meaningful and will confuse investors (because the order routeing system the data summarises is over-complex) and the compliance costs will greatly outweigh the benefits, (SEC, 2000f). Junius Peake (University of Northern Colorado) argued that what needs reform is the market structure.

The overall implication of these comments is that, by altering some of the details of what is proposed, a considerable increase in the transparency of US equity markets would be largely supported by market participants. In November 2000 the SEC (2000h) issued new rules requiring market centres and broker–dealers to publish the information specified in their earlier proposals discussed above (SEC, 2000e) (see Table 6.1). The only substantial change from the SEC's earlier proposals was a reduction in the information required in the quarterly broker–dealer reports. The SEC have concluded that 'increased public disclosure of

Table 6.1   Monthly and quarterly reports by market centres and broker–dealers

---

Market centre monthly reports

Data on each covered security[1] traded by the market centre must be classified into 20 groups using four trade size categories (100–499, 500–1,999, 2,000–4,999, 5,000 + shares) and five types of order (market, marketable limit, inside-the-quote limit, at-the-quote limit and near-the-quote limit).

For each of the 20 groups for a particular equity, the following 11 pieces of information must be provided:
1   Number of covered orders[2]
2   Cumulative number of shares of covered orders
3   Cumulative number of shares of covered orders cancelled prior "to execution
4   Cumulative number of shares of covered orders executed at the receiving market centre
5   Cumulative number of shares of covered orders executed at any other venue
6   Cumulative number of shares of covered orders executed from 0 to 9 seconds after the time of order receipt
7   Cumulative number of shares of covered orders executed 10 to 29 seconds after the time of order receipt
8   Cumulative number of shares of covered orders executed from 30 to 59 seconds after the time of the order receipt
9   Cumulative number of shares of covered orders executed from 60 seconds to 299 seconds after the time of order receipt
10   Cumulative number of shares of covered orders executed from 5 minutes to 30 minutes after the time of order receipt
11   The average realised spread for executions of covered orders.

For market orders and marketable limit orders the following 9 pieces of information must be provided:
1   Average effective spread for executions of covered orders
2   Cumulative number of shares of covered orders executed with price improvement
3   For shares executed with price improvement, the share-weighted average amount per share that prices were improved
4   For shares executed with price improvement, the share-weighted average amount period from the time of order receipt to the time of order execution
5   Cumulative number of shares of covered orders executed at the quote
6   For shares executed at the quote, the share-weighted average period from the time of order receipt to the time of order execution
7   Cumulative number of shares of covered orders executed outside the quote
8   For shares executed outside the quote, the share-weighted average amount per share that prices were outside the quote
9   For shares executed outside the quote, the share-weighted average period from the time of order receipt to the time of order execution.

Broker–dealer quarterly reports

Data must be provided on their routeing of non-directed orders in covered securities, divided into three sections: NYSE listed securities, NASDAQ securities and securities listed on AMEX and national exchanges.

For each of these 3 sections, 3 types of information must be provided:
1   The percentage of total customer orders for the section that were non-directed orders, and the percentages of total non-directed orders for the section that were market orders, limit orders, and other orders
2   The identity of the 10 venues to which the largest number of total non-directed orders for the section were routed for execution and of any venue to which 5 per cent or more of non-directed orders were routed for execution, the percentage of total non-directed orders for the section routed to the venue, and the percentage of total non-directed market orders, total non-directed limit orders, and total non-directed other orders for the section that were routed to the venue
3   A discussion of the material aspects of the broker or dealer's relationship with each market venue identified in the previous item, including a description of any arrangement for payment for order flow and any profit sharing.

Every broker–dealer shall, on request of a customer, disclose to its customer:
1   The identity of the market venue to which the customer's orders were routed for execution in the six months prior to the request
2   Whether the orders were directed orders or non-directed orders
3   The time of the transactions, if any, that resulted from such orders.

Notes: [1] Covered security means any NMS security and any other security for which a transaction report, last sale data or quotation information is disseminated through an automated quotation system as defined in various sections of the Act.
[2] Covered orders are orders received by a market centre during regular trading hours at a time when the NBBO is disseminated, and, if executed, is executed during regular trading hours. Orders for which the customer requests special handling for execution are excluded. These include orders to be executed at the market opening price or the market closing price, orders submitted with stop prices, orders to be executed only at their full size, orders to be executed on a particular type of tick or bid, orders submitted on a 'not held' basis, orders for other than regular settlement, and orders to be executed at prices unrelated to the market price of the security at the time of execution.

execution quality and order routeing practices is a minimum step necessary to address fragmentation' (SEC, 2000h). The SEC pointed out that the publication of order execution quality facilitates competition between market centres and between broker–dealers based on price improvement, rather than just commissions and execution speed. The SEC provided evidence of the substantial benefits that are expected to be received by traders from these transparency rules. If all the NASDAQ trades that are conducted at worse prices than those of the median effective spread traded at the median spread, traders would save $110 million per year. The SEC also found that effective spreads for small market orders on regional exchanges were 20%–39% higher than those on the NYSE. This again suggests there will be substantial cost savings for traders if they can obtain the prices available on the most competitive trading system.

The publication of similar data by 'market centres' and broker–dealers in the UK would be a welcome development. As the number of ATSs increases, such data would assist brokers in routeing orders to the trading system which has previously offered the characteristics desired by their client, e.g spread, immediacy, size, etc. It would also help investors in selecting brokers, and reveal any order routeing arrangements (e.g. internalisation, preferencing and payment for order flow). The European Commission (2001) has proposed that, each quarter, all authorised firms be required to disclose their order routeing practices.

Despite widespread support, the SEC consultation elicited a number of objections to the publication of such information which could also be relevant in the UK. These were the cost of producing and publishing the information, the possibility of law suits, the confusion of investors by the data from brokers, the interpretation of the data in a biased manner, the lack of any audit of the data, the concentration on speed of execution and price, which can be easily quantified, and the neglect of other aspects of best execution, and the avoidance by brokers and trading systems of 'difficult' stocks and trades as they will make the numbers look bad. The SEC was unimpressed by these objections, and chose to introduce the additional disclosure. These objections also appear to be unimportant for the UK, and it is likely that the benefits of this increase in information to market participants will outweigh the costs. Such transparency will play a large part in ensuring that the various trading systems function as a single market.

6.3 Conclusions

This study has argued that security market fragmentation *per se* is not a problem. A problem exists only if fragmentation results in worse execution. Provided the benefits of a consolidated market are preserved in a fragmented system, we can have our cake and eat it – we receive the benefits of competition and the benefits of consolidation. The challenge is to create such a fragmented market. Until recently, this was not fully possible as the linkages between markets were imperfect. However, developments in information technology have allowed cheap fast real time links to be implemented, and this is now revolutionising the structure and regulation of securities markets.[15]

For most of their history, owing to the powerful economies of scale and network effects associated with floor trading, securities exchanges have operated largely as monopolies. This monopoly situation, and the importance of their function, resulted in exchanges being closely regulated.

However, in the last few years technological developments (e.g. screen-based trading, instant electronic communication, etc.) have drastically changed this situation. Now the economies of scale in trading are much smaller, while the network effects can be largely preserved in a multi-trading system market. In consequence, the market for trading securities has become contestable, and new trading systems can easily enter to compete with existing trading systems.

In this new world, market forces play a powerful role in shaping the outcome, and the role of regulators changes substantially. The market for trading securities has moved a lot closer to the market for (say) trading houses (e.g. estate agent services[16]). In this new environment, the role of the regulator moves much more towards ensuring that there is a suitable infrastructure of rules which enable the competitive market in trading services to function. The CFTC has recently recognised this change in the role of regulators and is transforming itself 'from a front line to an oversight regulator' (William Rainer, Chairman of the CFTC, SBC, 2000). Mahoney (1997) also argues that trading systems should be freed from detailed regulation, and allowed to compete for business by determining their own rule book, while the regulators should concentrate on ensuring an absence of manipulation and negative externalities.

6.3.1   Some implications for regulators

This new situation has a number of implications for regulators:

1 *Inevitability of Fragmentation*
   Fragmentation is a necessary consequence of competition, and should be welcomed not be resisted. Indeed, given the ISD and the right of an exchange in one EU country to offer trading services in another, it is probably not possible to prevent fragmentation.[17]
2 *Differences in trading procedures*
   Diversity in trading procedures between trading systems can easily result from competition, as trading systems try to offer a superior service. This diversity is a healthy sign that competition is working and traders are being offered a choice.
3 *Price discrimination*
   The order flow is heterogeneous, and cross-subsidies between different types of orders are unsustainable in a competitive market. In consequence, different types of order flow will pay different prices for execution services. It may be difficult for regulators to distinguish between situations where a particular class of trader is excluded by a trading system on grounds of cost, and when a trading system

wishes to deny a group of traders access for some other reason. However, provided the market is contestable, any price discrimination or exclusion of traders on grounds other than cost will create an incentive for another trading system to enter the market and provide cheaper execution or access for the excluded traders.

4 *Penetration pricing*

Given the presence of economies of scale in trading, network effects for financial trading systems and the one-off costs of connecting to new networks, it is to be expected that new trading systems will initially price their services at below cost in order to compete with existing networks. However, as the network expands, this penetration pricing will be followed by a rise in price.

5 *Implicit mergers and alliances.*

Simple measures of market fragmentation based on the shares of order flow can overstate the level of fragmentation when trading systems have formed alliances and implicit mergers.

6 *Trading mechanism.*

There is no evidence that some types of trading mechanism (e.g. floor or screen, dealer or auction) are inferior from a regulatory viewpoint. Competition between trading systems can be left to decide the winners.[20]

7 *Trading system rules*

If a trading system decides to introduce rules which harm some of its customers, it will lose order flow to rival trading systems. Regulatory intervention is needed only when the behaviour of one trading system creates negative externalities, e.g. for traders or other trading systems. Such negative externalities are considered further in section 6.3.2.

8 *Linkage systems*

It is very important that the various trading systems in a fragmented market be linked together. While some support a formal consolidated system, e.g. NMS, for this purpose, others support informal competitive systems. Whatever, the decision regarding formal or informal systems, there are two policies:

(a) upper limits should be set on the prices charged for real time quote (and possibly trade) data, and

(b) the systems for data distribution and access to trading systems should not create barriers to new trading systems starting up.

It is not clear whether a consolidated best bid–offer should be established by regulatory action (as in the USA under the Vendor Display Rule), or whether a market solution will emerge. There appears to be no feasible way of ensuring time priority in the absence of some sort of CLOB.

9   *Different regulation for different securities or 'are metals different?'*
While one size does not fit all in terms of the details of the trading process,[19] it will be argued that it is sensible for the same basic regulatory framework of promoting contestable markets to be applied to all products and traders.[20] A bifurcation of regulatory treatment may occur between types of trader (e.g. professional and retail), or different regulatory regimes may be applied to different securities (e.g. metals are different), or a combination of both (e.g. the CFTC has introduced different regulations for different types of product (manipulable or non-manipulable) and different market participants (institutional or retail).

It has been claimed that some securities differ in terms of ease of manipulation and price discovery, and so require a different regulatory regime:

- *Manipulation.* Commodities may have a relatively inelastic demand and supply, and this makes them particularly susceptible to manipulative tactics, such as cornering and squeezing. However all markets are potentially vulnerable to some form of manipulation or insider trading, and so need rules against such behaviour. Some rules will 'bite' harder on particular securities, e.g. position reporting and metals markets, but the rules cannot be avoided or changed by redefining the security.
- *Price discovery.* While some trading venues may perform a price discovery function, this does not necessitate a set of rules which differ from those of other trading venues.

Having different rules for different securities has a number of drawbacks:

(*a*) *Multiple regimes.* If the basis for regulation is the product, each trading system which trades a variety of products (which may have a different mix of professional–retail traders) could be subject to a number of different regulatory regimes. For example, Jiway is to trade energy products, while LIFFE, CME and CBOT trade soft commodities, as well as financial securities. Multiple regulatory regimes increase the regulatory overhead of exchanges, and may lead to confusion.

(*b*) *Loopholes.* The use of different rules for different products will encounter the problem of defining products in a way that does not provoke the exploitation of loopholes. Deborah Lamb *et al.* (AMIR) (SEC, 2000b) argue that trading systems (equities, fixed income, futures, forwards, options, etc.) should be subject to the same rules. If not, loopholes will be created. For example, if the regulations differ between products, new securities may be introduced which exploit loopholes in the definition of products, e.g. new hybrids may be introduced along the lines of swaptions or equity linked bonds, and these may create definitional difficulties for regulators.

(c) *Instability*. It is unlikely that the situation will remain stable over time. The use of screen-based trading means that existing trading systems can easily start trading new products, possibly of a different type from their existing range of products. Indeed, it is quite possible that trading systems will increasing view themselves as specialists in providing execution services, with the underlying asset being of secondary importance. In which case general purpose trading systems will emerge using their screen-based systems to trade almost anything. Therefore, many trading systems could be subject to an increasing range of regulatory regimes.

(d) *Innovation*. A range of regulatory regimes could stifle innovation because new products and ways of trading may not fit easily into the regulatory system.

(e) *Lack of scrutiny*. The creation of MTEF and DTF by the CFTC could remove trading in some securities from public scrutiny. Daniel Rappaport (Chairman of NYMEX) stated in September 2000 that the Commodity Futures Modernization Act of 2000 would 'likely lead to a migration of energy trading to unregulated markets, thus depriving policy makers, regulators and the public of currently available information on market participation, concentration and financial performance'. It 'would remove a substantial portion of the energy marketplace from public scrutiny and regulatory oversight'.

Overall, it is simpler, clearer and probably cheaper to have a single set of rules applying to all securities markets. Given the changed role of the regulator in securities markets with its focus on ensuring the framework for competition and a withdrawal from detailed rule-making, there is much less need to be concerned about the minutiae of how trading systems operate. In this new situation financial market regulators are in a similar position to the OFT, which regulates a very wide range of industries according to the same basic rule book. Some rules will 'bite' harder on particular products, e.g. position reporting and metals markets, but the rules cannot be avoided or changed by redefining the product. This approach means that traders need become familiar with only one set of rules, and the scope for regulatory arbitrage is reduced.

10 *Different regulations for different traders*[21]

It has been proposed that the regulations for trading a particular security on a particular trading system should differ between types of trader. The FSA (2001) thinks that market infrastructure providers (MIPs)[22] that restrict access to professionals are unlikely to require the same degree of regulation as those that provide facilities to retail investors. However, the FSA also takes the view that the mainstay of protection for less sophisticated investors in fragmented markets is best execution (which does not require differential regulation by trader type). Such a situation has a number of disadvantages:

(a) *Lock-in.* LIFFE started trading universal stock futures on 29 January 2001. The expectation is that these futures contracts on individual stocks will be attractive to retail customers. On 17 October 2000 LIFFE introduced Mini FTSE 100 futures, which are one-fifth the size of FTSE 100 futures, and so are valued at less than £13,000 each. These new futures are designed to be used by retail customers. Regulations which differ according to the identity of the trader (e.g. retail, professional, institutional, market-maker, etc); risk locking a trading venue into dealing with a particular client type, and should be avoided in the interests of promoting access.

(b) *Distortions.* Different trading systems may be trading the same security according to different regulations, e.g. a retail exchange and a professional exchange. This can easily lead to market distortions, e.g. lower transparency requirements for the professional market.

(c) *Differentiation.* Many regulations apply to the trading process. If a trading venue has a mixture of different types of client trading the same security, it is impracticable (and probably unfair) to apply different rules to different traders, e.g. only institutional clients can see the size and price of the last trade.

(d) *Multiple regimes.* Each trading venue which is used by two or more types of trader could be subject to a number of different regulatory regimes. This will be expensive and potentially confusing.

(e) *Loopholes.* If there are different regulations for (say) retail and institutional traders, this will require:

• a careful distinction to be drawn between these two types of trader, and
• the monitoring of the type of trader to ensure that the trading venue still qualifies as professional (or retail).

(f) *Distortions.* The CFTC rules permitting Exempt MTEF and DTF mean that different exchanges will be trading the same security according to different regulations, e.g. a retail exchange and a professional exchange. This can easily lead to market distortions, e.g. lower transparency requirements for the professional market. When considering the possibility of separate regulatory treatment for retail and institutional investors, the SEC (1994) concluded that 'it would be difficult to provide completely different tiers of regulation and maintain fair and orderly equity markets'. 'Irreparable harm to the well-deserved reputation of the US markets could result from, for example, ... reducing the transparency for institutional trades.' 'Although removing these [regulatory] costs for larger investors could create a marginally more efficient operating environment for them, it would reduce significantly the fairness that makes the US markets so attractive to investors.'

11 *Different regulation for different trades*

While differentiation by security and trader type have been rejected, this does not mean that regulations cannot be differentiated in other ways. For example, most trading systems have rules which vary according to at least three criteria, (see Demarchi and Foucault, 1998, for a survey of five major European stock exchanges) The three criteria are:

- The size of the trade, e.g. special block trade procedures
- The liquidity or market capitalisation of the security, e.g. the London Stock Exchange trades shares in four different ways – SETS, SEAQ, SEATS-Plus and AIM – with securities moving between these trading systems as their liquidity changes
- The time of day – many exchanges have a call market at the open and close of trading, with a continuous market during the rest of the day.

Such rules recognise differences between *trades*, rather than differences between *traders* or *securities*.

6.3.2 Some policy recommendations

1 *Competition*

Regulators need to be concerned about the conduct of trading systems in the same way that the OFT is concerned about the conduct of companies. Are they colluding, are they competing unfairly, are they seeking to establish a monopoly (possibly by taking over their rivals), are they creating barriers to entry? Promoting competition fits well with the FSA's statutory obligations set out in the FSMA (2000, section 2). The regulatory role has changed fundamentally. Instead of trying to preserve consolidated trading on a single exchange, regulators are now trying to stop trading from consolidating, as this would constitute a monopoly supplier of trading services.[23] The regulation of trading systems has become much closer to that of any other service industry.

Some of the ways in which trading systems can behave uncompetitively include:

(a) *Creation of barriers to entry*. Barriers to entry may take the form of restricting access to trading systems, or restricting the availability of price and volume data, etc. For example, the NYSE blocked access by ATSs to the National Market System,[24] while NYSE Rule 390 prevented NYSE members from trading NYSE-listed stocks on an ATS. The IDB systems in the UK allowed only market-makers to see the quotes and trades on these systems.

(b) *Failure to share the network effects*. The dominant trading system in any market has an incentive to try to prevent rival trading systems from benefiting from its network effects (e.g. price discovery and liquidity). Therefore regulators need to ensure that a dominant trading system does not try to exclude other trading systems from its network benefits by failing to allow access, and by being non-transparent to outsiders (as did the IDB markets in London).

(c) *Corporate governance*. The change in the governance of exchanges (demutualisation and flotation) may lead to new problems. For example, once an exchange is owned by its major users, they have both the incentive and the means to change the way the exchange operates to suit themselves[25]. The demutualisation of exchanges also means that for-profit companies regulate other for-profit companies, who may be their rivals for order flow, e.g. RIEs may regulate ATSs. This could easily lead to conflicts of interest.

(d) *Lock-ins*. The only way a lock-in is likely to occur in financial markets is by regulatory action, e.g. prohibiting rival trading systems, or banning screen-based trading. Thus it is important that regulators do not, perhaps inadvertently, create a lock-in by creating some rule which prevents innovation and competition between trading systems. This fits with 'the desirability of facilitating innovation in the financial sector' (FSA, 1999b, page 6), which is one of the things the FSA bears in mind in pursuing its objectives.

In competitive markets firms will enter until the expected profit of the marginal entrant equals zero. There is a danger that some entrants will provide an inferior service, but this should be countered by the discipline of both the market and the regulator. There appears to be no way in which having a large number of service providers will, of itself, damage market quality. Of course, if there are, say, 20 rival trading systems, brokers will need to scan many prices. But the use of computers should solve this problem. The only regulatory concern over the number of service providers is that this number may become too small, so that the supply of trading services falls into the hands of only a few firms (oligopoly) or one firm (monopoly).

2   *Best execution*

In a competitive market, customers who are dissatisfied with the service they have received (e.g. from an estate agent) can take their business elsewhere. Therefore regulatory intervention (e.g. a best execution requirement) may be unnecessary. However, in the market for execution services, customers often lack the information to realise they have received poor execution. Even if they have the requisite information, they may not realise they have received poor execution. To deal with this situation, best execution is an important requirement, linked with the disclosure of execution quality by brokers to customers.

In a fragmented market, the requirement for best execution increases in importance, while the difficulty of enforcing best execution also increases. Therefore, as markets fragment, more attention needs to be given to ensuring that customers receive best execution. In the US it appears that some brokers regard the best execution obligation as applying 'on average' to the order flow they handle.

3   *Transparency*

In fragmented markets, transparency becomes even more important, and a key role for regulators is ensuring maximum transparency (both pre- and post-trade). The FSA (2001) thinks that fragmented trading may require common transparency standards for all significant venues in the price-formation process for exchange traded instruments. Transparency is one of the features (along with access and best execution) which links together a set of rival trading systems into a single market. In a fragmented market system, if one or more trading systems is permitted to offer a low level of transparency this could have a damaging effect on the price discovery process for the market. In such a situation, a key role for regulators is ensuring a high level of transparency. There is always a possible risk that a high level of transparency could damage liquidity, but there is no empirical evidence to support this view; and a substantial quantity of evidence to the contrary, particularly for liquid securities. If a high level of transparency is not required, there is a real possibility that opaque trading systems will be established and this will both damage price formation and create an advantage for those who are able to see the trading activity on this opaque trading system. It is suggested that the presumption is for maximum transparency, with the obligation placed on trading systems to argue the case for any reductions in transparency, e.g. pre-trade transparency for large trades. Transparency needs to encompass overseas trading if the transparency rules are not to be avoided by booking trades overseas.

4   *Linkages*
To obtain the advantages of competition without suffering the disadvantages of fragmentation, it is important that trading systems be linked together to create a single market. A linkage system provides pre- and post-trade transparency, as well as market access. It is recommended that reliance be placed on informal systems supplied by data vendors and information aggregators. However, the situation needs to be reviewed to ensure that such services are operating effectively, e.g. new trading systems can get their data displayed by the linkage system, the prices charged for the data are not excessive, and a consolidated best bid–offer across all trading systems is available.

5   *Access*
It is important that every trader can not only see what is happening on each trading system, but that they have the ability to trade on each trading system.[26] This can be achieved by a linkage system which allows traders to route orders to hit their chosen limit order or quotes on any trading system. Access does not mean that every retail trader can personally route their order to every trading system. But it does mean that those with direct access to a trading system are able to act as agents for those without such access, e.g. retail orders can be routed to a specified trading system via a broker.

6   *Manipulation and insider trading*
Securities markets require someone to look out for insider trading and market manipulation. Individual trading systems in a fragmented market have less incentive to spend money on these activities than a monopoly exchange because these activities generate a public good which benefits all trading systems, while the costs fall only on those trading systems who look for such abuses. In addition, in a fragmented system, spotting manipulation or insider trading may require information from most trading systems so that the aggregate market position can be seen. Therefore, responsibility for preventing market abuse is best placed with the regulators.

Since the prosecution of market manipulation is difficult, the opinion of Gilbert (1996) is that the emphasis should be on prevention, rather than prosecution; and prevention is achieved by increased transparency. Gilbert recommends that (a) UK derivatives markets be required to report client positions, and that (b) aggregate position data be published. Gilbert considered whether such reporting and publication should be extended to include the corresponding OTC and spot markets, and concluded that, while desirable, such a requirement would be infeasible. However, in some cases, e.g. stocks in LME warehouses, limited spot position reporting and publication could be required.

It may be sensible for traders with 'large' positions in a particular contract month (spot, futures, options and OTC markets combined) to be required to report them to the regulatory authorities.[27] A 'large' position can be defined with respect to the available supplies of the underlying asset, and so a modest number of contracts may be reportable for an obscure metal, but would be a long way short of the threshold for most interest rate products. It may also be sensible for regulators to have the power to require traders to unwind large positions if this is judged to be having an adverse effect on the market. Provided the threshold for reportable positions is high, very little reporting will actually take place, so minimising the regulatory burden.

Notes

1 There are some situations when links between trading systems will not preserve the network benefits of a consolidated market. Suppose that all trading in security U takes place on a trading system in the USA. Then a Japanese trading system also starts trading security U. If these two trading systems are not open simultaneously (time fragmentation), real time links are irrelevant. At any particular time the order flow is consolidated on a single trading system. The network benefits for traders will decline if the Japanese order flow is simply orders that would previously have gone to the US trading system because the same order flow is now spread over a longer period.

2 A trade-through occurs when an order is not executed against the best available price.

3 Many of the witnesses before the SBC (2000) were opposed to the introduction of a mandatory CLOB in the US, e.g. Harold Bradley (American Century), Antonio Cecin (US Bancorp), David Colker (Cincinnati Stock Exchange), David Downey (Interactive Brokers), Kevin Foley (Tradebook), Robert Forney (Chicago Stock Exchange), Richard Grasso (NYSE), Alan Greenspan (Fed), Kenneth Pasternak (Knight Securities), Gerald Putnam (Archipelago), Joe Ricketts (Ameritrade), Charles Schwab (Schwab) and Frank Zarb (NASD). The SEC (1994) also rejected a CLOB for equities, while the CBOE, Amex and International Securities Exchange rejected a CLOB for options. However, some witnesses before the SBC argued in favour of price–time priority, and

the obvious way to achieve this is by a mandatory CLOB; David Komansky (Merrill Lynch), Henry Paulson (Goldman Sachs), Philip Purcell (Morgan Stanley Dean Witter) and Allen Wheat (CSFB). In evidence to the SEC, a CLOB has also been rejected by Marshall Blume (University of Pennsylvania, SEC, 2000b), Meyer Frucher (Philadelphia Stock Exchange, SEC, 2000b), Dan Jamieson (investor, SEC, 2000b), Sam Miller (Orrick, Herrington and Sutcliffe, SEC, 2000b), Robert Wood (University of Memphis, SEC, 2000b) and Steve Wunsch (Arizona Stock Exchange, SEC, 2000b), while Hendrick Bessembinder (Emory University, SEC, 2000b) favoured a non-mandatory CLOB.

4 Such linkage systems can involve a very large number of messages. For example, OPRA, the options market linkage system in the USA, was running at 4,000 messages per second in 2000, and this was projected to rise to 38,000 message a second by about 2002 (Ed Joyce CBOE, SEC, 2000 g).

5 Companies which display information from a number of trading systems are termed 'information aggregators'.

6 In evidence to the SEC (2000 g) Rick Ketchum (NASD) said that NASDAQ must distribute prices 'so far away from the market as to be unhelpful' and 'auto-quoted prices on secondary markets for a small number of shares, usually 100 shares, which are effectively unhittable'. 'These two things generate a tremendous percentage of the total quotations.' In consequence, NASDAQ 'is putting out a lot of information that is literally ignored and thrown on the floor by everyone who trades in the whole country'.

7 The internet now offers a cheap method for price distribution.

8 Some trading systems offer old prices (e.g. with a 20-minute delay) for free, while real time prices are expensive.

9 The analysis of fees for quote information is similar to that for trading fees in section 6.2.2, and relies on network effects.

10 For example, before being required in 1975 to distribute its data, the NYSE severely restricted public access to its quotations (SEC, 1999).

11 The FSA expects PIPs to charge SIPs a percentage of any fees that the SIP receives when the information is sold on.

12 The market centres required to produce monthly reports include primarily specialists and market-makers on recognised exchanges, and also ATSs, exchanges and market-makers on OTC exchanges that trade NMS securities.

13 Reports would include any foreign equities traded by these US 'exchanges'.

14 The time of order receipt, type of order, limit price, size of order, time of order execution, price of execution, whether the order was cancelled, whether the order was routed to another trading system, the identity of such a trading system, the price of execution at another trading system.

15 A recent investigation of electronic trading in financial markets by the Committee on the Global Financial System (2001) concludes that 'the fragmentation of markets was not considered to be a major problem'.

16 Estate agents introduce buyers and sellers in an auction market for valuable pieces of real estate and charge the vendor a commission for their services. The market is highly fragmented both regionally, and between different types of property. It is subject to relatively little regulation.

17 It is possible that competition may ultimately lead to a few large trading systems; but these systems will operate in a competitive environment. There may also be niche trading systems serving particular needs.

18   Obviously some detailed rules will differ as between (say) screen-based and floor-based trading systems.

19   Regulations need to differ where there is (say) physical delivery, rather than cash settlement.

20   Metals may be different, but they should not be subject to a different regulatory regime. In their consideration of ATS, FESCO (2001) have come to some very different conclusions. According to FESCO regulations for ATS may differ according to client type (professional or non-professional), asset traded (metals are different), the size of the ATSs (volume, impact on price formation and market share), and the nature of the trading system (e.g. crossing network, semi-automated trading system, bilateral or multi-lateral trading).

21   This section deals with the rules concerning trading. It excludes the conduct of business rules, which clearly distinguish between various types of trader.

22   MIPs are RIEs, ATSs, Recognised Clearing Houses and market service providers generally.

23   In some markets, the primary trading system may remain a monopoly for some time. During this period, detailed regulation is probably required. However, once there is competition in the market to provide execution services, the failure of a single trading system will not lead to customers being unable to buy such services (Macey and O'Hara, 1999b).

24   Gerald Putnam (Archipelago) stated that the main barrier to entry for a new exchange in the USA is admission to the NMS, and he complained that, as a condition of entry to the NMS, the NYSE tried to impose restrictions on the way the Archipelago Exchange operates (CFS, 2001a).

25   Demutualisation often results in members of an exchange being allocated sufficient shares to reflect their rights in the mutual exchange, and so there is little change in who controls the exchange. However, when share ownership restrictions are removed and the shares become tradable, ownership may become concentrated.

26   This is subject to the qualification that some trading systems, e.g. institutional crossing networks, may exclude some traders on cost grounds.

27   Since it is proposed that a reportable position be defined with respect to a trader's net position across all trading systems and instruments; the appropriate person to receive and monitor these reports is the regulator, rather than the various trading systems.

7
Theory and Results on Transparency

7.1 Introduction

A trading mechanism can be thought of as a set of protocols that translates investors' latent demands into realised prices and quantities. Market transparency is essentially the ability of market participants to observe the information in the trading process, and transparency can be defined as 'the degree to which information about trading (both past and prospective) is made publicly available on a real-time basis' (IOSCO, 1993).This publication of trading information for transparency reasons is distinct from the confidential reporting of trades to the exchange and regulatory authorities for surveillance or settlement purposes.

It is often argued that transparency is important for the efficiency of markets. In part, the argument relates to the social welfare aspects of trading since, if investors know that some trades are being temporarily concealed, they may fear that the market is unfair, and this may reduce their willingness to trade, so reducing volume and market participation (Elwes, 1989; IOSCO, 1993). The SEC (1994) stated that it 'has long believed that transparency – the real time, public dissemination of trade and quote information – plays a fundamental role in the fairness and efficiency of the secondary markets ... transparency helps to link dispersed markets and improves the price discovery, fairness, competitiveness and attractiveness of US markets'.

However, transparency has also been linked to liquidity, for example by the Securities and Investments Board (SIB), which referred in 1994 to a trade-off between liquidity and trade transparency and stated that transparency in the case of the prompt publication of large trades might be restricted 'if this is necessary to assure adequate liquidity'.

Transparency is usually divided into *pre-trade* and *post-trade* components. The former refers to the information the market has about the order flow coming to the market, the prices of the orders being submitted, the identity of the traders and current dealer quotes, while post-trade transparency refers to the level of information about the last executed trades.

This chapter first considers the significance of market microstructure for the level of transparency in the market. Section 7.3 considers the theoretical literature on transparency. Sections 7.4 and 7.5 discuss the results of empirical work for the UK and other equity markets, while section 7.6 summarises the experimental evidence. Finally, section 7.7 considers the evidence for non-equity markets. Because many of the factors relevant to an examination of transparency also affect other aspects of market design and regulation, some of the same issues are also discussed in the chapters on fragmentation and consolidation of markets (Chapters 4 and 6). An overview of the major results and implications of this work appears in the first section of Chapter 6.

7.2   Market microstructure and natural transparency

One important issue is whether market microstructure really matters in terms of promoting one transparency regime rather than another. In this regard, caution must be exercised when applying the results of theoretical comparisons of stylised auction and dealership systems to the actual operation of real trading systems.

With most market structures, it is necessary to reveal some information in order to find a counterparty. This means that, in the absence of intervention by either an exchange or a regulator, there will be some market-led or 'natural' transparency (i.e. transparency generated by the market mechanisms themselves).[1] In addition, there may be voluntary publication of trading information; either publicly (e.g participants in various OTC markets may respond to surveys asking for their trading volume during past months, so that aggregate market volume figures can be published), or through specific vendors (e.g. Platts provide reports on prices and volumes for Brent crude and gas oil in the OTC markets, as does the Heron report) which make the information available for a fee. However, as a general rule, traders wish to keep their trading activity secret until it is no longer of much interest.

In terms of microstructure, different market types offer different degrees of natural transparency:

- *Open outcry or double auction market.* In an open outcry market, traders must reveal the price and quantity at which they wish to trade to other pit traders via hand signals and shouting. When a trade is consummated between two traders, the other pit traders can observe the price, volume and identity of the pit traders involved. Thus, pit trading has considerable natural pre- and post-trade transparency.
- *Screen-based auction market.* On a screen-based auction market, all traders can observe the prices (and possibly the size) of the best (and possibly other) limit orders. The disappearance of a limit order signifies that it has either been matched, or withdrawn. This higher transparency (compared to dealership systems) is required for efficient price discovery because there are no market-makers designated by the system to provide liquidity. In such markets, liquidity providers (in the form of limit order traders) will participate only in trading if sufficient information about the order flow is readily accessible.
- *Dealer market.* In some dealer markets, customers can see the quotes of some (but not necessarily all) dealers. In others (e.g. the foreign exchange market and other OTC markets), pre-trade transparency could be negligible. Customers are unable to observe trade volume or prices. Therefore, dealer markets have markedly less natural transparency than auction markets.

Although electronic order books could display all the details of all the orders submitted, almost every electronic order book displays far less information than this. For example, many such systems show only the best five orders on each side of the market. Other systems allow hidden, or 'iceberg', orders which may be placed on the system but which are not shown on the screen. Such orders, for example, can be placed on the Paris Bourse and are likely to be introduced on most European exchanges in the near future. Pagano and Steil (1996) argue that 'any trader, buy-side or sell-side, who slices up a block order and feeds pieces through the market over time is deliberately withholding valuable price-relevant information from the market and is therefore attenuating the market's transparency. But this allows him to lower his trading costs, and thus affords him an incentive to trade actively. This explains why the Paris Bourse's CAC system actively assists traders in shielding their full trading intentions: traders may submit 'hidden orders' into the system, and the Bourse allows them to do this because it is believed to be worthwhile sacrificing some measure of transparency in order to attract more turnover.' Thus the purpose of such hidden orders is to provide protection for larger orders, and this highlights the perceived negative relationship between the transparency regime and liquidity provision, at least for larger orders. Even if quotes are published in dealership systems, their usefulness is often limited as market-makers are often prepared to trade at prices better than those that they, or other dealers, quote.

The issues related to post-trade transparency are very much related to the incentives of the providers of liquidity. In an electronic limit order book, immediate publication occurs whenever orders match and this matching is easily made public. Is there any reason to reduce this level of post-trade transparency in auction-based markets? Pagano and Steil (1996) argue that there is no incentive to lower transparency in such markets because limit order traders are more likely to be attracted to a market place that offers high levels of transparency that can provide information on the price discovery process. 'Indeed, such markets have a strong positive incentive to ensure that post-trade price and volume information is quickly and widely disseminated, since this information attracts the interest, and limit orders, of other traders.' Of course, this argument will apply only if the market concerned is seeking a wide participation; other markets might seek trade by restricting access to small groups of traders (e.g. the UK IDB systems), in which case wide dissemination of prices would be an unattractive commercial option.

On the other hand, in a dealership system in which market-makers are required to commit capital to provide liquidity, restricting transparency is often argued to be particularly important to encourage market-makers to participate in large trades and to reduce the price impact of such trades. This arises because participation in a large trade will cause the market-maker's inventory to become unbalanced and to deviate from their desired position. This deviation could be costly as the market-maker is forced to trade on their own account to regain their desired inventory and publication of the large trade would reveal the market-maker's immediate future trading objectives.[2]

7.3   Theoretical models

The typical market microstructure model used to analyse transparency hinges on two classes of traders: informed and uninformed. The informed traders are assumed to receive a private signal about the true value of the asset and they have discretion as to whether or not to trade. In contrast, uninformed (or liquidity) traders trade for purely liquidity reasons with no information about the asset and, depending on the type of model being considered, they could have discretion where and when to trade, but normally they have no discretion on this decision. In such models, these traders interact with liquidity providers, usually market-makers who observe the order flow and adjust prices based on the net order imbalance observed.

7.3.1 Gains of uninformed and informed traders

One major issue addressed in the theoretical literature is the allocative effect that transparency arrangements have on the welfare of the universe of traders. Pagano and Röell (1996) examine this question within a framework that contemplates batch markets, dealer markets and continuous auction markets which also differ both in their structure and in their levels of transparency, defined as the degree to which the current order flow is visible to the competing market professionals involved in setting prices. Market-makers set their spread so as to protect themselves against the losses which they incur by trading with informed traders. Inventory holding costs are not assumed to be an issue. Seen from this perspective, market liquidity in this model is limited by the presence of adverse selection in the market and the ability of the market-makers to distinguish informed traders from liquidity motivated traders. Pagano and Röell then analyse how the ability of price-setting agents to observe order flow affects the expected transaction costs of uninformed traders. Since the losses of uninformed traders provide the gains to informed traders, this analysis focuses on the distributional effects of market transparency.

Pagano and Röell show that the expected trading costs of uninformed traders in the transparent market are always less than or equal to their expected trading cost in the dealer market. This occurs because the ability of the single informed trader to 'hide' differs in the two market settings. The larger is the trade information available in the transparent market, the larger is the reduction in the informed trader's profit. The trade information available in the transparent market allows greater exposure of informed traders, and this results in the uninformed traders facing smaller expected losses.

Pagano and Röell argue that, in general, uninformed traders do at least as well in trading in a continuous market as in a dealer market, and they can do even better trading in a transparent market. These results suggest that uninformed traders are typically better off in a more transparent market. However, their model does not explain why, in practice, dealer markets are popular with large traders. One possible explanation is that traders care not only about expected trading costs but also about the probability of an order executing. The dealer market provides a firm price quote for each order size, while in an auction market there is execution risk, so that traders who are averse to execution risk might therefore prefer the implicit insurance offered by the dealer market. Other explanations rely on aspects of transparency which are not part of these models. For example, in a dealer market large trades are negotiated via personal contact so that there is scope for directly distinguishing between information-motivated and noise traders. Another explanation is that market-makers gain something from trading with informed traders, for example by obtaining or inferring the trader's private information which can be used in their subsequent trading.

Fishman and Hagerty (1995) argue that informed traders will not voluntarily disclose their trades. Therefore, if there is to be post-trade transparency, it must be mandated. However, they argue that mandatory transparency allows informed traders to manipulate the market. When potentially informed traders reveal that they have just traded, the market will be unsure whether this was an informed or an uninformed trade. Therefore, the market price will tend to rise on the disclosure of buy trades, and fall on the disclosure of sell trades. If the trade was, in fact, uninformed, the potentially informed trader can now reverse their initial trade at a gross profit, although such profits may be insufficient to cover the transactions costs. In addition, this strategy requires the market to know the identity of traders, or at least that the published trade was initiated by a potentially informed trader.

Another, related, aspect of transparency that has received some attention is the announcement of pending orders. Admati and Pfleiderer (1990) provide a model of sunshine trading where some liquidity traders can pre-announce the size of their orders while others cannot. They show that those investors who are able to pre-announce their trades enjoy lower trading costs. This happens because the market correctly recognises that these trades are not information motivated. The question then arises as to what happens to the welfare of traders who cannot pre-announce their orders. The model shows that the costs for liquidity traders who are unable to pre-announce their trades rises. In this way, pre-announcement identifies the trade as informationless but increases the adverse selection costs for other traders.

7.3.2   Impact of transparency on market-makers' behaviour

Lyons (1996) addresses the trade-off between transparency and market participation which arises because, although greater transparency can accelerate revelation of information in the price, it can also impede dealer risk management. Lyons shows that dealers prefer incomplete transparency, so that other traders only observe the order flow with noise. Slower price adjustment provides time for non-dealers to trade, thereby sharing risk otherwise borne by dealers. At some point, however, further reduction in transparency impedes risk sharing: too noisy a public signal provides non-dealers too little information to induce them to trade.

Another question that has been addressed is whether market-makers use the information they obtain from their order flow to make trading profits in subsequent periods. If they do, then the models reviewed above can be extended to a two-period setting. In such a two-period setting, the first-period market for large and informative orders is more liquid under an opaque publication regime. In the second period, the market as a whole is less liquid because market-makers must defend themselves against the possibility that their competitors are better informed. Broadly speaking, models predict that adoption of a more transparent regime harms informed traders, benefits small liquidity traders and may have an ambiguous effect on large liquidity trades.

7.3.3 Opaque versus transparent markets

One major issue is the role of transparency in a fragmented market where trading systems have to compete for the order flow. Will trading systems want to set higher standards to send a signal that trading on their system is 'clean', or will they apply the 'race to the bottom' type of regime where trading systems compete on the basis on the lowest transparency levels?

Madhavan (1995) examines the relation between fragmentation and market transparency where transparency is the disclosure of post-trade information to market participants. In his model, Madhavan provides an argument for having less rather than more disclosure. The trading universe in Madhavan's model consists not only of informed and uninformed traders, but also of large liquidity (i.e. institutional) traders. These traders are not motivated by information, but their trades are large and, to minimise the price impact, they break up their trades over time. The implication of this analysis is that, faced with a choice between a high disclosure trading system and a low disclosure trading system, an uninformed institutional trader will prefer to direct trades towards the more opaque trading system because a large trade can successfully be broken up without attracting too much attention and hence moving the price in the direction of the trade. This imposes costs on short-term noise traders. Here, non-disclosure benefits dealers by reducing price competition. This model suggests that one danger of too much transparency is that traders might migrate to other trading platforms, perhaps even to off-exchange avenues and this will lead to even less information being released to contribute to the price discovery process.

There may, however, be other factors that may induce dealers to desire greater transparency in other forms. Whereas most of the models reviewed so far deal with mandatory disclosure, Chowdhry and Nanda (1991) provide a model where market-makers voluntarily provide information. The model may explain why some markets desire greater transparency. This happens because making trading information public can discourage insider trading while making the market more attractive to uninformed traders. By revealing trades and providing information on trader identities, dealers can discourage or reduce trading by insiders or other informed traders. This allows dealers to charge lower bid–ask spreads because they face lower adverse selection costs, attracting more liquidity traders from trading systems that are more opaque. This suggests that a trading system with a reputation of being highly transparent may benefit from reduced adverse selection costs. In a multi-trading system context, this gives rise to 'race to the top' regulation, and trading systems will compete for order flow by offering high levels of disclosure.

In terms of competition between transparent and opaque trading systems, it can be noted that, irrespective of the relative comparative static merits of the two transparency regimes, dealers on opaque trading systems can always bid for order flow because they have the advantage of keeping information confidential. Pagano and Röell (1992, 1996) argue that the more transparent the trading system, the more order flow information market-makers have at their disposal on which to condition their quote-setting behaviour. Other papers based on this argument include Röell (1990) and Naik, Neuberger and Viswanathan (1994, 1999), who argue that if dealers can analyse the information contained in the order flow they can give better prices to information-intensive orders relative to the rest of the market. Such models are based on the concept of learning – market-makers can learn about the security's fundamental values from informed traders and thus they can use this information while trading with smaller traders.

One policy issue of interest is whether transparency has any impact on the volatility of the price discovery process. By going for maximum transparency, the noise produced by the trading process will be rendered fully public without any discrimination between the different trades. Madhavan (1996) considers this question and shows that greater transparency in the form of disclosure of retail order flows can exacerbate the price volatility. Disclosing information about noise in the market system increases the effects of asymmetric information, thereby reducing liquidity. Essentially, noise is necessary for markets to operate and disclosure robs the market of this lubrication. Madhavan shows that transparency is more beneficial in a market with large numbers of traders that provide sufficient noise trading and he concludes that the potentially adverse effects of transparency are likely to be greatest in thin markets.

7.4   Empirical evidence from the London Stock Exchange

Before proceeding to analyse the research carried out on the impact produced by the different transparency regimes which have been used at the London Stock Exchange, it is useful to summarise the various transparency regimes used on the London Stock Exchange. Before examining the empirical evidence in detail, it is useful to note that for over two years (1986–9) the London Stock Exchange operated successfully with complete post-trade transparency (Table 7.1).

Table 7.1   Summary of the London Stock Exchange transparency regimes

Start of regime[1,2,3]	Rule	Delay[5]
27 Oct 1986	All trades in *alpha* stocks	5 min
27 Feb 1989	Trades in *alpha* stocks over £100,000	24 hour
	Other trades	5 min
29 Jan 1990	Trades in *alpha* stocks over £100,000	24 hour
	Other trades	3 min
14 Jan 1991	Trades larger than 3×normal market size (NMS)[4]	90 min
	Other trades	3 min
13 Dec 1993	Trades larger than 75 × NMS: the equity market-maker may opt for a delay in publication of five business days, or until 90 per cent of the position has been unwound, whichever is the sooner	5 days
	Trades larger than 3 × normal market size (NMS)	90 min
	Other trades	3 min
1 Jan 1996	Trades larger than 75 × NMS: the equity market-maker may opt for a delay in publication of five business days, or until 90 per cent of the position has been unwound, whichever is the sooner	5 days
	Trades larger than 6 × NMS	60 min
	Other trades (including IDB trades of any size)	3 min

Table 7.1 (Continued)

Start of regime[1,2,3]	Rule	Delay[5]
1 Oct 1997	SETS stocks: trades through order book	0 min
	SETS stocks: telephone trades below $8 \times$ NMS	3 min
	SETS stocks: telephone trades over $8 \times$ NMS	5 days
	Other stocks	Unchanged

[1]Until 14 January 1991, the volume of large trades was published immediately. Subsequently, publication of large trade volume was also delayed and published at the same time as the trade price.
[2]There is no publication of an individual trade if it is a SEAQ bargain under £1,000, a bargain in a stock with an NMS of under 2,000 shares, or a bargain on SEAQ International.
[3]When a company is the subject of a takeover bid all trades, regardless of size, are published immediately.
[4]NMS is approximately 2.5 per cent of the stock's average daily volume over a previous interval
[5]The delay in publication operates in calendar time, and so a trade at 4.29 pm, which is subject to a 90-minute delay, is published at 5.59 pm the same day.

7.4.1 Elwes (London Stock Exchange)

The Elwes Committee (1989) analysed shares that were promoted from beta to alpha status on the Stock Exchange. For the period under consideration, all *alpha* trades were published within five minutes, while *beta* trades were not. Thus, trading in *alpha* stocks was subject to substantially greater transparency than was trading in *beta* stocks. Elwes concluded that this increase in transparency did not lead to a significant change in the volume of trading of these shares. This result is consistent with the view expressed by the OFT (below), that the rapid publication of large trades does not harm volume.

7.4.2 Director General of Fair Trading (1990)

The Director General of Fair Trading (1990) conducted a comparison of the period with only a five-minute delay in the publication of all trades in alpha stocks (27 October 1986 to 26 February 1989), and the subsequent period when the publication of large trades was subject to a 24-hour delay. He found that after the introduction of a 24-hour delay in publication:

- the average bid–ask spread for all trades rose slightly
- the average touch for all trades rose slightly
- there was a small drop in volume
- the percentage of large trades rose
- the average size of equity market-makers' quotes on SEAQ in excess of 50,000 shares fell
- inter-market-maker trading, as a percentage of total trading, fell.

While these results are based on only a few months of trading after the change in publication regime, and other factors have not been controlled for, they do *not* support the case that the maintenance of the delayed publication of large trades ensures:

- small bid–ask spreads, and a small touch for all trades
- a small touch for large trades
- a high total volume of trading
- equity market-makers quoting for a large size of trade.

7.4.3 MacIntyre (1991)

The purpose of this study was to compare trading before and after the change in the Stock Exchange transparency regime on 14th January 1991. Data for December 1990 and April 1991 on 169 stocks that were previously classified by the Stock Exchange as *alpha* stocks, and subsequently had an NMS of 2,000 shares or larger was used. In December 1990 the transaction price of trades in *alpha* stocks over £100,000 was published with a delay of 24 hours, although the volume was published immediately. In April 1991 the price and volume of trades above $3 \times$ NMS was published after 90 minutes. Thus, price transparency was increased, while volume transparency was decreased.

After allowing for a general rise in share prices, the change in the touch between the two periods was insignificant. There was also little change in quote sizes while the volume of trading, as a proportion of total SEAQ volume, fell. Finally, the proportion of trades valued at over £1 million fell. The expectations were for a widening of the bid–ask spread for large trades, and a narrowing for small trades, a reduction in quote size and a reduction in the volume of large trades. Only the last of these effects was supported by the data.

7.4.4 Neuberger (1992)

Neuberger (1992) uses transactions data on 14 UK stocks from September 1987 to February 1988 to test a model of aggregate market-maker profits. During this period there was no delay in trade publication. While he could not successfully measure the separate effects on the bid–ask spread of information asymmetries and inventory control, he did find that the total inventories of equity market-makers in each of these stocks followed a mean reverting process (i.e. they tended to return to some desired level over a period of a few weeks).

7.4.5   Breedon (1993)

Breedon (1993) analysed transactions data on three UK companies (Marks and Spencer, Lloyds Bank and Rolls-Royce). This data covered two time periods: November 1988–January 1989, when large trades were published after five minutes; and August 1991–October 1991, when large trades were delayed by 90 minutes. Using regression analysis, Breedon estimated the measured (or traded) spread (i.e. the difference between the transactions prices of buy and sell trades). He found that the move to delayed publication increased the measured spread for large trades, relative to that for small trades, particularly for buys from the equity market-maker.

Breedon suggested this result may be due to a decline in the information content of large trades between the two periods, rather than the change in transparency regime. Breedon does not mention whether this change in the relative measured spread is statistically significant. He also found that the change in transparency regime had no effect on the speed of the price reaction to large trades, nor on the size distribution of trades.

7.4.6   Snell and Tonks (1995)

They did not test transparency directly, but looked at two related questions: whether trades contain information, and whether equity market-makers control their inventories. For 10 UK stocks over a two-week period in September 1990, they used the extent to which all market-makers in a particular stock were net buyers or sellers over half-hour periods as a measure of the volume of trade (this excludes inter-market-maker dealing). The average of the mid-point of the touch over each half-hour period was used as a measure of the quoted price.

They found some evidence that net volume contains information, and stronger evidence that equity market-makers (in aggregate) try to control their inventories. The inventory effect was examined in two different ways. First, an increase in inventory was found to have a negative effect on the mid-quote. Second, aggregate inventory had a negative first order autocorrelation coefficient, and the average period for an inventory imbalance to be halved was 12.4 trading hours, or about two days. This period is well beyond the 90 minutes by which the publication of large trades is delayed. This result is consistent with some of the US work on equity market-makers' inventory control which are reviewed below.

7.4.7   Board and Sutcliffe (1995a, 1995b)

Board and Sutcliffe (1995a, 1995b) examined the effect of the London Stock Exchange's reduced transparency for large trades on prices and trading patterns of equity trading, the use made by equity market-makers of the transparency rules and the IDB systems to unwind the inventory arising from their obligation to offer immediate execution of large trades, the price impact of block trades and the effect of the regime on the equity options market. They argue that while delayed publication and the IDB systems allow market-makers the opportunity to offset their risks are potential costs to allowing market-makers these facilities. Generally speaking, these costs arise from the information asymmetry created by these arrangements. After a large customer sale, the market-maker knows that there is an excess supply of stock, which is likely to lead to a long-term price reduction once the deal is published. Thus the offsetting activities of the market-maker are on the basis of superior information and the costs of this are likely to fall on the counterparties to the market-maker's positioning trades. To the extent that these information asymmetries are significant, the customer demanding immediacy is indirectly subsidised by the counterparties to the market-maker's positioning trades.

The Board and Sutcliffe report was based a sample of firms from the FTSE 100 and FTSE 250 indices for the period 1 April 1992–31 March 1994. Over the sample period, the London Stock Exchange's trade publication delayed the publication of trades of over $3 \times NMS$ for 90 minutes. Over the period considered, Board and Sutcliffe find that although trade publication was delayed for only 3 per cent of customer trades, this represented over 55 per cent of the value of such trading. Larger proportions of IDB and other Inter Market-Maker (IMM) trades were delayed. Overall, almost half of the value of trading was subject to delayed publication. For the FTSE 250 sample, the percentage of trading subject to delayed publication was substantially higher at 75 per cent.

Another analysis carried in the report is the relationship between traded spreads and the transparency regime. It was found that substantial proportions of all trades, at all but the largest sizes, were executed inside the current best quoted prices. It was found that IDB trades were consistently at more favourable prices than were customer trades of similar size. In addition, traded spreads for customer trades were asymmetric about the mid-quote in that customer sells were further inside the touch than are customer buys. These findings imply that knowledge of currently quoted prices is not a perfect substitute for knowledge of the last trade price.[3]

In terms of the trading behaviour, Board and Sutcliffe find that SEAQ market-makers often engage in pre-positioning before a large trade is executed. In the case of liquid stocks, the pre-positioning took more than three hours to be completed. They report that prices for *alpha* purchase orders following a large *alpha* purchase trade are found to increase until the 12th trade and the same number of sell trades are needed to fully adjust the price following a large (*alpha*) sale order. In clock-time, this adjustment takes about 45 minutes for *alpha* buy trades and 42 minutes for *alpha* sell trades. This represents a time-interval which is significantly less than the 90-minute publication delay allowed by the London Stock Exchange at the time.

Board and Sutcliffe also argue that the issue of transparency on equity markets should not be restricted to its impact only on the equity market but also on the impacts generated on other markets whose products are denominated in terms of the equity instruments. A case in point is the traded options markets where the correct pricing of the options depends, among other things, on the knowledge of the current equity price. If there are trades whose publication is delayed, the current equity price is harder to observe. Indeed, the market-maker who was party to the large trade has the possibility of making arbitrage profits by entering the options market during the period of delayed publication. When the authors analyse the relationship between trading volume on the LIFFE market and the patterns of equity trading in the underlying stocks they find that there is a significant relationship between the two. However, this association is attributable to fully transparent equity market transactions which are essentially those with sizes less than $3 \times$ NMS. For equity market trades in greater volumes than this, they find no strong relationship. The intra-daily analysis suggests that there are few measurable effects during the 90 minutes for which trade publication of large equity deals is delayed. Thus there is an increase in options volume when 1,000,000 shares are traded in 1,000 deals each of 1,000 shares, while there would be no impact on options volume if the same number of shares were to be traded in two deals each of 500,000 shares.

This result seems inconsistent both with the use of traded options for the hedging of large trades, and with the exploitation of superior information by equity market participants. One of the explanations for these results is in terms of a lack of interest in the use of options by equity market participants. Another is that equity market-makers would use traded options for hedging but cannot because of the relative illiquidity of the options market. A third possibility is that options market-makers are reluctant to trade at times when they believe that large equity trades at unobservable prices or volumes are occurring, and it is likely that their counterparty has superior information about recent equity trades.

7.4.8 Gemmill (1996)

Gemmill (1996) conducted an analysis of the price reaction in the UK to large trades in three different transparency regimes. He used transactions data on 26 of the 50 highest volume stocks traded on the Stock Exchange, and analysed the data for the month of May in the six years 1987–92. This data has two months in each of three different transparency regimes. Considering only customer-initiated trades, Gemmill identified the 20 largest purchases and the 20 largest sales for each share in each month.

He adopted an event study methodology for each large trade, using event time, rather than clock time. He defined the benchmark return for each large trade as the average return for the preceding 20 trades, excluding the last 10 trades. He then analysed the returns on the 10 trades that preceded the large trade, and the 20 subsequent trades. For these 30 trades he computed excess returns, i.e. the actual return minus the benchmark return.

Gemmill used these excess returns to test five different hypotheses:

1 *Large trades have a temporary, but not a permanent, effect on prices.* This hypothesis was rejected. Large purchases led to a permanent rise in price, while large sales led to a smaller and almost statistically insignificant fall in price. This is consistent with large trades having an information content, suggesting that knowledge of such trades may confer an advantage.
2 *The delayed publication of large trades leads to smaller spreads.* This hypothesis was rejected. Spreads for large trades were not smaller during the period when publication was delayed for 24 hours. A reduction in spreads was one of the cited benefits of delayed publication.
3 *Delayed publication affects only the temporary, not the permanent, price effect of a trade.* This hypothesis was rejected. There was no clear relationship between delayed publication and the size of either the temporary or the permanent price effects. Thus the permanent and temporary price responses appear to be unaffected by delayed publication.
4 *Delayed publication leads to less price volatility following large trades.* This hypothesis was rejected. The variance of returns was not smaller during the period of 24-hour delays in publication. Again, this casts doubt on the usefulness of publication delays in dampening volatility, as suggested in the Agnew Report (SIB, 1994).
5 *Delayed publication does not reduce the speed with which prices reach their new permanent level after a large trade.* This hypothesis was accepted.

Delayed publication does not reduce the number of transactions required for the new permanent price to be reached.

Gemmill also investigated whether the spread and permanent price effect were affected by the size of the large trade. For purchases, he found a significant U-shaped relationship between spreads and size, but no relationship between permanent price effects and size. For sales he found a weak reverse U-shaped relationship between the spread and size, and a U-shaped relationship between the permanent price effect and size. In general, the size of a large trade had only a small effect on the permanent price response.

Gemmill found that, for all three transparency regimes, the prices of these very large trades were well inside the SEAQ touch. This is consistent with Board and Sutcliffe's findings, but contrasts with some previous empirical findings (e.g. Wells, 1993), that very large trades usually take place outside the touch. Gemmill's result implies that equity market-makers do not require a bid–ask spread that is wider than for NMS trades, even when publication occurs after 5 (or 3) minutes.

Overall, the size of the permanent and temporary price effects for large trades, the spread, the volatility of returns, and the speed of the price response were all unaffected by the transparency regime. Thus delayed publication had little effect. Gemmill argues that, since large trades (particularly purchases) have a permanent price effect, delayed publication creates an information asymmetry that can be exploited by equity market-makers. However, the asymmetry was short lived in that his results for large trades indicate that 'prices have fully adjusted at least after three–five trades' (Gemmill, 1994). Indeed, Gemmill's results show that most of the adjustment occurs in the next trade. Under all the transparency regimes studied, publication of large trades was delayed by at least three minutes. Therefore, provided the next few trades occurred within three minutes, delayed publication did not alter the informational advantage derived by equity market-makers from knowledge of the large trade.

This suggests that different results on the effects of delayed publication might have been obtained if the data set had included a transparency regime with the instantaneous publication of large trades. However, given that trade execution is not screen-based, such a transparency regime is impractical.

The implications of these results are that the benefits of delayed large trade publication accrue in the short period immediately after the trade. Thus, there is little support for the 90-minute rule, which in practice seems to offer few benefits. Equally, they suggest that effort be put into reducing the three-minute reporting requirement.

7.4.9 Saporta, Trebeschi and Vila (1999)

They analysed trades in seven UK stocks for the three months before, and the three months after, the change in transparency regime on 1 January 1996. They found no evidence of a change in the distribution of trade size, and no change in the realised spread. They fitted the Huang–Stoll model to split the realised spread into two components – adverse selection costs plus inventory costs, and order processing costs. They found no evidence of a change in either type of cost, and concluded that the increase in transparency did not result in any adverse effects on the market characteristics investigated.

7.4.10 Board and Sutcliffe (2000)

Board and Sutcliffe returned to the issue of transparency to analyse the possible impact on trading behaviour caused by the change of the transparency regime introduced on 1 January 1996 when the trade publication rules of the London Stock Exchange were changed to increase transparency. The main changes were that the publication of intermediate sized customer trades and all inter-market-maker trades were no longer delayed; and that the period of delay for larger customer trades was decreased to 60 (from 90) minutes. They investigate whether these changes in trade publication affected market behaviour by examining data on 60 firms from the FTSE 100, FTSE Mid 250 and the FTSE Small Cap indices before and after this rule change.

The questions addressed in this paper include:

1 *Did trade sizes change so as to retain delayed publication?*
For the largest FTSE 100 stocks which account for over 60 per cent of both the number and value of trades in both periods, the value of trades for which publication was delayed is slightly below the 25 per cent target established by SIB (1995). For the larger stocks in the FTSE Mid 250 sample, with more market-makers, the delayed percentage in 1996 was over 40 per cent, while for the group of stocks in the FTSE Small Cap index which had fewest market-makers, the percentage delayed in 1996 was 88 per cent.

One of the most important issues is whether trade size has been affected by the changed transparency regime. If delayed publication is valuable, the number of trades in the 3–$6 \times$ NMS band, which were delayed under the old but not the new regime, should have fallen substantially; while the 6–10 category will have risen if traders increased trade size to benefit from delayed publication. However, the analysis shows that there is little evidence of traders seeking to retain delayed publication by switching to trades above 6×NMS. In 1995, 32 per cent of trading value was above 6×NMS, while in 1996 this figure had risen to 34 per cent.

2   *Were spreads adversely affected?*

An analysis of the traded bid–ask spreads revealed that there was little change in the prices available. At almost all trade sizes, the 1996 bid and ask prices were as good as or slightly better than those for 1995. For trades in the 3–6×NMS region (i.e those most affected by the increase in transparency), the 1996 prices were superior to the 1995 prices. This price improvement is inconsistent with market-makers increasing their bid–ask spread to cover the increased inventory risk owing to the loss of delayed publication for these trades.

3   *How did market-makers' behaviour change?*

Market-makers' handling of single customer block trades over 3×NMS and any-sized inter-market-maker trades were analysed. Two types of inventory positioning were considered: pre-positioning, which takes place before the block trade is executed; and post-positioning, which occurs in the period of delayed publication (i.e. 90 or 60 minutes) after the block trade. Since pre-positioning requires knowledge of a pending block trade, the ability to pre-position will be directly linked to market-makers' ability to engage in protected trading or Worked Principal Agreements.

The main implications of the results are that the amount of total positioning was generally rather low, and is consistent with that documented by Board and Sutcliffe (1995a, 1995b). The average positioning was under 40 per cent of the block volume for FTSE 100 stocks, but only 8 per cent for the FTSE Small Cap stocks. This difference probably reflects the much thinner market in FTSE Small Cap stocks and consequently fewer opportunities to trade. The average amount of total positioning of 3–6×NMS trades (for which publication delays were removed altogether in 1996) in FTSE 100 stocks fell only slightly (from 38 per cent to 32 per cent) between 1995 and 1996 (however, the numbers of fully positioned and unpositioned trades did not change), and the level of total positioning for stocks outside the FTSE 100 did not change. For 6–10×NMS trades (for which the period of delayed publication was reduced to 60 minutes), the average amount of total positioning decreased by 1.5 per cent between 1995 and 1996 for the FTSE 100 stocks, by 1.3 per cent for the FTSE Mid 250 stocks, and by almost 7 per cent for the FTSE Small Cap stocks. Given the thinness of trading in the FTSE Small Cap stocks, this modest reduction in total positioning may be unrelated to the changed transparency regime.

The average amount of post-positioning for 3–6×NMS trades in FTSE 100 stocks fell by 6.3 per cent between periods, but was little changed for the other groups of stocks. The average degree of post-positioning of 6–10×NMS trades also dropped by 4.4 per cent for FTSE 100 stocks, with smaller declines for the other indices. Although it is possible that market-makers switched to using protected trades when delayed publication ceased on trades between 3 and 6×NMS, the average level of pre-positioning was unchanged between regimes which is inconsistent with the use of protected trading to circumvent the new publication rules.

For 6–10×NMS trades, the average amount of pre-positioning rose from 17.7 per cent in 1995 to 23.6 per cent in 1996 which is consistent with a greater use of trade protection, and a greater propensity to pre-position such trades. However, these trades were not directly affected by the removal of delayed publication for 3–6×NMS trades, and so the explanation for this change may well lie elsewhere, particularly as there was no change in the average degree of pre-positioning for the FTSE Mid 250 stocks at both 3–6 and 6–10×NMS.

Finally, for the FTSE Small Cap sample there has been a decline in pre-positioning for 6–10×NMS trades from 8.5 per cent to 3.7 per cent. In summary, these results indicate that for 3–6×NMS trades in FTSE 100 stocks, there was a modest decline in average post-positioning, with no change in pre-positioning. There was no change in average pre- or post-positioning of such trades for the other two indices. For 6–10×NMS trades, while the total positioning for the FTSE 100 stocks was unchanged, there was a modest switch from post- to pre-positioning. For the other two indices, the only change was been a drop in both pre- and post-positioning for the FTSE Small Cap index.

Lastly, market-makers often attempted to offset one block with one or more further block trades, as an alternative to unwinding through smaller trades, and it is possible that the change in transparency regime altered this process. However, the distribution of the number of customer block trades per day was very similar in 1995 and 1996. The large samples and similarity of the trading frequencies suggests that the increase in transparency has not been associated with a major change in market-maker behaviour in undertaking customer block trades, including the extent to which one customer block trade is used to position another.

4 *Conclusions*

Overall, the Board and Sutcliffe (2000) results show that while the rule changes have led to a substantial increase in transparency and, as predicted, they appear to have had little adverse effect on the market characteristics examined. Thus the size of trades, the traded bid–ask spread, inter-market-maker trading, offsetting blocks and pre- and post-positioning all appear to have been largely unaffected. The findings of this paper support the view of the SIB (1997) that 'neither the Exchange nor member firms have suggested to us that these higher levels of transparency have had any adverse effect on liquidity'. The fears that greater transparency would harm the market have not been borne out in practice.

This analysis of the London Stock Market suggests that increasing the transparency of a dealer market by reducing or eliminating trade publication delays is largely beneficial, in that information asymmetries are reduced, while the bid–ask spread and volume are not adversely affected.

7.5 Empirical evidence from non-UK equity markets

While the potential for studies exists, there appear to be very few empirical studies of the effects of changing the level of transparency on equity markets outside the USA and UK. The exceptions are studies for Canada and Korea, which are considered below. Because of differences in structure between markets, the results of the studies reviewed in this section may not apply directly to the UK.

7.5.1 USA – National Association of Securities Dealers (1983)

On 8 February 1983 NASDAQ introduced its National Market System (NMS), which involved the immediate publication of trades. A study of the effects on 49 shares that were chosen to trade on tier 2 of the NMS was reported in NASD (1983). Data for the initial period of immediate publication (8 February 1983–29 April 1983) were compared with data for preceding months (November 1982–February 1983) for three groups of shares: the shares chosen to trade on tier 2 of the NMS; shares that applied to trade on tier 2 of the NMS, but were not chosen; and shares that did not apply for tier 2 of the NMS.

The study found that the move to immediate publication of trades:

- led to a rise in volume
- possibly resulted in a slight drop in the bid–ask spread
- had no effect on volatility
- had no clear effect on the number of equity market-makers.

While this change in transparency regime applied to all trades, not just large trades, the consequences were generally beneficial: higher volume and lower bid–ask spreads. These results are consistent with those found in the UK studies discussed above.

7.5.2 USA – Holthausen *et al.* (1987, 1990)

One approach adopted by academic literature to study the impact of transparency has been to analyse the price impact following the execution of a large trade and investigate whether different publication regimes matter. The idea behind such an approach is that large orders are expected to be transmitted to the market by traders acting on price sensitive information. Although this argument has received subsequent revisions (for example, informed traders could in fact submit medium-sized orders in order to camouflage their information), the literature seems to converge to the view that a large buy trade signifies good news while a large sell trade signifies bad news. In view of this, the literature has investigated whether the publication regime affects the price discovery process taking place after the large trade has been executed.

Although most markets have facilities for the execution of unusually large ('block') trades, the mechanisms for achieving this vary substantially. For example, on the NYSE, large customer orders are negotiated (i.e. brokered) off the trading floor in the 'upstairs market'. These orders are not published until counterparties have been found (i.e. until the negotiation is complete and the obligation to trade is created). When the order is taken to the floor, outstanding limit orders between the current and block prices are given priority.

Holthausen *et al.* (1987, 1990) investigate how quickly prices attain new equilibrium levels after large-block transactions, and measures the associated temporary and permanent price effects. They find that prices adjust within at most three trades, with most of the adjustment occurring in the first trade. The temporary price effect for seller-initiated transactions is related to block size, but the temporary price effect observed for buyer-initiated transactions is no larger than that observed in 100 share trades. Most of the price effect associated with block trades is permanent and is related to block size, regardless of the initiating party. (These results are consistent with those for the UK reported by Board and Sutcliffe, and Gemmill).

7.5.3   USA – Porter and Weaver (1998)

The Porter and Weaver (1998) paper is essentially focused on post-trade transparency on the NASDAQ market and compares it with centralised exchanges such as the NYSE, American Stock Exchange (AMEX), Boston, Chicago and Pacific. As of 1 June 1982, NASD members began reporting all equity trades on the NMS within 90 seconds of trade execution and in-sequence. Violation of these rules is permitted only in the cases of a lost trade ticket, a computer problem, or if the stock experiences abnormal volume. Clearly, out-of-sequence reporting could also be used by dealers to manage the release of information to other dealers and investors.

The authors find substantial out-of-sequence reporting during 1990. Out-of-sequence dollar volume reported on NASDAQ exceeds out-of-sequence dollar volume reported on the combined centralised exchanges in virtually every minute of the trading day. The difference between NASDAQ and the centralised exchanges becomes even bigger (about 13 times larger) after the market closes. The paper investigates whether the NASDAQ-permitted reasons for late reporting can explain the patterns and magnitude of out-of-sequence reporting, but find no evidence consistent with the NASDAQ-permitted explanations. On the other hand, they find that if a transaction is a block trade, the probability that it will be reported late increases by 107.3 per cent. In addition, controlling for the individual firm's percentage of trades on odd eighths, the probability of a trade being reported late increases 94.2 per cent if the trade is on an odd eighth.

If the volume weighted average of the out-of-sequence trades reported after market close is above the mid-point of the closing bid and ask, then trades reported late can be useful in predicting both the direction and magnitude of the following day's return. This suggests that dealers could be using some out-of-sequence reporting to manage the flow of information. In fact, the paper finds evidence that late trades reported after the market closes have some ability to predict the following day's return. This finding adds substantial power to the conjecture that trades reported after the market close are informationally motivated and that delayed reporting of some trades is strategic. Thus, the findings suggest that late-trade reporting is beneficial to NASDAQ dealers.

7.5.4 Canada – Madhavan, Porter and Weaver (2000)

Madhavan, Porter and Weaver (2000) examine the issue of pre-trade market transparency on the Toronto Stock Exchange (TSE) before and after the limit order book was publicly disseminated in April 1999. The TSE applied the new transparency rule both to the securities traded on the TSE's floor system (these are the more actively traded stocks) and to the less actively traded stocks trading on the TSE's Computer Aided Trading System (CATS).[4] Since some Canadian securities are cross-listed in US markets, the authors were also able to analyse the effects of changes in disclosure on cross-border spreads without the complications arising from time-zone effects.

After controlling for the effects of changes in price levels, volume and the variance of returns, Madhavan, Porter and Weaver found that the increase in transparency had no effect on the quoted and traded spreads for CATS stocks, no effect on effective spreads for floor stocks, but did lead to a widening of quoted spreads of $0.026 for floor stocks. Execution costs are determined by traded spreads, and these did not widen for either CATS or floor traded stocks.

Data on the depth of floor trading before the increase in transparency is not available, and so the change in depth for the floor cannot be computed. The depth of CATS trading decreased by 2 per cent after the increase in transparency when the depth was revealed to the general public, in addition to members of the exchange. This change in depth is small and may be due to other factors, e.g. differences in volume, price levels and the variance of returns before and after the transparency change.

After controlling for changes in the number of trades, return volatility increased for both CATS and floor trading. As the authors point out, increased return volatility could be associated with greater price efficiency because the greater transparency speeds up the price discovery process. The increased transparency had no significant effect on the profits of specialists in either the floor or CATS markets. Nor did the increase in transparency have any effect on the size distribution of trades on either the floor or CATS. Fifty-six of the floor stocks were also traded on other Canadian and US exchanges, and the increase in transparency had no effect on the proportion of the order flow directed to the TSE. This suggests the increase in transparency did not lead to the order flow being directed to other exchanges (i.e. overseas).

The conclusions are that the greater transparency led to an increase in return volatility (which may have been associated with an improvement in price discovery), and to a small decrease in depth. It had no effect on traded spreads, specialist profits, the size distribution of trades, quoted spreads for stocks cross-listed in the USA, nor the order flow of the TSE.

7.5.5   Korea – Lee and Chung (1998)

In 1992 the transparency of stocks traded on the automatic trading system of the Korean Stock Exchange was increased. After July 1992 the system published not only the best bid and ask prices, but also the volume of the best bid and ask prices and the price and volume of the rest of the limit order book. Stocks traded on the non-automated system that did not experience any increase in transparency were used as a control. It was found that the increase in transparency led to a reduction in the variance of daily returns, and an increase in volume.

7.6   Experimental evidence

Research that deals with the issue of transparency aims at conducting the impact of changes in transparency on some variables, like the price of block trades. One problem that such research faces is the any change in transparency appears to be an endogenous process and, considering that the different regimes stretch over a decade, this type of research is bound to be influenced by the changes in the trading environment. These problems complicate the results and their interpretation.

Four research projects, carried out by Flood *et al.* (1997, 1999) and Bloomfield and O'Hara (1999, 2000), have tried to depart from these 'natural experiment' exercises and use developments in experimental economics to address the issue of transparency.

7.6.1   Flood *et al.* (1997)

This paper considers post-trade transparency using nine professional traders from four Dutch banks, and two computerised traders (who may be informed or uninformed). Market-makers in the transparent market can see all the trades of the two computerised traders, as well as their own trades, while in the opaque market traders can see only their own trades. In both types of market the level of pre-trade transparency is low, and the quotes of market-makers are available only one at a time, on request. Flood *et al.* find that post-trade transparency has no effect on volatility. In the transparent market price discovery is faster, and spreads are generally narrower. However, spreads are narrowest at the start of trading in the opaque market. The authors conclude that uninformed traders gain from post-trade transparency, while informed traders lose.

7.6.2 Flood *et al.* (1999)

They analysed the effects of pre-trade transparency on spreads, volume and price discovery using seven human subjects (professional securities traders from five Dutch banks) and two computerised traders (who may be informed or uninformed). In the transparent market, the quotes of all seven market-makers were disclosed immediately. In the opaque market no quotes were publicly disclosed, and market-makers had to call each other to obtain quotes. There is no post-trade transparency. The volume of trading in the transparent market was much higher than that in the opaque market, while spreads in the opaque market were initially much higher than for the transparent market, but then dropped to reach a similar level. This indicates that pre-trade transparency (in the absence of any post-trade transparency) tends to increase market liquidity by increasing volume and narrowing spreads. However, price discovery is slower in the transparent market, and this is attributed to market-makers altering their quotes gradually because they can see the quotes of their rivals.

7.6.3 Bloomfield and O'Hara (1999)

In this experiment there were two human market-makers, two human traders, two computerised informed traders and two computerised uninformed traders. The humans were mostly MBA students from Cornell University. Three levels of transparency were examined involving differences in both pre-trade and post-trade transparency. In the transparent market the quotes and trades of the two market-makers were publicly disclosed. Neither quotes nor trades were publicly disclosed in the opaque market, although traders received private quotes. Finally, in the semi-opaque market quotes were disclosed, but trades were not. The authors found that pre-trade transparency had little effect, while the disclosure of trades improved price discovery, and caused wide spreads at the opening of trading. Post-trade transparency also increased the profits of the market-makers at the expense of traders who could delay their trades (informed and liquidity traders).

7.6.4 Bloomfield and O'Hara (2000)

This paper investigates the effects of two exchanges trading the same security, but with different levels of transparency. They conducted two laboratory experiments to investigate this question. In the first experiment two dealers published their trades, and two did not. In the second experiment, the four dealers were allowed to choose whether or not to publish their trades. It was found that transparent markets do not thrive in competition with less transparent markets, and that individual dealers prefer opacity. Opaque dealers were found to be more profitable than transparent dealers, even though they were trading at smaller realised spreads. When taken in conjunction with the findings of Bloomfield and O'Hara (1999), this finding suggests that dealers face a prisoner's dilemma – if they are all transparent, they make higher profits than when they are all opaque. However, given that every other dealer is transparent, a single dealer will increase their profits if they became opaque. One way of resolving such a prisoner's dilemma, and to allow dealers to maximise their collective profits, is by regulatory intervention.

7.7   Evidence from non-equity markets

There is very little literature on the impact of transparency on markets other than those for equities in the USA and UK. However there are a few studies of the effects of information asymmetries, and some of these can be viewed as studies of transparency.

7.7.1   US Treasury notes and bonds – Umlauf (1991)

In the USA, IDB systems exist for trading Treasury notes and bonds. Primary dealers (and aspiring primary dealers) are able to see all the IDB screens, while secondary dealers (e.g. retail investors) can see the screens of only two of the nine IDB vendors. Umlauf (1991) found that prices on the IDB systems accessed only by the primary dealers led those open to secondary dealers by about two to five minutes; while the bid–ask spreads of the IDB systems for primary dealers were narrower than those on the IDB systems open to secondary dealers. These results are consistent with primary dealers being better informed than secondary dealers, so that information is reflected first in the non-transparent or 'closed' IDB market. Since primary dealers try to exploit this information asymmetry in the transparent or 'open' IDB market, bid–ask spreads in this market are wider. Thus the differences in the transparency and access of these two IDB markets leads to a transfer of wealth from the secondary dealers to the primary dealers.

7.7.2   Bund futures on LIFFE and the DTB – Kofman and Moser (1997)

Kofman and Moser studied the effect of a different level of transparency on two exchanges trading an identical security. Bund futures were traded on LIFFE using open outcry, where the identity of the pit traders involved in each quote and trade can be observed, while the DTB uses screens, where traders are anonymous. Kofman and Moser argue that market-makers on the DTB require wider spreads to compensate them for the anonymity and the risk of being picked off by informed traders. This study used time and sales data for a six-week period to compare the performance of LIFFE and the DTB in trading bund futures. It was found that realised spreads on the two exchanges were very similar, and Kofman and Moser concluded that the increase in the DTB spreads owing to its lower transparency was offset by the lower order processing costs of a screen-based exchange.

7.7.3 Indian Inter-Bank Deposits – Shah (2000)

The Indian inter-bank deposit market operates as an OTC telephone market with indicative quotes on Reuters screens, but with no trade publication. In 1998 the level of transparency of this market increased when the National Stock Exchange started collecting prices from dealers and publishing the average. Publication of the 14-day rates began on 10 November 1998, while the 30-day and 90-day rates were published from 1 December 1998. After controlling for changes in factors which affected the bid–ask spread for 1-day rates, it was found that publication of the average rate led to a clear reduction in the bid–ask spreads for 14-day, 30-day and 90-day rates.

7.7.4 Italian Treasury bonds – Scalia and Vacca (1999)

As from 14th July 1997 there was a decrease in the transparency of the screen-based inter-dealer market in Italian Treasury bonds (Mercato Telematico dei Titoli di Stato, MTS) – the names of market-makers posting bid and offer quotes were no longer revealed. Scalia and Vacca (1999) used data on every MTS trade for the 213 days before and 221 days after this transparency change to study its effects. After the decrease in transparency there was a 22 per cent fall in the number of small traders, and a rise of 14 per cent in the number of large traders. Scalia and Vacca argue this is because the suppression of identities harmed the uninformed (small) traders, while benefiting the informed (large) traders. There were also proportionately more large daily changes in inventory after the change (which could be due to the drop in the number of small traders).

After the change the estimated bid–ask spread, market depth and volatility were lower, while the MTS market became more likely to lead LIFFE's BTP futures. These results are difficult to interpret because, as well as the change in transparency, there were a number of other important changes at this time. Throughout the data period, the Italian government was monitoring the turnover of dealers, and there is evidence that dealers inflated their turnover by about 30 per cent. In addition, during the data period the Italian economy was being managed to meet the criteria for entry to the Exchange Rate Mechanism (ERM). Finally, from December 1997 repo contracts were traded on MTS and this reduced the cost of establishing short positions. Scalia and Vacca show that a large proportion of the changes in the bid–ask spread, market depth and volatility are due to macroeconomic effects, rather than the decrease in transparency.

Notes

1   Angel (1998) has suggested that in buying and selling some securities, traders face a prisoner's dilemma. They wish to trade but, in a market with asymmetric information, revealing that they wish to trade is valuable information which may move the price against them. Traders wish others to reveal their trading intentions without revealing their own. This prisoners' dilemma is overcome by creating markets in which all traders are required to reveal information about orders and trades. This dilemma is likely to be much more acute in equity markets, than in interest rate or forex markets, because there is much more information asymmetry in equity markets. Therefore, the incentive to form organised equity markets with required levels of transparency is greatest for equity markets. This argument is consistent with organised markets in equities and equity options, but OTC spot markets in interest rates and forex. However, it does not explain organised markets in index futures and options, nor in bond (and forex) futures and options. (although forex futures have low volumes on exchanges, and a very high OTC volume. There is also a large OTC market in interest rate futures – swaps).
2   It should be noted that the market-maker could also use derivative instruments to hedge this imbalance position or use the IDB systems as alternatives to own account trading, thus reducing the amount of own account trading required.
3   For more evidence on this, see also Bloomfield and O'Hara (1999).
4   The TSE's floor resembles the NYSE in that only the specialist (in TSE's jargon the specialist is called a 'registered trader') observed the limit order book. Other traders could see only the best bid and ask prices and their size. From 12 April 1990 the limit order book for up to four price levels above and below the touch was published, including their size. In addition, trades were reported more quickly by moving from a punched card to an electronic system. In contrast, CATS members could already see the limit order book including the size of the orders, and the change allowed the general public to see this information.

8
The Regulation of Transparency

The purpose of this chapter is to offer suggestions to help regulators in setting transparency standards. The FSA is required by the FSMA[1] to ensure that each RIE has appropriate arrangements for relevant information (information that is relevant in determining the current value of the investments) to be made available to persons engaged in dealing in investments on the exchange. This requires the FSA to ensure that markets are transparent. In addition, the FSA has a duty to maintain confidence, promote public understanding, protect consumers, reduce financial crime and facilitate competition. All of these objectives are advanced by transparent markets.

Much of the previous academic debate concerning transparency has concentrated on the effects of delayed publication in dealer markets. However, the transparency questions facing regulators are wider than this because transparency can be compromised in ways other than delaying trade publication, and there are other types of market than dealer markets. Therefore the following analysis takes a more general and pragmatic approach to the question of transparency.

The theoretical evidence surveyed in Chapter 7. generally suggests that increased transparency is beneficial. The bulk of the published empirical papers on the effects of transparency have examined the London Stock Exchange, which has changed its transparency regime several times since 1986. It is useful to note that, in one of these regimes which lasted for over two years, the London Stock Exchange operated successfully with complete post-trade transparency. These papers are summarised in Table 8.1 which shows that almost none of the adverse effects predicted for increased transparency has been found.

Overall, the results in Chapter 7 suggest that high transparency is theoretically desirable and that, empirically, increased transparency

Table 8.1 Summary of the major results of empirical studies of the delayed publication of large trades

Predicted change[1]	Elwes	DGFT	MacIntyre	Breedon	Board and Sutcliffe	Gemmill	Saporta et al.	Board and Sutcliffe	NASD	Madhavan	Lee and Chung	Flood et al.	Bloomfield and O'Hara
	1989	1990	1991	1993	1995	1996	1999	2000	1983	2000	1998	1997 1999	1999 2000
	UK	UK	UK	UK	UK	UK	UK	UK	USA	Canada	Korea	Experiment	Experiment
Bid – ask spread Increase	–	No	No	–	No	No	No	No	No	No	–	Experiment	Experiment
Size of quotes Decrease	–	No	No	–	–	–	–	–	–	No	–	No	No
Reduce	No[2]	No	–	No	No	–	–	–	No	No	No	–	–
Price Efficiency Increase	–	–	–	–	–	–	–	–	–	–	–	Yes	Yes
Number of Market-makers Reduce	–	–	–	–	–	–	–	–	No	–	–	–	–
Price volatility Increase	–	–	–	–	–	No	–	–	No	Yes[3]	No	No	–

Notes:
[1] 'Predicted change' shows the direction of the effect of increasing transparency suggested by those resisting an increase in transparency.
[2] 'No' indicates that the change shown in the 'Predicted Change' column was not found.
[3] 'Yes' indicates that the predicted change was found.
'—' indicates that the predicted change was not examined.

seems not to be accompanied by reductions in either market quality or liquidity.

8.1 The policy dimensions of transparency

The transparency of a market has a number of different characteristics. Full transparency involves the immediate publication to all interested parties of all the available information, and so is seldom encountered. There are a number of dimensions in which markets fail to achieve full transparency, and regulators need to consider markets along each of these dimensions.

1 *Which type of transparency is concerned?*
Two main types of transparency have been identified – pre-trade transparency and post-trade transparency.
Pre-trade transparency is concerned with the publication of information that becomes available before a trade, and involves such matters as market-makers' quotes, details of unfilled orders, etc.
Post-trade transparency is concerned with the publication of the details of a trade that has occurred (e.g. the name of the company whose shares have been traded, the time of the trade, the price and quantity of shares traded, and the identities of the buyer and seller). Of course, information on previous trades provides useful information when making subsequent trades, and so pre- and post-transparency are both aspects of the information set relevant to market participants. Another aspect of this is the degree of post-trade anonymity allowed.
2 *What conditions must be met before trade publication occurs?*
(a) *Time.*
The time lag before publication can range from instant publication to a one-week delay (e.g. for trades larger than $75 \times$ NMS UK market-makers could opt for a delay in publication of five business days). The time lag may be in trading time or calendar time.
(b) *Trade type*
The London Stock Exchange applied different trade publication rules to trades of different types, and crossed trades, broker to broker trades and riskless principal trades all required immediate publication.
(c) *Trade size*
In some markets, only trades above some threshold size are subject to delayed publication, e.g eight NMS in the UK.

(d) *Inventories*
Some large London Stock Exchange trades were delayed until 90 per cent of the position has been unwound by the market-maker concerned
(e) *Security type*
The identity of the securities to which the transparency rules apply. For example, the rules could be that only trades in UK listed companies traded on the London Stock Exchange need be published within 3 minutes, while trades in non-UK stocks, or overseas trades in UK stocks need not be published for 24 hours. The London Stock Exchange did not require immediate publication of trades on SEAQ International. When a company was the subject of a takeover bid the London Stock Exchange required that all trades, regardless of size, be published immediately.

3 *To whom is the 'published' information made available[2]?*
(a) Market participants (e.g. pit members, those allowed to trade on screens)
(b) Those present (e.g. includes those permitted to observe the pit or screen, but not participate)
(c) Subscribers to a vendor licensed to distribute quote or trade data (e.g. Reuters)
(d) The public (at no charge).

4 *What information is to be published?*
(a) *Pre-trade.* Quoted price, the identity of the market-maker posting the quote, the size up to which the quote is firm, is this quote on the inside spread (or yellow strip), the depth of the order book.
(b) *Post-trade.* Trade price, individual or aggregate volume, the counterparties to the trade, the time of the trade, the type of counterparties involved in the trade (e.g. IDB, market-maker, customer), the trade type (e.g programme trade, worked principal agreement, basket trade, etc.), the inventories of the market-makers involved.

5 *Charges*
Data vendors charge for their services, and this may exclude some traders from seeing the quote and trade information in real time.

6 *Choice*
The transparency requirements may offer traders some element of choice, e.g the specified period of delayed publication is only a maximum, and traders can choose earlier publication if they wish (as was the case for very large London Stock Exchange trades).

To the extent that OTC markets do not trade standardised products, information on OTC trading becomes difficult to aggregate and compare because these trades may be non-commensurable (Rappell, 1998). In order to permit the interpretation of OTC data these markets might be asked to publish, not only price and quantity information, but also details of the conditions and terms of the different contracts. However, this may breach the confidentiality of the agreements negotiated between the counterparties, and would also make disclosure very lengthy as the contract terms would need to be specified. In some cases, OTC markets have moved towards a high degree of standardisation of the products traded, and here transparency would be much easier to implement.

8.2 Alleged benefits of increased transparency

This section outlines the various ways in which increasing the transparency of a market can be beneficial.

8.2.1 Efficiency will increase

A high level of transparency means that more information is available to all traders because every trader can see the full picture, rather than having access to only their part of the picture. This extra public information tends to improve the efficiency of the market (Director General of Fair Trading, 1994). The information content of the quote and trade data is fully impounded into prices immediately, rather than waiting until the information generating these quotes and trades is revealed, and so price discovery is improved. This gain in efficiency assumes that traders do not simply switch to alternative non-transparent methods of trading when transparency is increased (this possibility is considered below).[3]

With immediate disclosure, any widening of the bid–ask spread for large trades may mean that some information will not immediately be reflected in the share price because these large trades no longer occur. On the other hand, if options are substitutes for equities in information trading, and as equity bid–ask spreads widen, the role of price discovery may simply pass to the derivatives markets.

8.2.2 Asymmetric information will decrease

If there is less than full transparency, some traders will have superior information that other traders do not have. For example, if there is delayed publication the counterparties to each trade know the price and quantity of the trade, while other traders do not. If this information is price sensitive, even if only in the short run, the counterparties concerned can profit from this private knowledge. For example, if prices are expected to fall on the announcement of a large sell trade, the traders concerned can aim to have a short position by that time. The Director General of Fair Trading (1990) concluded that such an information asymmetry represents a market distortion because this advantage is not the result of superior trading efficiency.

An opaque market favours insiders who have some access to private information (i.e. who are able to see part of the order flow), at the expense of outsiders who do not have access to this private information. In consequence, a move to increased transparency results in a redistribution of wealth from the informed to the uninformed. It is not, therefore, surprising that market insiders are generally strongly in favour of retaining opacity.

Thus, when there is delayed publication, gaining access to such price sensitive information will increase the attractiveness to equity market-makers of large trades, and this may induce the market-maker to offer a better price for the large trade. The empirical evidence summarised above tends to support this argument.

Of course, if the immediate publication of large trades resulted in an increase in the volume of pre-arranged trades (such as protected trades, Worked Principal Agreements and block trades) an information asymmetry between the market-maker and potential counterparties would remain while the market-maker searches for a match.

8.2.3   Cross-subsidies will be eliminated

An increase in the transparency of a dealer market which involves a move to the immediate publication of large trades means that traders who require immediacy for large trades may have to pay more for this service (Director General of Fair Trading, 1994). This is because the inventories of market makers can no longer be liquidated at the more favourable prices that prevailed before there was public knowledge of the previous large trade. Immediate trade publication reduces the risk for market-makers of trading with someone who is better informed (e.g. knows about unpublished large trades). This may actually lead to a small reduction in the bid–ask spread for small and medium sized trades, although the bid–ask spread for large trades may rise.

8.2.4   Investor confidence will increase

If investors know that transparency is compromised (e.g. that some trades are being temporarily concealed), they may fear that the market is unfair and this may reduce their willingness to trade, so reducing volume and market participation (Elwes Committee, 1989; IOSCO, 1993). In which case, a move to greater transparency could generate new order flow, and attract order flow from other (less transparent) exchanges.

8.2.5 Price volatility will be reduced

There have been a range of suggestions concerning the effect of increased transparency on price volatility.

One view is that increased transparency leads to reduced price volatility. Because trade and quote information is a very noisy signal, it is likely that the price response to fundamental information is more gradual than when the information is released in a single public announcement. If this is true, a transparent market is likely to have more small price changes than a non-transparent market, while a non-transparent market will have fewer, but larger, price changes. Which type of market is the more volatile depends on the definition of volatility. However, the variance of returns for a transparent market will probably be less than the variance for a non-transparent market.

A different view is that increased transparency increases price volatility. If publication is not delayed, market-makers may require a wider bid–ask spread for large trades to compensate for the inventory risk, even when the large trade is known to be liquidity-based. This will create temporary price movements, unrelated to any change in the fundamental value of the stock (i.e. bid–ask bounce). These price movements will increase measured volatility. Wells (1993) draws a distinction between fundamental information (e.g. news which affects forecasts of the company's subsequent performance) and information on temporary market conditions. Price movements caused by temporary market conditions are argued to create excess volatility and be undesirable (Director General of Fair Trading, 1994). Delayed publication is argued to prevent the price volatility caused by temporary liquidity pressures, and so the abolition of delayed publication would increase volatility.[4]

There is a different argument concerning price volatility and delayed publication. If publication is not delayed, equity market-makers may require a wider bid–ask spread for large trades to compensate for the inventory risk, even when the large trade is known to be liquidity-based. This will create temporary price movements, unrelated to any change in the fundamental value of the stock.

8.2.6 Competition between market-makers will increase

Small market-makers (e.g. new entrants) may be more dependent on published information than are large market-makers (Wells, 1993). It is possible therefore, that delayed publication discourages the entry of new market-makers, and encourages the exit of small market-makers. On the other hand, if immediate publication causes a fall in the net profits of equity market-makers, this will encourage an increase in the concentration of equity market-makers. In addition, the increased risk associated with supplying immediacy for large trades when there is immediate publication may mean that market-makers need a larger capitalisation, and this will tend to favour large market-makers, or those who are part of a large company. Therefore, increased transparency will reduce the barriers to entry into market-making.

8.3 Alleged costs of increased transparency

This section considers a number of effects of increased transparency that may be seen as undesirable.

8.3.1 Bid–ask spreads will widen

The bid–ask spread in a dealer market is determined by three different factors:

(a) a liquidity or inventory effect, which is the cost to market-makers of increasing the size of their positions
(b) an information effect, which reflects the risk that the counterparty is better informed than the market-maker[5]; and
(c) an order processing cost, which represents the administrative costs involved in processing the trade.

Both the inventory and information components of the bid–ask spread are especially relevant for large trades.

Inventory costs in auction and dealer markets

There is an important difference between dealer and auction markets so far as transparency is concerned. In any market, the inventories of the counterparties are altered by the trade, with large trades having a bigger inventory effect. In an auction market, the two parties to the trade are usually content with their new inventory position (i.e. the seller wanted a lower inventory and the buyer wanted a higher inventory[6]). However, in a dealer market, the market-maker is merely taking the opposite side to the order flow. In which case, large trades (or a succession of small trades in the same direction) may move their inventory away from its target level (Board, and Sutcliffe, 1997). This inventory position exposes the market-maker to unwanted price risk, as well as tying up capital. Therefore, market-makers adopt inventory control policies to stabilise the size of their inventories at low levels. In consequence, it is claimed that the immediate publication of large trades is particularly harmful in dealer markets.

Information effects

Because it is claimed that large trades which leave a market-maker with a substantial inventory can be unwound only at unfavourable prices, and because a large trade may imply an information asymmetry, market-makers are argued to quote less favourable prices for trading large blocks of shares. This suggests that the touch (the difference between best ask and bid prices) for large trades will tend to be wider than for small trades.[7] If all trades were published immediately, traders requiring immediacy for large trades would have to pay for this service.[8] Although some uninformed traders (e.g. arbitrageurs and index tracking funds) might demand immediacy, market-makers would now have more reason to suspect that those traders who require immediacy are trading on the basis of time sensitive information, and the bid–ask spread may widen further for this reason.

Order processing costs

Franks and Schaefer (1991) also suggest that, if they knew another market-maker had recently been involved in a large trade, other market-makers might act so as to penalise the market-maker concerned. For example, if a market-maker is thought to have acquired a large long position, other market-makers may lower their bid quotes, leading to a widening of the touch. This will not only reduce the profits of the market-maker with the large inventory, but will also reduce the price received by other traders who sell during this period.

As noted above, a case can also be made that the immediate publication of large trades will actually lead to a slight narrowing of the spread. This could arise if market-makers as a group benefit from the increased disclosure of the activities of their competitors, which leads to a reduction in risk. As the risk of any trade might be argued to have fallen, the need for a large risk premium will also fall, and the spread could be expected to narrow. In addition, any increase in competition between market-makers arising from a more uniform distribution of trade information might be expected to narrow the spread. As well as affecting the bid–ask spread for large trades, a move to immediate publication may also change the bid–ask spread for smaller trades. Since market-makers would now be informed immediately about large trades, the risk of trading with someone who has superior information will fall (Kyle and Röell, 1989). This may lead to a reduction in the bid–ask spreads for smaller trades, and reduce the increase in the spreads for large trades (Director General of Fair Trading, 1990).

8.3.2 Immediacy and volume will be reduced

One of the principal reasons offered for the delayed publication regime on the London Stock Exchange was the need to ensure that market-makers can offer immediacy at a low price. If transparency is increased and all trades, whatever their size, are subject to immediate publication, there are a number of possible changes in trader behaviour:

1 *Splitting.* One alternative to a market structure designed to allow very large numbers of shares to be traded in a single bargain is for traders, particularly those who do not need immediacy, to split large trades into a sequence of smaller trades, as is commonly done in other markets (Hodson, 1994). These smaller deals might be expected to be at more attractive prices than would be offered for a single large trade. It seems, however, that practice on the London Stock Exchange militated against this as traders using this strategy are asked by market-makers whether the smaller transaction is part of a larger trade. If the answer is yes, the market-maker will quote a wider spread because the associated transactions will make it harder for the market-maker to liquidate their position. If the trader lies and answers no, the market-maker will penalise him or her in subsequent transactions (Pagano and Röell, 1992).

2 *Worked Principal Agreements.* An alternative response is for traders who do not require immediacy to use Worked Principal Agreements (WPA), in which the market-maker does not acquire an inventory. In a WPA, the market-maker undertakes to complete the trade at a later time on the same day at a price more favourable than that immediately available. This gives the market-maker a chance to pre-position their inventory, and the price given will reflect the success of the market-maker in the pre-positioning exercise. The trade, when executed, will be reported to the London Stock Exchange in the usual way.

3 *Shop the block.* Instead of pre-positioning the large trade via a WPA, the market-maker may attempt to find counterparties with whom to match the large trade. As Burdett and O'Hara (1987) pointed out, 'shopping the block' informs those contacted that a large trade is about to take place and its direction, and gives them a rough idea of the likely price.

4 *Crossing networks.* Uninformed traders who wish to trade in size and do not require immediacy may wish to use a crossing network (e.g. eCrossnet).

Given these various alternatives to demanding immediacy in size from market-makers, the volume of large trades might fall; but the total volume of trading could be unaffected by a move to the immediate publication of large trades.

8.3.3 Related markets will be damaged

An increase in transparency in one market may have good or bad consequences for related markets. For example, increased London Stock Exchange transparency could have implications for the traded options market (see Board and Sutcliffe, 1998) or the OTC markets, for which no information on individual trades need be published.

It should be noted that the effect on LIFFE's options market of increased equity transparency was predicted to be positive (i.e. that increasing London Stock Exchange transparency would benefit LIFFE's traded options market). The fact that low transparency might impose an externality on other markets forms another reason in favour of mandated transparency.

8.3.4 Flight overseas

It has often been claimed that, if there is an increase in the transparency of a UK market, the order flow will be transferred to a non-transparent overseas exchange.[9] If trading does move elsewhere to circumvent the immediate disclosure of large trades, delayed publication effectively remains in operation (Kyle and Röell, 1989). In these circumstances, it could be argued that the market would become less transparent than before, since the off-exchange activity need never be published (or ever become available to London investors). However, the available evidence is that this is an empty threat. There do not appear to be any examples of increased transparency causing financial institutions to move their trading overseas.[10] However, there are many examples of increased transparency not leading to an exodus overseas, e.g. the dramatic increase in the transparency of the UK equity market in the 1990s. This lack of flight is despite the direct costs of avoiding the UK transparency rules being very low. For example, to avoid UK transparency regulations, financial institutions would not have to shut down their trading operations in London and move overseas. Under the EU passport, they could route their trading through a subsidiary office in another EU country, and be subject to that country's reporting (and hence transparency) rules. The traders could stay in London, and these trades would be subject to UK regulation. However, despite the low cost, financial institutions have chosen not to do this, which suggests that increased transparency does not lead to flight overseas.

The lack of examples of overseas flight to avoid increases in transparency is supported by a general lack of flight overseas. There are only a couple of examples of government behaviour causing financial markets to move offshore (eurobonds and Swedish equities). However, there are many situations where financial markets have not fled because of some local adversity. For example, equity purchases in the UK, are subject to a 0.5 per cent stamp duty. While this tax is unwelcome, the UK equity market has not moved overseas. This suggests that there are powerful reasons for financial institutions wishing to trade in London, and that increases in regulatory requirements, such as increased transparency, are unlikely to cause them to move overseas; despite repeated protestations to the contrary.

Even if there is a real risk of flight overseas, it is also possible that the immediate publication of large trades may attract some trading currently done elsewhere because of the current lack of transparency on the Stock Exchange.

8.4   Access and transparency

The discussion of transparency so far has largely been in the context of a single trading system. With the possible emergence of competing trading systems, two new issues arise:

- Will transparency affect the degree of price fragmentation?
- Will transparency affect the fairness of the market?
- Will transparency affect barriers to entry?

To explore this, Table 8.2 shows a simple model where there is an incumbent trading system *TS*1 and a new entrant *TS*2. Note that the term 'trading system' is not confined to formal trading structures – a negotiated telephone market is a trading system as well. *TS*1 and *TS*2 could also be parts of a 'single' trading system operated by an exchange (for example an order book and telephone market or an order book and IDB market). There are also two types of user, *A* and *B*. Type *A* users have access to the incumbent *TS*1. They may or may not have access *TS*2. Type *B* investors have access to *TS*2 and may have access to *TS*1.

Table 8.2 The effects of transparency on fragmentation, fairness and entry barriers

Summary	
Price fragmentation	Only if user bases are strictly segmented and even then leakage will probably eliminate price differences
Fairness	This will depend on the degree of access of type *B* investors to the opaque *TS1*; at the least they will incur extra costs, at the worst they will trade at a disadvantage
Barriers to entry	Risks and costs will deter Type *B* users from accessing the market through *TS2*; Type *A* users will probably stick to *TS1* Success of *TS2* will be less assured than if *TS1* were transparent

Cont. overleaf

Table 8.2 (Continued)

	TS1	TS2	Aspect	Conclusion
Situation 1 – segmented users	A only – *TS1* denies access to Type *B* because they are not professionals or not otherwise part of the inside group	*B* only – perhaps type *B* users are reluctant to participate when the better-informed Type *A* users can participate.	**Price fragmentation**	If the split is truly complete then there is no mechanism to bring prices in the two mechanisms together
				If *TS1* is opaque to some extent and there is no user overlap there will be period when prices diverge significantly – unless Type *B* users rely on Type *A* users for their market access – i.e. abandon *TS2*.
				If *TS1* is transparent then users of *TS2* can see the 'main market' price and act accordingly.
			Fairness	Opaque *TS1* will oblige Type *B* users to employ Type *A* users in order to find out what the market price actually is
				By doing this Type *B* users will avoid the risks of mispricing (assuming Type *A* users do not front-run or otherwise abuse the market) but incur costs for a service they could do themselves if the market were open or transparent
			Barriers to entry	Opaque *TS1* will make it difficult for *TS2* to compete for business since users risk mispricing and will be forced to revert back to intermediated use of *TS1*

Situation				
Situation 2 – one-way unsegmented market	A	AB – TS2 accepts any type of users probably in the interests of maximising liquidity – unless it deters Type B users, this is a rational choice	Price fragmentation	Type A users will have access to both TS1 and TS2 and will arbitrage any price differences irrespective of whether TS1 is transparent or opaque. However, if TS1 was transparent then Type B users would be able to avoid being on the wrong side of the arbitrage
			Fairness	Type B users will experience better pricing than in the opaque, segmented situation but the arbitrage profits earned by Type A users will be at the expense of Type B users. If the market is competitive then these need not be large but are still positive. Type B users will, however, always be trading is situation of inferior information. Again, if the market is competitive these need not be large
			Barriers to entry	With opaque TS1, type B users have the choice of employing Type A users to access TS1 (Type A users will probably not use TS2 except for arbitrage) or suffering from the arbitrage and other uncertain but possible information asymmetries
Situation 3 – common user base	AB	AB	Price fragmentation	Irrespective of the level of transparency, arbitrage will eliminate price discrepancies

Cont. overleaf

Table 8.2 (Continued)

TS1	TS2	Aspect	Conclusion
		Fairness	In theory there should be no difference but the probability is that Type *A* users will have access to more of the private information in *TS1* than will Type *B* users Therefore, in practice, Type *B* users will tend to employ Type *A* users as a source of market information
		Barriers to entry	In theory no barriers but superior access to private information for Type *A* users will make it hard for *TS2* to attract business

*TS*1 is assumed to be less than fully transparent. If it is an incumbent trading system it may have reduced its transparency in order to prevent the 'parasitic' new systems from, as it sees it, free-riding on its price discovery process. Alternatively it may just be an OTC trading system with little or no natural transparency.

8.5   The interaction between OTC markets and exchanges

If related securities are traded on an exchange and an OTC market, the transparency regime for the exchange has implications for the OTC market, and vice versa. The possibility of arbitrage means that there will generally be a very close relationship between the prices in the OTC market and the exchange. Participants in the OTC market can price their trades using the published exchange quotes and trades. Therefore, price discovery is performed largely by the exchange, as any information content in the OTC order flow is not made public. However, some participants in the OTC market will have access to this information. This creates an information asymmetry which OTC traders can exploit in their exchange and OTC trading. If traders can choose where to trade, *ceteris paribus*, they may prefer to use the opaque OTC market for some trades as this minimises the information they reveal to others. To analyse further the possible effects of such market fragmentation, a small thought-experiment will be conducted which looks at three possible situations. The logical transparency possibilities to be examined for the two exchanges are:

1   Both exchanges are opaque
2   Both exchanges are transparent
3   One exchange is transparent, while the other is not.

In each case, the exchange is a dealer market, and this fits well with an OTC interpretation for one of the exchanges. Transparency means that every traders can see every quote and trade. Opacity is interpreted as a dealer market where traders can only see some dealer quotes, and their own trade price. Every trader has access to both exchanges:

1   If both exchanges are opaque, whether there is one or two exchanges makes little difference – trading is opaque on both exchanges
2   If both exchanges are fully transparent, whether there is one or two exchanges makes little difference – trading is transparent and customers can see all quotes and all trades on both exchanges

3 If one exchange (*T*) is transparent, while the other exchange (*O*) is
   not, then all customers will be able to see trades and quotes on
   exchange *T*, but only a few dealer quotes and their own trades on
   exchange *O*. It is likely that the exchange has high transparency
   standards (i.e. *T*), while the related OTC market is opaque (i.e. *O*).

Exchange *O* may well attract an order flow with a high information
content, e.g. large trades, trades based on information (as opposed to
liquidity trades). This is because informed traders seek to exploit their
information without revealing they are informed, while market-makers
seek protection while unwinding large trades. In this case some market-
makers and traders in exchange *O* will acquire private information from
seeing part of the order flow. They are then free to exploit this information by trading on either exchange *T* or exchange *O*. In consequence,
traders on both exchanges risk trading with a better-informed counter
party, not just those on the opaque exchange (negative externality of
exchange *O* for exchange *T*).

Public prices in this market will be largely provided by exchange *T*.
However, exchange *T* will be dealing with an atypical slice of the order
flow – that from uninformed traders. Hence, its published prices may,
on occasion, not reflect private information that has been revealed to
some traders in exchange *O* (negative externality of exchange *O* for
exchange *T*). Thus, exchange *O* will play an important, although hidden,
role in the price discovery process; and prices on exchange *T* will tend
to lag behind those on exchange *O*.

Traders will compare the public quotes on exchange *T* with the private
quotes they receive on exchange *O*. This suggests that exchange *O* quotes
cannot be worse than the public quotes on exchange *T*, and that quoted
spreads may generally be smaller on exchange *O*, despite the risks of
information asymmetries between customers and market makers (positive externality of exchange *T* for exchange *O*). Market-makers may be
willing to accept smaller spreads on exchange *O* to acquire the private
information contained in this order flow, which they can then exploit
in both exchanges.

Price fragmentation may occur as between the two exchanges. However, arbitrage should prevent wide price disparities, provided potential
arbitrageurs can discover the current prices on exchange *O*. This need
for information on prices in exchange *O* may restrict arbitrage to institutional traders and market makers. This means that they can make
arbitrage profits, while other traders (on both exchanges) get to trade
with them at inferior prices (negative externality of exchange *O* for

exchange *T*). The prevention of those with access to opaque market segments making continuous arbitrage profits at the expense of the uninformed is another reason for mandated transparency. The prevention of those with access to opaque market segments making continuous arbitrage profits at the expense of the uninformed is another reason for mandated transparency. Equally, from the perspective of retail participants, it will be difficult to be sure that best execution has been achieved if the prices in one exchange (*O*) are opaque.

The coexistence of two trading mechanisms with different transparency rules risks a 'race for the bottom' in transparency standards, although there is not much evidence of such an outcome.[11] Indeed, higher transparency may actually attract order flow.

8.6 Cost-benefit analysis of transparency

Any cost-benefit analysis (CBA) faces a number of difficult problems:

- *Population*. For whom are the costs and benefits being computed – traders, market makers, the UK population, or the world? The answer to this question can have a considerable effect on the results. For example, if the analysis is conducted with respect to the world then, ignoring any side effects, driving trading offshore has no effect on total costs and benefits.[12]
- *Redistribution*. Even if there is agreement on the group for whom the costs and benefits are being assessed, there may be distributional effects within the group. For example, increased transparency might harm market-makers, while benefiting traders. Is this desirable or undesirable?
- *Risk*. Any figures for the costs and benefits from some possible course of action are just estimates. Some figures may be reasonably certain, while others may be liable to considerable error.[13] How should such forecasting risk be handled within the CBA? If the costs and benefits used in CBA represent the expected values, it is being assumed that decision-makers have a neutral attitude to risk, which may not be the case.

1 *Direct costs*
   The direct costs of an increase in transparency are small. The increased use of information technology means that the costs of capturing and publishing this information in real time have fallen to low levels. For trades on recognised exchanges, much of the information is already reported to the FSA. The additional costs of

immediate publication would be low, and probably offset by increased revenue from the sale of this information. For transactions that are not reported to the FSA, authorised bodies are required to record the details of each trade for possible inspection by the FSA (as well as for their own commercial purposes). In such cases, increased transparency involves the additional cost of transmitting this data to the Transactions Monitoring Unit (TMU) of the FSA and subsequent publication. Given the use of information technology, these costs are thought to be small.

2   Indirect costs

- It has been claimed that bid–ask spreads in dealer markets will widen if there is increased transparency, although there is no empirical evidence to support this statement. Given an assumed change in realised spreads, this could easily be costed by multiplying by the number of securities traded.
- It has been asserted that immediacy and volume will be reduced by an increase in transparency.
- Related markets may be damaged by an increase in transparency, although there is no evidence of such an effect.
- An increase in transparency may lead to a flight overseas of trading, although there is no evidence of such an effect.

3   Benefits

- An increase in transparency may lead to an increase in market efficiency, with prices reflecting information more quickly.
- Information asymmetries will decrease if transparency increases, and this could lead to a narrowing of bid–ask spreads.
- Cross-subsidies between traders in a dealer market will be eliminated.
- Investor confidence will increase as transparency increases.
- Price volatility may decrease as transparency decreases, although it has also be argued that volatility will increase
- Competition between market-makers in a dealer market will increase as transparency increases.

The indirect costs and benefits are subject to the problems of population, redistribution and risk noted above. In addition, some costs and benefits may be difficult to quantify, e.g. the increase in customer confidence because the market it is more transparent. Even when the effects of increased transparency have been quantified, they may be difficult to value. For example, if the abolition of delayed publication means that information is reflected in the price an average of x minutes faster than previously, what is this worth?

Given the problems noted above of population, redistribution and risk, in addition to those of quantification and valuation, any CBA is likely to be inconclusive. If this state of affairs is used to argue that no change to the transparency rules should be made because a CBA cannot demonstrate an improvement in welfare, it risks locking society into a status quo in which no changes are made.

8.7 Empirical evidence – demonstrable harm?

The extent to which greater transparency damages or benefits the market is an empirical question. Since every market can be argued to be unique in some way, it is not possible to demonstrate conclusively that greater transparency will, or will not be harmful before any such change is made, ignoring the problems mentioned above of actually computing a meaningful net benefit or cost figure.

A review of the available empirical evidence reveals no documented cases of increased transparency being harmful. Empirical studies of transparency in the UK and USA have generally concluded that changes in the speed of publication have little effect on the market characteristics studied (Board and Sutcliffe, 1995a, 1995b, 1996b, 2000; Breedon, 1993; Director General of Fair Trading, 1990; Elwes Committee, 1989; Gemmill, 1994, 1996; MacIntyre, 1991; NASD, 1983; Neuberger, 1992; Snell and Tonks, 1995). In particular, a number of the negative effects (e.g. on the bid–ask spread, liquidity and trading volumes) that have been suggested as likely to follow increased transparency have not been found.

Using data for 1992–4, Board and Sutcliffe (1995a, 1995b, 1996b) conducted an extensive empirical investigation of the London Stock Exchange. Large trades were found to have a permanent price impact of about 0.2 per cent, which was realised about 45 minutes after the large trade, suggesting that knowledge of a large trade offers potentially valuable information to the market-maker concerned. Two types of inventory positioning were considered by Board and Sutcliffe (1995a, 1995b, 1996b). The first was pre-positioning, which takes place before the large trade is executed; and the second is post-positioning, which occurs during the delay between trade execution and publication. They found that, of the volume of large trades, 26 per cent was pre-positioned, 15 per cent was post-positioned, while 59 per cent was neither pre- nor post-positioned. These results strongly suggest that market-makers did not consistently use the opportunity offered by the transparency regime to offset the excess inventory acquired as a result of a large trade. Board and Sutcliffe (1995a, 1995b, 1996b) also found that the amount of positioning tended to fall as trade size rose. This surprising result implies that market-makers do not perceive very large trades as riskier than smaller ones; which substantially weakens the justification for delayed publication. Finally, it was found that market-makers complete such post-positioning as they undertake in less than 45 minutes. Based on the analysis of actual trade practice, the overall recommendation in Board and Sutcliffe (1995a, 1995b, 1996b) was that transparency on the London Stock Exchange should be increased and they argued that, contrary to practitioners' arguments, the adverse consequences from a reduction in the publication delay for large trades would be minimal.

8.8 Summarising the arguments

The bias of regulators has always been towards more rather than less transparency. However, in the light of the less than conclusive discussion of empirical evidence and theoretical arguments above it is worth re-examining this inclination.

The apparently painless shift to near full transparency with SETS while dealer trading remains the dominant form of trading offers some useful insights. It is possible that the nature of the market changed with the reduction in the danger of the exposure of dealers' positions caused either by the removal of the requirement to quote or by the lower chance of a trade requiring dealer capital.

The SEC (1994, p. VII-3) conclude that 'the evidence shows that transparency has improved the liquidity of the equity markets in the US, and that it has not led to an exodus of large traders to alternative market's. In the context of overseas equity trades, the SEC (1994, p. VII-2) take the view that 'regulatory reporting cannot substitute for transparency and its benefits of fair and accurate price discovery'.

In sections 8.2 and 8.3, we examined six arguments that are commonly expressed in favour of greater transparency and four against. As the discussion showed, there is some redundancy in these arguments – some are merely alternative or opposite formulations of others. In fact, the discussion seems to revolve around six key arguments which are summarised in Table 8.3. Summarising the five arguments about the favourable effect of transparency on markets we have: one true, three probably true and one possibly true with no contrary empirical evidence. This suggests that transparency seems, on the balance of probabilities, to be a good thing for markets and that regulators' traditional preference for transparent markets is well founded.

Table 8.3 Summary of the transparency arguments

	Key argument	Conclusion
1	Transparency leads to better price discovery	This is probably true but since it is impossible to measure the quality of price discovery (i.e. was a price the best estimate of value at the time) the conclusion is based on the proposition that if people know what is going on then they will act in a rational manner This argument requires only that 'enough' people know what is going on, not that every body knows
2	Transparency improves investor confidence and attracts new users	Probably true in theory, and discussions with practitioners over the years have confirmed that the most worrying thing for them is the fear that they will be disadvantaged through lack of information that is available to others. Avoidance of this lies behind the regulation of corporate disclosure and insider trading and market transparency seems like an extension of that
3	Limiting transparency improves liquidity by encouraging commit-ment of risk capital to facilitate customer orders	Possibly true, but only in the limited circumstances where risk capital is being committed frequently (i.e. dealer markets) and only then when dealers are required to make public quotes and there is little other (i.e. non-dealer positioned business) That is, in theory, dealers' willingness to commit capital may be adversely affected but only when there is: • a very high probability that any large trade has caused an inventory movement • when dealers are obliged to trade at published prices and so, to avoid further inventory movement, a quote change is required. In practice, however, there is no empirical evidence to support this Studies have shown that dealers' behaviour is not significantly changed when transparency is increased
4	Limiting transparency rewards one group of users at the expense of others	True, as the insider group is potentially able to exploit its advantage It may profit from its ability to arbitrage using superior information on true values, or by trading against other users or by offering its unique access to superior information to other users for a fee

Table 8.3 (Continued)

	Key argument	Conclusion
5	Limiting transparency may create barriers to entry for new entrants, alternative trading systems or damage related markets	Probably true, as limiting transparency advantages the insider group
		Typically these are the same people as the dominant players on the incumbent trading system
		They are not motivated to try alternatives and other users are cautious about trading directly with the insider group and therefore will be less likely to use competing systems
		However the empirical evidence for harm to related markets is inconclusive
6	Greater transparency may drive markets OTC or overseas	Possibly true other things being equal, but they rarely are and the advantages of staying on exchange or within a credible national regulatory regime are strong
		Few documented movements and none driven by transparency changes
		Many moves to greater transparency have not driven markets away.

8.9 Policy formulation

When regulating the degree of transparency in a market, regulators may wish to

- establish the current level of transparency,
- form a view on the appropriateness of this level of transparency, and then
- develop a transparency policy for that market.

Having decided to alter the level of transparency, the FSA is required by the FSMA (2000, section 2.3.c) to conduct a CBA before moving on to change the regulations.

8.9.1 Establishing the current level of transparency

There can be less than full transparency along the six dimensions detailed above. In an attempt to quantify the current level of transparency in a market, regulators can ask the questions such as:

1 *Pre-trade transparency*
  (a) What proportion of traders and potential traders could, if they wished, see in real time:
      (i) the best available prices (e.g. the touch, yellow strip, inside spread, top of the book)
      (ii) the identities of the traders offering the best prices
      (iii) the size up to which the prices are firm
      (iv) the quotes and limit orders away from the touch, and their size?
  (b) What is the charge for seeing the pre-trade data?
  (c) Are hidden orders permitted?
2 *Post-trade transparency*
  (a) What proportion of traders and potential traders could, if they wished, see in real time:
      (i) Individual trade prices
      (ii) volume of each trade
      (iii) the identities of the counterparties to each trade
      (iv) the type of counterparties involved in each trade
      (v) the trade type of each trade?
3 Possible measures of the extent of lack of transparency owing to delayed publication for each security include:
  (a) The proportion of total volume that is subject to delayed publication. This has a scale of 0 per cent–100 per cent, and is directly affected by the trade size and trade type required to qualify for delayed publication.
  (b) The volume-weighted average delay in publication. This can be measured in minutes, and has a scale from 0 to infinity. It is affected by the size, trade type, inventory position and time delay in the publication rules.
  These numbers can be compared across securities, e.g. different stocks traded on the same exchange.
4 Do traders have any choice in whether publication of their trade is delayed? If desired, the proportion of volume where there is choice can be computed.
5 What is the charge for seeing the post-trade data?

8.9.2 Judging the appropriateness of the current level of transparency

The simple answer is that, if there is less than full transparency, the burden of proof should be on justifying the opacity. Unfortunately, the burden lies with the FSA to justify a regulatory change. There are no easy answers to judging whether an opaque market is acceptable. What follows are some thoughts relevant to this debate.

1 *Related trading systems*

In some cases similar securities may be traded on several exchanges and trading systems. This situation provides three arguments for judging the level of transparency:

(a) While there are always microstructure differences between trading systems, if there is higher transparency on systems trading similar products, this strengthens the case for requiring the same level of transparency on the trading system under consideration because it shows that a higher transparency level is possible.[14]

(b) An opaque trading system may result in the problems created by the IDB systems for the UK equity market, so strengthening the case for removing any difference in transparency between trading systems in a fragmented market.

(c) If one trading system is transparent, then this could provide a lot of information about trading conditions for use by traders in the opaque trading system.

Thus, if there is a similar but more transparent trading system, this strengthens the case for increasing the transparency of the opaque trading system. However, the presence of related trading systems may increase or reduce the benefits from increased transparency. If there is no existing 'benchmark' trading system (e.g. an OTC market is moving onto an organised trading system), then this 'related trading system' argument cannot be used to establish a lower bound on the level of transparency for the new trading system.

2 *Transparency history*

The exchange may have previously altered their level of transparency. If they had a higher level of transparency than at present, this may provide evidence that an increase in transparency would not damage trading. For example, it was suggested in *Quality of Markets* (1990) that the immediate publication of large trades would make it 'virtually impossible' for equity market makers to take on large trades. However, between 27th October 1986 and 26th February 1989 (28 months) all trades in *alpha* shares on the London Stock Exchange were published within five minutes, providing evidence against this statement. If an exchange have previously increased their level of transparency without adverse effects, this may also evidence that increasing transparency is not harmful. There may be an upward time trend in transparency, possibly owing to market pressures and changes in the trading process. In which case, the trading system will easily accept a high level of transparency.

3 *Identity of end users*

What proportion of people at the end of the investment chain are institutional investors; market-makers; producers, wholesalers and processors of commodities; or retail investors?[15]

If almost all of the end users are not retail investors or non-financial businesses, this indicates that, at least at the moment, this is a professional market, and participants are able to look after themselves.[16] In a professional market traders are aware of most of the trading information because they are active participants in the market. In which case, the formal publication of this information does little to increase their knowledge, and the publication of trading information to increase transparency is seen as pointless as 'everybody knows'. If the end users are non-professionals, then there is a stronger case for a high level of transparency as they are not party to the same information as market participants.

However, using the proportion of non-professional participation in a market to judge transparency standards may run into a chicken and egg problem. Without transparency there will be no non-professional participation; and without non-professional participation, there will be no transparency. In consequence, transparency may get stuck at a low level. This suggests that basing a long-term transparency regime on the current proportion of non-professional business may be ill-advised, unless there is no prospect of retail or producer – consumer interest in the market. If non-professional users are taken to include businesses which need to manage their forex and interest rate risk, then it is hard to think of markets which do not have a nascent non-professional interest.

4 *Trading mechanism*

Does the trading system use a dealer or an auction trading mechanism? The choice of trading mechanism determines the minimum amount of pre-trade transparency. In a dealer system investors know at least some dealer quotes, while in an auction market investors know at least the best current limit orders. In a dealer market, the absence of transparency may not be as damaging to efficiency as in an auction market because the quotes are set by market-makers who have some access to the available quote and trade information. Therefore, the prices at which customers are invited to trade with the dealers reflect this private information.[17]

The choice of trading system also affects the alleged adverse effects of increased post-trade transparency. It is only in dealer markets that the inventories held by dealers must be unwound, and so in auction markets this argument for reduced transparency should not be used. Some trading systems use a hybrid dealer – auction system, e.g. the London Stock Exchange uses SETS in conjunction with a telephone dealer market, while many trading systems with an auction system, also have an 'upstairs' dealer system for large trades.

5 *Private information*

What is the information content of trade and quote information?

The level of private information available differs from market to market. In some markets (e.g. equities) there can be considerable information asymmetries, and so the quote and trade information is very informative. However, in other markets there is less private information (e.g. government bonds and forex) and the flow of orders and quotes is less informative. Transparency is more important in markets where there are considerable amounts of private information.

Although the importance of private information will probably be higher in manipulable markets, this does not imply that transparency should be increased only if the security, or underlying security, is easily manipulable. Even if there is little private information, a well-functioning market which meets the four statutory obligations of the FSA requires transparency to ensure confidence, best execution and non-manipulation (although manipulation is unlikely in the government bond and forex markets).

6 *Materiality*

If a trading system has an immaterial effect on the market, it may be argued that it need not be required to meet minimum transparency standards.[18] In the USA, trading systems with a market share below a specified percentage (5 per cent and 20 per cent) are exempt from various rules. However there are a number of reasons why market share may be an inappropriate materiality criterion:

- A particular trading system may have a disproportionate importance in the price formation process, e.g. it sets a reference price at which many other trades take place. In which case transparency for this trading system is important, even though it has a low volume.
- A particular trading system provides information to the participants which is not available elsewhere, e.g. the IDB systems, and transparency is again important.

- A crossing system has a substantial volume, but very little influence on the market, and so transparency is less important.

For these reasons, a simple market share criterion for materiality is rejected. Hasbrouck (1995) has implemented an empirical approach for measuring the contribution of a particular trading system to the price formation process, and this might provide a means for judging materiality (for trading systems for which a time series of trading data is available).[19]

Any materiality test should be applied separately to each security on a trading system. This is because a particular trading system may play an important role in price formation for one security, but be irrelevant for price discovery in another security.

7   *End user dissatisfaction*

Is there evidence that end users are dissatisfied with the current trading arrangements (e.g. companies and the foreign exchange market)? If so, it is possible that an increase in transparency will lead to customers being able to insist on a better deal from their brokers, or that the greater transparency will reduce the barriers to entry for a new exchange.

8   *Level playing field*

Does the trading system make available the same information to the market as a whole as it makes available to any one participant?

This question concerns whether information asymmetries are created by the transparency policies of the trading system, i.e. is the playing field level? If one market participant can see the entire order book, then so should everyone else. While desirable on the grounds of fairness, there may be some situations, e.g. shopping a block trade, or a market-maker negotiating over the phone with a potential counterparty, when some participants are given access to information not possessed by others.

9   *Voluntary disclosure*

While the voluntary adoption of disclosure rules by trading systems is to be welcomed, caution should be exercised concerning trading system rules which allow traders to choose whether or not their trades are disclosed. For example, London Stock Exchange market-makers involved in trades above $75 \times$ NMS can choose to have a delay in publication of five days, or until 90 per cent of the risk has been unwound (whichever is sooner).

Fishman and Hagerty (1993) constructed a theoretical model in which they compared the mandatory and voluntary disclosure of trades by insiders.[20] They argue that, if traders can choose whether or not their trade is published, this choice can be used to manipulate prices to their own advantage. Therefore there are risks in a post-trade transparency regime where traders can choose whether or not a particular trade is published.

10   *Block trades*

Most trading systems have special rules concerning block trades. It appears that large trades require a dealer system; and auction trading systems are usually supplemented with an upstairs market where dealers are able to 'shop the block'. The rules of dealer systems may also allow large trades to be treated in a special manner, e.g. Worked Principal Agreements on the London Stock Exchange. In view of this situation, it appears sensible to allow less stringent transparency requirements for block trades.

Special arrangements to facilitate block trades usually involve a reduction in pre-trade transparency. Block trading rules which permit other relaxations of the normal rules of the trading system are hard to justify, e.g. reduced post-trade transparency or permitting trades at prices that would be attractive to, but do not interact with, outstanding limit orders in the main market.

11   *Pre- versus post-trade transparency*

These dimensions of transparency are not independent because what a trader already knows affects the information content of an additional piece of information. For example, if quotes are published in real time, the information content of trade publication is reduced. This issue of the interaction between different sources of information has important implications for interpreting the results of empirical studies of transparency. A study of a switch to the publication of quotes (in a situation where trades are not published either before or after the change in pre-trade transparency) may find that it reduces the search costs of traders seeking the best price, and traders offer narrower spreads to get order flow. However, if trade prices were already published, the introduction of the publication of quotes may have much less effect on spreads as much of this information is already available to traders. Thus empirical studies of a change in transparency need to be interpreted in the light of the other information available to traders.

Mandating a high level of post-trade transparency is both desirable and straightforward, e.g. immediate publication of the trade size, price, time and security traded. Pre-trade transparency is different in two ways. First, both dealer and auction markets must reveal some pre-trade information if customers are to trade (e.g. the price and size at which they can trade), and so there is some minimal level of natural pre-trade transparency. Second, it is more complex to specify the pre-trade information to be published. The pre-trade information differs with the type of market, e.g. dealer quotes or limit orders. In addition, there are more choices for a pre-trade transparency regime, e.g. top of the book only, the best five orders on each side of the book, order size, special procedures for block trades, hidden orders, etc. While a high level of pre-trade transparency is desirable, regulators may need to be more flexible than on post-trade transparency.

8.9.3 Changing the level of transparency

If there is less than full transparency then, unless substantive arguments can be produced to justify this situation, the regulatory aim should be to eventually remove this opacity.

1 *Status quo*
   Regulators should not seek to impose a new set of transparency standards without regard for the existing transparency rules and trading habits in the market. Regulators should start from the existing position in each market and move gradually towards the goal. This implies the initial acceptance of differences in transparency rules between trading systems, even if logic might suggest they should have the same transparency.
2 *Scales not boxes*
   The regulatory aim should be to permit reduced transparency only along dimensions that can be gradually altered, e.g. the length of a publication delay or the size of trade. If a whole class of trading (e.g. OTC trades) or type of information (e.g. volume) is exempt from publication, it is harder to adjust some slider to gradually include these trades or information. For similar reasons, there is a danger that if markets are classified by the type of end user they will become 'stuck' with a particular user base, i.e. stay a professional market.
3 *Sliders*
   Regulators can gradually move the sliders in the direction of increased transparency for each market. This gives them the option to stop if there is clear evidence of demonstrable harm. The only concern about such a gradualist policy is that, if the markets expect that eventually that the slider will be moved from, say, a 60-minute delay before publication to immediate publication; there may be an apparently large response to the first small reduction (e.g. from

60-minute to 50-minute delay). However, this large reaction occurs because the first small reduction creates the expectation that the publication delay will ultimately be abolished, and the market reacts accordingly. A gradualist approach may also mean that a fresh consultation and CBA is required for each movement of the sliders, possibly leading to annual reviews of transparency.

Notes

1 Treasury (2000, section 4(2)c).
2 This is closely related to the question of 'natural' transparency which is discussed further below.
3 Increased transparency may tend to reduce the benefits of being an informed trader, so reducing the incentives for traders to acquire information. This would harm the price discovery of the market. However, even in a very transparent market, powerful incentives still remain to acquire fundamental information about the underlying asset.
4 However, with delayed publication large trades may take place inside the touch, so increasing temporary price volatility.
5 Easley and O'Hara (1987) have constructed a theoretical model in which large trades take place at less favourable prices than normal-sized trades because of the increased probability that the counterparty is better informed than the market-maker.
6 An exception are traders who provide market-making services in an auction market, e.g. locals.
7 This assumes that the higher risk borne by the equity market-maker when they accept a large inventory leads to wider spreads rather than a refusal by the equity market-maker to provide immediacy for large trades (i.e. it is assumed that there is no market failure).
8 Ball and Finn (1989) have questioned the view that a large trade will cause the bid – ask spread to widen for purely liquidity (or inventory or immediacy) reasons. Since the market-maker concerned receives all the benefits of ownership, an extra reward is unnecessary. Such an argument implies that a market-maker is ready and willing to immediately add a long or a short position of any feasible size to their portfolio at the current bid or ask price. However, such action may give market-makers a poorly diversified portfolio, and may exhaust their capital available for market-making. It is more plausible to expect that the price of liquidity rises with the demand. There are problems in empirically testing this matter because large trades may also involve information effects, which may cause the bid – ask spread to widen.
9 There are two reasons why a move to immediate publication might increase the amount of business conducted in other markets. First, some participants might prefer the current lack of transparency and would move to their home, or other, market if fuller transparency were to be implemented by the Stock Exchange. Second, if spreads widened in response to the change, traders may choose to trade in ways which avoid these higher costs, either by engaging in domestic off-exchange trading, or by using foreign exchanges which allow delayed publication of such trades.

10 Although it has been suggested that one reason why SEAQ International has attracted trading in foreign equities from their home exchanges because it has no publication requirements for individual trades (Röell, 1992). SEAQ-I also offered a degree of liquidity not generally available on the home markets of the stocks concerned. It is noticeable that the volume of trade on SEAQ-I has diminished sharply following the increased liquidity of the home markets – even though SEAQ-I is now relatively opaque relative to the home markets.

11 Some of the experimental evidence considered in in Chapter 7 report laboratory situations designed to test for the existence of such tendencies.

12 So far as UK customers wishing to trade the security are concerned, whether the trade occurs in the UK or overseas is of secondary importance. If they are concerned about the legal jurisdiction under which the trade occurs, they can continue to trade in the UK and effectively stop the move offshore. If trading does move overseas, the UK economy may lose the economic benefits of hosting the exchange, but this is a separate issue from that of creating an attractive exchange on which UK customers can trade.

13 For example, how can the increased risk of illiquidity arising during periods of market turbulence, caused by an increase in transparency be measured and valued?

14 The 'bench marking' should be based on the level of transparency of the trading system, rather than the quality of the market, e.g. spreads.

15 Note that this is not considering the parties to each trade, but rather it is looking at investment chains where dealers and brokers are not end users and so do not count.

16 In the case of commodities, some producers, middlemen and consumers may also be non-expert traders.

17 Of course, the strength of this argument, traditionally advanced to support reduced transparency in dealer markets, depends on the informativeness of dealers' quotes. In particular, if dealers quote wide spreads (but are prepared to trade inside them) and do not revise them frequently, the usefulness of current quotes will be sharply reduced.

18 Existing trading systems might be unhappy about offering low transparency standards to new (and small) entrants into the market. It is possible that some entrants may wish to run an opaque trading system, so damaging the price formation process. Transparency is an important aspect of market quality, and should not be compromised to allow entrants to run opaque trading systems.

19 Hasbrouck (1995) investigated price discovery in the 30 shares in the Dow Jones Industrial Average for the 3 months in 1993 using quote data time stamped to the nearest second. Using a cointegration approach, he found that, across his 30 stocks, 91 per cent of the price discovery took place on the NYSE, and 9 per cent took place on the six regional exchanges combined. For AT&T, the NYSE accounted for 98.9 per cent of price discovery, while for another company this figure was only 76.1 per cent.

20 Insiders are traders who are thought by the market to be trading on the basis of private information.

9
Over the Counter (OTC) Markets

OTC markets are part of the total market for a security, and so have been considered in the Chapters dealing with transparency and fragmentation. OTC trading tends to be a hidden aspect of financial markets whose importance is large and growing, but where regulation and disclosure are small. For these reasons, this chapter brings together the material on OTC markets from elsewhere in this book to highlight the importance of these markets to regulators.

It will be argued in this chapter that OTC trading is as much a part of the market in a financial security as is trading on an exchange,[1] and so should be included within the ambit of 'orderly markets'. Second, the consequences of OTC trading for exchanges will be examined. Third, the case for trade reporting and pre- and post-trade transparency in OTC markets will be considered. Finally, some possible policies for increased trade reporting and transparency in OTC markets are presented.

9.1 Background on OTC markets[2]

OTC markets grew up to meet some specialised needs that exchanges could not meet, or where the circumstances of the market (e.g. type of user) was such as to render an exchange unnecessary. The following factors have encouraged their growth:

- The transaction is in a customised contract – e.g. for a different duration to the standard exchange contract
- There is no organised exchange for the asset – e.g. swaps or forex
- OTC trading is cheaper than exchange trading because there are no exchange fees, though these are small, larger savings are made from the avoidance of brokerage fees

- The trade is too large for the exchange. In some markets these large trades are brought on-exchange through block trade facilities
- OTC trades avoid the transparency or other regulations applying to exchange-traded products.

The existence of OTC trading has a number of advantages for the functioning of a market:

- Provides more capacity to handle trading during periods of peak order flow, or when the exchange is unable to trade – e.g. owing to a system failure
- Provides a choice of trading venue and contract design for traders
- Provides a source of competition and innovation for the exchange.

OTC markets have traditionally been distinguishable from exchange markets on a number of features:

- OTC markets are multiple dealer markets, while exchanges can be auction markets or use just a single specialist
- Regulation and surveillance is much lighter in OTC markets
- OTC markets offer products that can be tailored to user specifications
- OTC market-makers usually have direct contact with their customers without the intervention of brokers
- OTC market-makers deal in both primary and secondary issues
- OTC markets are generally much less transparent than exchanges
- OTC markets are professional markets, while exchanges mainly cater to both professional and retail users
- Most OTC markets do not have a clearing house operation, while every exchange has an associated clearing house.

OTC markets often involve a fairly small number of participants. Moessner (2001) reports that in April 1998 the largest 10 banks accounted for 71 per cent of trading in interest rate options in the UK. Just as exchange trading is moving onto screens, a similar process is underway in OTC markets (Committee on the Global Financial System, 2001). OTC markets are moving from bilateral telephone trading to multilateral screen trading, with an increased use of clearing services (FSA, 2001b). For example, in the foreign exchange market there are Reuters' Dealing 2000–2 and Electronic Broking Services (EBS) for inter-dealer trading; while portals such as Atriax and FxAll offer customers the ability to trade with many rival dealers. In government bonds, there are inter-dealer systems (BrokerTec, eSpeed and MTS) and multi-dealer sites for customers (BondClick and TradeWeb). It is likely that these OTC electronic systems will develop to look more and more like electronic exchanges.

9.2   The size of OTC markets

The level of transparency of OTC markets is generally very low, and there is little hard published information on their size. Table 9.1 presents the nominal value of OTC and exchange trading in derivatives in the G10 countries for the year ended June 2000, as estimated by the Bank for International Settlements (BIS). This shows that for every £1 traded on a derivatives exchange in 2000, £6.76 was traded in an OTC derivatives market. Thus, 87 per cent of total volume in these derivatives is in OTC markets. In addition to derivatives, there are also large OTC spot markets, and so total OTC trading in financial products is well over $94 trillion per year.[3]

These numbers suggest that in London the financial OTC markets are probably many times larger than the corresponding exchange markets.[4] While no authoritative data is published on OTC volumes, in recent years the size of OTC markets has increased very considerably in absolute terms, and it is probable that the importance of OTC trading has also increased, relative to the corresponding exchanges.

9.3   The interaction between exchanges and OTC markets

If the exchange and OTC markets were distinct, each type of market could be analysed and regulated separately. In some cases, trading in

Table 9.1   Nominal value of OTC and exchange trading in derivatives in the G10 countries, year ended June 2000

	$US billion	
	OTC	Exchange
Foreign exchange	15,494	51
Interest rates	64,125	12,313
Equities	1,671	
Commodities	584	1,540
Others	12,163	
Total	94,037	13,904

Source: BIS, 2000.

a new security may arise in the setting of an OTC market, with no trading in a closely related exchange-traded security. In this case, the OTC trading has no negative effects on exchange trading (other than possibly discouraging retail involvement and preventing the transfer of trading to an exchange). In this situation (analogous to an infant industry) the embryonic OTC market can be lightly regulated. The FSA could develop criteria for determining which OTC markets merit a light touch in terms of transparency and access (e.g. a lack of close substitutes that are exchange-traded, no evidence that the OTC market is stopping the creation of exchange trading in the security[5]). Even if an OTC market receives a light touch in terms of transparency and access, the regulators may still be interested in other aspects of such markets, e.g. manipulation and barriers to entry; particularly where an OTC market generates substantial risks to the FSA's statutory objectives. The FSA's view is that 'there is likely to be little case for regulatory intervention in OTC markets that are predominantly inter-professional. Regulatory intervention will only be contemplated where material risks are identified that the FSA does not believe can be adequately addressed through the operation of market forces. However, the FSA would be concerned if inter-professional OTC market infrastructure providers (MIPs) erode existing transparency standards or have a negative impact on the price formation process of retail markets' (FSA, 2001b).

However, for most securities trading on exchanges and OTC markets is very strongly connected, to the extent that they are really different aspects of the same market: in which case the analysis and regulation has to be of the entire market, not just the exchange-traded portion, if orderly markets are to be maintained. In some cases an OTC market trades a product that is almost identical to an exchange-traded product, e.g. forex forward contracts or interest rate swaps. In these cases the degree of substitution between the OTC and exchange products is extremely high and they are effectively one market. In other cases, there are differences between the two markets, but the OTC traders use the related exchange to hedge their risks, and probably price their OTC contracts off the exchange prices. In such cases, strong links between the exchange and OTC market exist.

9.4 Consequences of OTC markets and exchanges forming a single market

There are a number of markets where there is both exchange and OTC trading. Given that exchanges are more transparent than OTC markets, there are a number of ways in which the presence OTC markets affects the related exchange:

1 The possibility of arbitrage means that there will generally be a very close relationship between the prices in the OTC market and the exchange.
2 Participants in the OTC market can price their trades using the published exchange quotes and trades. Therefore, much price discovery is performed by the exchange, and any information content in the OTC order flow is not made public.
3 The OTC market may well attract an order flow with a high information content, e.g. large trades, and trades based on information (as opposed to liquidity trades). This is because informed traders use the OTC market to exploit their information without revealing they are informed, and market-makers on the exchange may seek to unwind large trades via the OTC market. In this case some market-makers and traders in the OTC market acquire private information from seeing part of the order flow to the OTC market. They are then free to exploit this information by trading on either the exchange or the OTC market. In consequence, traders on either the exchange of the OTC market risk trading with a better informed counterparty.
4 The exchange receives an atypical slice of the order flow, with a higher proportion of its order flow from uninformed traders. Hence, its published prices may, on occasion, not reflect private information that has been revealed to some traders in the OTC market. Therefore, the OTC market plays an important, although hidden, role in the price discovery process; and prices on the exchange sometimes lag behind those on the OTC market.
5 Traders with access to the OTC market will compare the public quotes on the exchange with the private quotes they receive in the OTC market. This suggests that quotes in the OTC market cannot be worse than the public quotes on the exchange, and that quoted spreads may generally be smaller in the OTC market, despite the greater risks of information asymmetries between customers and OTC market-makers. OTC market-makers are willing to accept smaller spreads to acquire the private information contained in this order flow, which they can then exploit in both the exchange and OTC market.
6 Price fragmentation may occur as between the exchange and the OTC market. However, arbitrage will prevent wide price disparities, provided potential arbitrageurs can discover the current prices in the OTC market. This need for information on prices in the OTC market

may restrict arbitrage to institutional traders and market-makers. These traders make arbitrage profits, while other market participants trade with them at inferior prices. In consequence, those with access to the OTC market make continuous arbitrage profits at the expense of the uninformed traders on the exchange. Those who have access to the OTC market are very happy with this situation.

7 The continued maintenance of substantially different regulations for these two types of trading (exchange and OTC) of essentially the same security invites regulatory arbitrage.

8 OTC markets may provide a way in which insider traders and market manipulators can operate without the regulatory restrictions that apply to exchanges.

9 The requirement for a broker to obtain best execution for a client needs to incorporate the possibility of trading in the OTC market. Therefore, if best execution is to obtained, brokers need access to the OTC market, while if best execution is to be monitored, customers (and the FSA) need to know what prices are available in the OTC market.

10 A trader may default on delivering the underlying security in an OTC deal when their counterparty had been relying on receipt of the underlying security to fulfil their delivery obligations under an exchange-traded derivative contract on the same asset. In this case the OTC market can have an adverse effect on the corresponding derivatives exchange.

9.5 OTC markets and trade reporting

It has been argued that many OTC markets are very big (and growing), effectively in the same market as the corresponding exchange, and are lightly regulated (relative to exchange trading), with very low levels of transparency. This situation has a number of negative consequences, which have been mentioned above – e.g. information asymmetries between traders, delayed price discovery in the exchange, inferior prices on the exchange, arbitrage profits for some OTC traders, regulatory arbitrage, problems in ensuring best execution and the possibility of manipulation and market abuse, etc. Therefore, OTC trading (as currently regulated) creates a considerable risk that the four statutory objectives of the FSA will not be met.

While no information on OTC trading is published, trade reporting to the FSA does take place for some categories of OTC trading by SFA Authorised Firms (AFs):

- *Equities and debt.* The SFA rules require that all trades by UK AFs in the gilt, fixed interest and equity markets, whether in exchange-traded or OTC markets, be reported. The FSA receives reports of OTC trades in spread betting and contracts for difference trades in equities, equity swaps, equity and bond options and credit derivatives (which are based on the price of a reportable instrument). However, repo and reverse repo trades are currently not reported, and are specifically exempted in 17.4.1 (1) of the draft *FSA Supervision Manual* (FSA, 2000b).
- *Interest rates.* OTC interest rate trades are not reportable. Thus interest rate swaps, forward rate agreements are excluded from the reporting requirements, although the FSA does receive reports of some of these OTC trades because they are mixed up with other reportable trades.
- *Currency and commodities.* Neither on-exchange trades, nor OTC trades in currencies and commodities (softs on LCE, oil and gas on IPE, and metals) are reportable to the FSA, although they may be reportable to the exchange concerned.
- *Primary transactions.* In addition, there is no reporting of primary market trades, i.e. the initial transfer from the issuer to the first taker as principal. However, this exemption does not apply to derivative trades. Thus, initial public offerings of shares or bonds are not reported to the FSA, unless the instrument ranks equally with an existing issue. While reporting of primary market transactions is not required, some are reported voluntarily because they are mixed up with reportable trades.

In addition to the above exclusions from the trade reporting regime, the passported activities of all incoming European Economic Area (EEA) firms are exempt.

The reporting rules for OTC trades aim to ensure that where there is a reportable exchange-traded product, the OTC trades in this product or its derivatives are reported. However, Table 9.2 shows that there are gaps in this policy. First, there is the exemption for repo and reverse repo trading. Second, there is the omission of all trading in softs, metals and oil and gas from the FSA trade reporting regime. The omission of softs and oil and gas may be because these products do not fall within the scope of financial securities, as defined by FSMA (2000). However, FSMA (2000) does specifically cover palladium, platinum, gold and silver; and the London Metal Exchange (LME) currently trades silver futures and options. Currencies are also specifically mentioned by FSMA (2000), but OTC trades in currencies and currency derivatives are not reported to the FSA.

Table 9.2 OTC reporting to the FSA

Product	Is there exchange trading?	Is OTC trading reported to the FSA?
Equities	✓	✓
Debt	✓	✓except repo and reverse repo
Interest rates		
• Traded on LIFFE	✓	✓[1]
• Others	✗	✗
Credit derivatives	✗	✓
Currencies	✗	✗
Softs	✓	✗
Metals	✓	✗
Oil and gas	✓	✗

Note:
[1] This refers to the OTC trading of products referenced to LIFFE instruments, and is minimal.

The FSA receives about 800,000–1,000,000 trade reports per day; of which around 350,000 are OTC transactions. If an AF participates in a reportable OTC trade as buyer or seller, it must report it to the FSA. Therefore, trades are reported by both parties, unless one of the parties is not an AF (e.g. they are a company, an individual, an overseas fund, an investment manager or a personal investment firm). In consequence, there are more than 175,000 OTC trades reported per day. After FSMA came into force (i.e. post-N2 on 30th November 2001), only SFA firms have to report their OTC trades, with investment managers and personal investment firms being exempt. However, OTC trades between two such firms are relatively rare.

9.6 OTC markets and regulation

There are two strongly related areas where increased regulatory intervention in OTC markets may be appropriate – trade reporting and transparency. In the UK the boundaries for trade reporting and publication are somewhat inconsistent between the UK RIEs. Trades that would be transacted on-exchange at LIFFE would be transacted on a telephone market on the London Stock Exchange. The London Stock Exchange trades would, however, be reported and published; however, essentially identical trades on the LME would not be published.

The benefits of bringing OTC markets into the transparency and trade reporting regime include:

- Preventing regulatory arbitrage between OTC markets and exchanges
- Eliminating possible ambiguity of regulation between similar products
- Improving transparency and so enhancing the quality of price formation and market confidence
- Removing a possible source of information asymmetry
- Limiting the scope for future investor scandals
- Facilitating the monitoring of market quality
- Improving the monitoring of best execution and market manipulation
- Reducing the scope for arbitrage profits being made by those able to trade in the OTC markets, at the expense of those only able to trade on the exchange.

A *Trade reporting*. Reports of individual trades provide regulators with information with which to detect and investigate various aspects of market abuse. They can also be used to monitor market quality and best execution. All trades conducted on-exchange must be reported. At present some 15–20 per cent of the trades currently reported to the FSA each day relate to OTC activity. However, despite the fact that many OTC trades are a very close substitute for on-exchange trades, there is no general requirement that OTC trades be reported. In the absence of trade reporting, regulators have very little information on what is happening in the relevant OTC markets.

A number of arguments against increased trade reporting for OTC markets have been made:

1 *It would be costly*. Reporting involves the one-off cost to firms of altering their in-house systems to generate the required reports, and the continuing cost of a reporting charge for each trade – the FSA currently charges 2p per trade for direct reporting. However, these costs do not appear onerous; some OTC markets are already required to report their trades (equity and debt), some OTC traders currently choose to voluntarily report trades, and all trades on an exchange must already bear the costs of being reported (and published).

2 *If OTC markets were required to report their trades*, they would object to RIEs being the reporting agents. However, there are precedents for

this, e.g. the London Stock Exchange used to act as a reporting agent for some Eurobond reports to the SFA through its SEQUAL system. Alternatively, an OTC market can choose to report their trades direct to the FSA.

3 *The OTC markets may move offshore* if they are subject to greater trade reporting. Regulation Q and the setting up of OM London show that regulation can lead to a move offshore, though the examples are often from the distant past, and do not concern to trade reporting. However, moving offshore is rarely as simple as it sounds, and clients are suspicious of offshore entities. It has been threatened at every regulatory change, and has yet to happen in response to UK regulatory changes. The UK OTC equity and debt markets have not moved offshore because they are required to report trades.

4 The reporting of trades to the FSA (or an RIE) is useful only if the FSA is able to adequately monitor these reports. If this is not the case, reporting may create a false impression of security from market abuse. While there may be some initial resource problems for the FSA in processing the additional trade reports, if trade reporting is an effective measure for on-exchange trades (and equity and debt OTC trades), then it could also be made effective for the remaining OTC trades. This step would also permit the FSA to see the overall picture by scrutinising the relationships between exchange and OTC trades, and provide the FSA with OTC trading data that could trigger an investigation and measure market quality.

B Transparency. There are two different reasons for wanting a high level of transparency in OTC markets:

• First, as argued elsewhere in this book, there is a strong case for financial markets being highly transparent.
• Second, if the exchange has a high level of transparency, having a lower level of transparency in the corresponding OTC market will have damaging effects on the market as a whole (as described above). Indeed, it is possible that an increase in the transparency of the exchange, without a concomitant increase in the transparency of the corresponding OTC market, will increase the negative effects of this differential transparency.

There is an additional argument (in addition to those listed for trade reporting) against increasing transparency for OTC markets. OTC contracts are customised and therefore there is little point in increasing transparency from trade publication since the information gain would be slight.[6] However there is a trend towards increased standardisation within the OTC markets and there seems little justification for treating OTC replicas of exchange contracts and the exchange contracts differently. Conceivably increased transparency might only be applied to OTC replicas, but if only OTC contracts that replicate exchange-traded products are regulated, close look-alikes (e.g. the FTSE 99) also may have an effect on the market, even if they are not exactly the same as the exchange-traded product. As a practical matter therefore, all products traded on an OTC market that are close substitutes for an exchange-traded security should be included in the regulatory regime.

9.7   Policies on trade reporting and transparency

There are moves in other countries towards increasing the trade reporting and transparency of OTC markets. The SEC has recently required market centres to produce monthly reports (see Chapter 6). In this context, market centres include specialists and market-makers on recognised exchanges, ATSs, exchanges and market makers in OTC markets that trade NMS securities. The FIBV is in discussion with the Basle Committee on Banking Supervision on the acceptability of reporting and publishing OTC trades in instruments traded on their members' exchanges. The European Commission (2001) has proposed that investment firms which execute off-exchange transactions in instruments traded on a regulated market must report those trades to a regulated market immediately after completion. These trades will then be published by the regulated market.

In the USA, Freddie Mac requires the group of banks who act as dealers in its bonds to produce weekly reports about trading volumes and prices. The incentive for the banks to do this is that they want to be appointed as underwriters for future bond issues by Freddie Mac. Bond trading systems such as EuroMTS have compulsory reporting requirements, and this information is available to bond issuers listed on the system:

A *Trade reporting*. The final objective could be for all OTC markets to report their trades. There are a variety of ways of moving towards this desired final position on trade reporting. Here is one possibility.

The difficulty of defining an exchange for regulatory purposes suggests that responsibility for trade reporting should lie with the AFs themselves, although if their trade is on an exchange, they may choose to delegate this responsibility to an RIE. In OTC markets the responsibility for trade reporting, where trade reporting is required, already lies with the AFs. The FSA could require that all trades involving an AF be reported, but the FSA may initially choose to exempt OTC trading in some products. Over time the requirement for trade reporting by OTC markets could be extended beyond the equity and debt markets to cover all OTC markets. Because most of their trading is currently on appropriate exchanges, and OTC trading in equity and debt instruments must already be reported, the change in focus from RIEs to AFs need have no immediate impact on AFs.

B *Transparency.* The current levels of transparency in the OTC markets are very low. For example, for non-participants there is no pre-trade transparency, no post-trade transparency, and almost no public information on the general nature of these markets, e.g. volume, products traded, etc.[7] Therefore, there are many different dimensions along which the transparency of OTC markets can be increased. The final objective could be for comparable transparency standards for both exchanges and OTC markets.[8] However, it is unrealistic to expect OTC markets which trade securities that are a close substitute for an exchange-traded product to move immediately to the same level of transparency as prevails in on-exchange trading.

Some possible ways forward include the following:

1 Rather than publish individual trades, *aggregate data for OTC markets* could be published. Where trade reporting to the FSA is already mandatory (equities and debt), this could be undertaken by the FSA using the existing data sources.[9] For those markets where trade reporting is not required, market-makers could be asked to supply aggregate data per time period to the FSA for publication. The SEC have recently introduced rules under which each market centre must publish monthly aggregate information on their trading activity, and these rules could be used as a source of ideas in specifying the definitions used in collecting this aggregate data. It is suggested that OTC markets be required to publish much less information than required by the SEC, but much more frequently, e.g. daily. This would start to open up the opacity which surrounds OTC markets.

2 *Pre-trade transparency in OTC markets* might be increased by publishing some information on quotes, possibly anonymously, but preferably in real time. A start could be to copy the procedures in the Indian inter-bank deposit market, where such an increase in pre-trade transparency has been beneficial. The Indian inter-bank deposit market operates as an OTC telephone market with indicative quotes on

Reuters screens, but with no trade publication, (Shah, 2000). In 1998 the level of transparency of this market increased when the National Stock Exchange started collecting prices from dealers and publishing the average. Publication of the average rate led to a clear reduction in the bid–ask spreads.

3 *Post-trade transparency in OTC markets* revolves around the anonymous publication of trade prices, sizes and trade times. There are a number of different ways in which these requirements could be phased in, e.g. delayed publication of prices, publication of trade prices but not volumes, etc.

Notes

1 Because of the creation of ATS, there is not a simple dichotomy between exchanges and OTC markets. For simplicity, throughout this chapter OTC markets are compared with RIEs. However, many of the same points could be made when comparing OTC markets with ATSs.

2 For background material on OTC interest rate options see Moessner (2001).

3 The dominance of OTC trading in derivative markets also has importance for spot markets, since it is generally accepted that spot, futures and options markets in the same underlying asset are effectively one market.

4 There appears to be no published hard data on the size of OTC trading in London.

5 Often there is a natural move for securities from being initially traded on an OTC market to being traded on an exchange.

6 To the extent that OTC markets do not trade standardised products, information on OTC trading becomes difficult to aggregate and compare because these trades may be non-commensurable (Rappell, 1998). In order to permit the interpretation of OTC data these markets might be asked to publish, not only price and quantity information, but also details of the conditions and terms of the different contracts. However, this may breach the confidentiality of the agreements negotiated between the counterparties, and would also make disclosure very lengthy as the contract terms would need to be specified. In some cases, OTC markets have moved towards a high degree of standardisation of the products traded, and here transparency would be much easier to implement.

7 In order to function, markets need some minimal level of transparency, e.g. natural transparency. Thus, in a dealer market customers need to be able to see the quotes offered by rival market-makers. In some OTC markets (e.g. where an OTC market has moved onto a computer screen) participants are able to see the quotes posted by other participants, and also the price and size of trades. In such a situation it is not possible to argue that allowing non-participants to see this information will damage the competitive position of OTC traders by revealing their quotes and trades to other market participants. However, revealing the prices available on this market to non-participants, who are indirect participants in this market via their trades with market participants, may harm the position of market participants. With increased

transparency, customers can now see the prices available to market insiders, and they may insist on receiving better prices. In this situation, increased transparency results in a wealth transfer from OTC traders to their customers, and so is strongly resisted by OTC market participants

8   Where there is no exchange-traded product (or close substitute) the transparency standards could be less demanding.

9   Such data would permit an investigation of claims that various rule changes at the London Stock Exchange led to the switch of trading to the OTC market.

10

A New Regulatory Framework

In this chapter we put forward a regulatory structure that we believe may be more suited to the environment as it is likely to develop.

10.1 Investor protection

It will become increasingly difficult to define an exchange for regulatory purposes, and attempting to monitor trading activity by focussing on only one or two of many competing trading venues is increasingly unlikely to be effective. However since investor protection is concerned with ensuring that those acting for investors fulfil their fiduciary obligations, the correct focus of regulation is the Authorised Firm (AF). In fact, a focus on AFs has long been the thrust of UK regulation.

While the responsibility for best execution regulation is clear, the current regulations are not well suited to the new environment. In a sense they fall between being too prescriptive, as in the equity market, and too vague. The best execution rule in the equity market probably has the effect of disadvantaging new entrants, particularly for retail business, and not providing an incentive for innovation or improvement. Elsewhere it is unclear whether the rules have much effect as they do not seem to be well monitored or robustly enforced. As best execution becomes more complex, with alternative trading venues and a wider range of trading strategies, prescriptive rules will work less and less well. Hence the shift must be towards more general obligations, but with stronger monitoring and enforcement. We note that the FSA has initiated a debate into this question.

In this context, the rules recently introduced by the SEC to assist market users in monitoring execution quality are helpful. The first requires the regular publication by market centres[1] of summaries of execution quality using algorithms defined by the SEC, and the second requires the regular summary disclosure by brokers of which market centres they use (with potential for disclosure of the routeing of individual orders). The basic idea is that, armed with this information, market users can judge which market centre best suits their orders and whether their broker routed them accordingly.

We are attracted to some elements of these SEC rules, in particular:

- The emphasis on market centres rather than exchanges is consistent with a fragmented market
- The design of the summaries attempts to capture the complexity of order execution and the differing requirements of different order sizes
- The extension beyond single-order execution to consideration of orders over a period, which does not focus on those orders which, with hindsight, have been wrongly routed
- The continued refusal to define exactly what is best execution.

The cost to market centres and brokers of providing the information required by the SEC will be modest, given the IT resources at their disposal. However, the SEC rules generate a very large amount of information, and a likely future development will be the entry of commercial providers to analyse and customise this information for users.

10.2   Barriers to entry

In other industries, regulators have actively sought to force the incumbents to open the market. The view has been that, although new entrants might be free to enter, they would be unlikely to succeed without some form of positive discrimination. In financial markets the cost of transferring business is relatively low (though inertia is high) and users and intermediaries are very aware of the alternatives on offer. The stickiness comes from the fact that the most valuable asset of a trading system is liquidity. Unless those who trade on new trading venues have low cost and unfettered access to trading and information on the incumbent trading system, there is little chance that users will risk incurring a massive illiquidity premium, or the possibility of mispricing by trading away from the main trading system.

A common user base and transparency should ensure that prices are aligned across market venues (although there will be a loss to those on the wrong side of the arbitrage). Thus, new entrants are unlikely to succeed unless those who trade on these venues have good access to the current state of play on the main trading system. This argument applies equally to markets that are currently OTC, where alternative trading systems (ATSs), perhaps available to a wider range of users, are trying to set up. This suggests that policies encouraging transparency, reasonable cost access to current information and non-discriminatory access to infrastructure, such as settlement, are necessary if effective competitors are to emerge.

We recognise that information on trading activity represents one of a trading system's principal assets (and is often a major source of revenue). This suggests that trading systems will generally be prepared to make this information available, albeit at a price, and that price and trade information will, therefore, be widely available. We believe that competition between the information vendors and the trading systems is likely to keep the costs of this information at reasonable levels. This means that the only likely regulatory involvement is to specify the minimum level of information which is to be disclosed and to monitor the cost at which this information is made available to ensure that it is not excessive. We envisage few situations in which direct intervention to enforce the required disclosure, or to reduce its cost, would be necessary.

10.3   Implementing transparency

Whatever the evidence, there are strongly entrenched views about transparency. While our predisposition is towards higher rather than lower transparency, we accept that it is not realistic to suddenly impose transparency on exchanges or OTC markets that have long been opaque. We propose an approach based on three steps:

- establish the current level of transparency,
- form a view on the appropriateness of this level of transparency, and then
- develop a transparency policy for that market.

The first step suggests metrics to calibrate transparency levels so that a base level can be established for future comparison. The view on appropriate levels will be assessed largely qualitatively but with regard to:

- *Transparency of related trading systems.* If there is a similar but more transparent trading system, this strengthens the case for increasing the transparency of the opaque trading system.

- *Transparency history.* If the trading venue previously had a higher level of transparency than at present, this may provide evidence that an increase in transparency would not damage trading.
- *Identity of end users* – intermediaries versus others. If the end users are non-professionals, then there is a stronger case for a high level of transparency as they are not party to the same information as market participants.
- *End user dissatisfaction* – including likely potential users and other participants in the trading chain who may not currently be direct users.
- *Trading mechanism.* The choice of trading mechanism determines the minimum amount of pre-trade transparency. In a dealer system investors know at least some dealer quotes, while in an auction system investors know at least the best current limit orders. The choice of trading mechanism also affects the alleged adverse effects of increased post-trade transparency. It is only in dealer systems that the inventories held by dealers must be unwound, and so in auction systems this argument for reduced transparency should not be used.
- *Extent of likely private information.* What is the information content of trade and quote information? Transparency is more important in markets where there are considerable amounts of private information.
- *Level playing field between traders.* Does the trading system make available the same information to the market as a whole as it makes available to any one participant?
- The possibility that *selective or voluntary disclosure* could be used manipulatively.
- *Block trading.* Most trading systems have special rules concerning block trades.
- *Materiality.* If a trading system has an immaterial effect on the market, it may be argued that it need not be required to meet minimum transparency standards.[2]

We do not believe that the current level of retail participation or possibility of manipulation should be determinants of transparency policy. Retail participation is only likely in transparent markets, so to an extent the level of retail involvement is a consequence of transparency rather than a determinant of it. This does not mean that regulators should ignore the degree of retail involvement, rather that they should not be persuaded that the absence of current retail involvement is a sufficient reason to limit transparency.

If there is less than full transparency then, unless substantive arguments can be produced to justify this situation, the regulatory aim should be to eventually remove this opacity. Regulators should have a predis-position towards increasing transparency as conditions allow. We suggest a gradual process allowing small increases in transparency along specified dimensions, such as the length of any publication delay. This would have the advantage of not frightening any market users, and of giving the regulators the opportunity to make reasoned judgments based on incremental changes.

There are two ways of ensuring a gradual movement by trading systems towards increased transparency – a sequence of regular reviews, or an ad hoc approach based on representations from competitors and users, together with the FSA's own market quality monitoring.

10.4   Regulation of OTC trading

The thrust of this book is that regulators do not need to, and should not try to, mandate the functioning of trading systems, but should focus on over-arching principles to be applied to all trading. Therefore, for OTC markets, the appropriate regulations concern the publication of trades to inform the market, unless participants are able to show demonstrable harm to the market; and reporting of trades and positions to monitor possible manipulation.

This proposal is controversial for OTC markets and, while it is an important component of the most consistent solution to the challenges raised by recent developments in financial markets, we recognise that increases in transparency must be made with care. The process we have suggested above should therefore be applied to OTC markets – but with sensitivity.

The FSA already receives trade reports from various OTC equity and debt markets and these procedures could be extended to a wider range of OTC trading. However, the reporting of trades to the FSA is useful only if the FSA is able to adequately monitor these reports. If this is not the case, reporting may create a false impression of security from market abuse. While there may be some initial resource problems for the FSA in processing these additional trade reports, if trade reporting is an effective measure for on-exchange trades, it could also be made effective for off-exchange trades. This step would also permit the FSA to see the broader picture by scrutinising the relationships between on- and off-exchange trades, and provide the FSA with OTC trading data that could trigger an investigation.

Since OTC and exchange markets are converging, the recommendation is that the principles of market transparency should be deemed applicable to OTC markets, just as they are for exchanges. The discussion of transparency above sets out a framework for making decisions about increasing (or reducing transparency) and our conclusion is that these should apply to all trading, whether on-exchange (which will become increasingly hard to define) or OTC.[3] However this should be done with great sensitivity and seen as a long-term goal as the OTC market situation evolves ever closer to that of exchange markets, rather than as an immediate objective.

10.5 Summary of the regime

We have identified three main risks to meeting the FSA's statutory objectives:

- the segmented trading of the same security in a number of venues, leading to low liquidity, price fragmentation, poor price discovery, difficulty defining an exchange, and the like
- best execution becoming hard to achieve and harder to monitor and enforce
- an increasing risk of systemic risk and market abuse, as no single entity has an overall picture of trading activity.

Our proposals form a package in which lightening regulation in some areas (the RIE/AF distinction, the detailed rules adopted by trading systems, market fragmentation, and the distinction between asset classes and types of trader) is contingent on regulation being strengthened in others (competition, transparency and best execution). Overall, the proposed regime of a single set of rules is simpler, clearer and probably cheaper than the existing rules.

The main thrust of the proposals is to move regulation from a concern with how particular trading systems operate to regulating how the market place as a whole functions. In this new situation, the regulatory emphasis shifts from a concern about the minutiae of how existing trading systems function to one of creating the environment for competition in the supply of trading services, which puts the emphasis on competition, transparency (or information) and best execution.

We believe that in a future regulatory regime:

1 The focus of *trade regulation and monitoring* should switch from *RIEs*, which are no longer the sole marketplace for trading to AFs which participate in most trading, whatever the venue. (Of course, AFs may

delegate this responsibility to an RIE or another reporting agent.) This will potentially cover a much greater proportion of trading than at present and will allow more detailed monitoring and investigation of trading behaviour and positions, particularly in markets which are susceptible to manipulation. This does not necessarily mean that the current regulatory distinction between RIEs and AFs need be abandoned. Trading systems will make the choice based on a range of factors, but as the regulatory focus shifts away from RIEs the regulatory relevance of the distinction will diminish.

2 Recognition that one focus of regulation should be to maintain a *competitive system of trading systems*, rather than detailed supervision of a monopoly exchange, with the consequent requirement for rules promoting entry to the market and preventing restrictive practices. This reliance on competition is in line with FSMA (2000, section 2) which requires that regulation should facilitate innovation, maintain the competitive position of the UK, minimise the adverse effects of regulation on competition, and promote competition between those who are subject to regulation by the FSA.

3 Market fragmentation should be welcomed as a *symptom of competition*, while barriers to the entry of new trading systems should be resisted. Rules of incumbent trading systems which prevent some traders having access to a trading system should also be resisted. Again, this recommendation is in line with the emphasis on innovation and competition in FSMA (2000, section 2). Informal linkages between trading systems and traders should be relied upon to create an integrated market with the benefits of competition, without the costs of a fragmented market.

4 The *trade publication regime* should be based on the principle of high transparency, unless demonstrable harm from such trade publication would result. This proposal is consistent both with the four statutory objectives of the FSA and with the importance of transparency as stated by both the SIB and the SEC. A structured process should be adopted when assessing possible changes to trade publication parameters. An implication of this is that the regulators should carefully appraise the arguments advanced against expanding the transparency regime to OTC markets.

5 A more sophisticated definition of *best execution*, possibly based less on explicitly rule-based systems, such as that used in UK equity markets, and more on codes of practice expected of brokers. The rules should recognise the diversity of order requirements. The rule should be drafted in a way that permits innovation and encourages

investors to take responsibility for their own decisions. Best execution also has transparency and access implications.

6 Since transparency has implications for competition, the prices charged for *real time quote (and possibly trade) data* should be monitored, and the systems for data distribution and access to trading systems should not create barriers to new trading systems starting up. This means that some form of affirmative action may be required, as has happened in other industries to make a monopoly into a contestable market. In particular, this may mean that the prices charged for real time quote and trade data should be monitored and, where necessary, regulated, and that the systems for data distribution and access to trading systems should not create barriers to new trading systems starting up.

Notes

1 The concept of a market centre is different to that of an exchange since each NASDAQ dealer or NYSE specialist is a market centre.

2 Existing trading systems might be unhappy about offering low transparency standards to new (and small) entrants into the market. It is possible that some entrants may wish to run an opaque trading system, so damaging the price formation process. Transparency is an important aspect of market quality, and should not be compromised to allow entrants to run opaque trading systems.

3 If there is an OTC market, with no trading in a closely related exchange-traded security; the OTC trading has no negative effects on exchange trading. In this case the OTC market may be exempted from a requirement to be transparent.

11

The Evolving Regulation of Financial Networks

James J. Angel
Georgetown University, USA

11.1 Introduction

It is no secret that financial markets are changing rapidly and that regulation needs to change to keep up with the changes in the industry. In order to understand the evolution of market regulation, it is important to understand not only the many trends affecting financial markets, but also the network economics that dominate the industrial organisation of the industry. This leads to many similarities between the stock exchange industry and other network industries such as telecommunications, transportation, and computer operating systems.

In studying markets, and in particular equity markets, it is all too easy to fall for the trap of concentrating on only one institution or country. Academics such as myself are prone to this error because we can often get data from one particular institution, such as the NYSE. However, a market is a network that connects all the potential buyers and sellers in an instrument. In recent years, Sun Microsystems has successfully made the point that 'The network is the computer'. Similarly, in equity markets it is extremely important to understand that 'The network IS the market'. This approach yields an enormous amount of insight, because the economics of networks indicate where barriers to entry arise, and the problems that arise in regulation.

In this chapter, I start off by enumerating the trends affecting the industry, and then discuss the impact of network economics on regulation, and finally discuss the US experience in regulating the equity market as a financial network. This brief chapter is not meant to be a complete treatise on network economics.

11.2   Trends in the financial markets

11.2.1   Technology

Technology has affected financial markets in several ways. First, it has led to a dramatic collapse of communication costs. In the old days, high communications costs created natural barriers between stock exchanges which reduced the competition between them. Thus, the Paris Bourse mainly traded different stocks at different times than the NYSE. Stock exchanges viewed each other more as colleagues rather than competitors. First the telegraph, then the telephone, and now the internet have made communication costs almost vanish. This has reduced the natural barriers between exchanges, leading to a steady and long-term consolidation in many countries.

Technology has not only brought communication costs down, but it also makes new trading technologies possible. The closing of old stock exchange floors is one obvious example. Most countries have closed their old physical trading floors and replaced them with computerised limit order matching systems. Nevertheless, in many such countries these central limit book systems have captured only a fraction of the total volume, with the rest of the business upstairs or offshore.

However, trading technology means much more than cheap telecoms and matching of limit orders. New technologies are under development that go far beyond the crude, first generation limit order matching systems that some countries call stock exchanges today. There are many trading strategies that are much more complex than the 'limit' and 'market' orders matched in some markets, which is one reason for the very high level of trading outside the pure limit order matching systems. Furthermore, pure limit order matching systems lack incentives for market makers to provide liquidity into those systems. Several countries have implemented or are implementing what I call 'second generation' electronic systems. These hybrid systems such as NASDAQ not only match customer limit orders, but also incorporate dealer functionality.

But there is much more that can be done with technology. Many firms are working on third generation electronic trading platforms that incorporate 'push' technology. First and second generation systems depend upon traders to actually put their order into a particular trading platform. However, there is a lot of liquidity that chooses not to reveal itself to particular platforms. For example, an institution may work a large order in small chunks to avoid tipping its hand. A trading system that can find the natural counterparty for that order can provide a huge value. Liquidnet does this with a Napster-like system whose software sits inside an institution's order management system and, like a trusted spy, seeks out natural counterparties inside other institution's internal order books. When a potential match is found, only the two institutions involved find out about it and can negotiate privately and electronically. NASDAQ's planned Liquidity Tracker similarly works to sniff out liquidity outside its system.

11.2.2 Entry

There have been many attempts at entry into these businesses. There have been many failed attempts at entry, such as Optimark's attempt to incorporate artificial intelligence and fuzzy logic into trading systems. There have also been successful attempts at entry, such as POSIT's match system that provides complete anonymity to its participants through periodic crosses. New attempts at entry into the cross-border trading business include Jiway, Virt-x, and various attempts by other markets to expand internationally.

11.2.3 Consolidation

As mentioned above, the decline in communication costs has led to a consolidation of stock exchanges within many countries, leading to only one stock exchange in many countries. The major question is what the consolidation will look like across national borders. Regulatory and political barriers make it difficult to consummate cross-border mergers, even when the economics make sense.

11.2.4 Demutualisation

In the old environment, exchanges were organised as co-operatives owned by their members. This made sense because of the peculiar nature of the exchange business. Exchanges essentially operate dating services that match buyers and sellers. This means that the suppliers of the firm are also the customers of the firm. These supplier–customers are the brokers who seek to execute their customers' orders as well as intermediaries who seek to make money through providing liquidity to the market. Because the actions of a trading platform operator such as a stock exchange have a huge impact on the profits of the participants, those participants naturally desire influence over the decisions of the trading platform operator. Co-operative ownership is one means of using such influence.

Although co-operative organisations often work well in stable environments, co-operative governance is very slow and prone to political paralysis. In a fast-changing environment, cooperative exchanges may not be able to move quickly enough to respond to competitive threats. Indeed, many of the most severe competitive threats to co-operative exchanges are from their own members. As one executive at an exchange confided to me 'Our biggest competitors are on our board of directors'. Thus, in the 1990s exchanges began converting away from co-operative governance into standard for-profit corporations. This trend is now largely complete, with the NYSE being the only large equity market that has not yet demutualised.

11.2.5 Deregulation

Deregulation is a world-wide trend affecting not only financial services but many other industries as well. As I view it, there have been three basic eras of financial regulation. In the first era, *Pre-regulation*, financial markets were left alone with fairly minimal regulation beyond the commercial code. The *Regulation era* was ushered into the USA through the Securities Act 1933 and the Securities Exchange Act 1934. In the regulated worldview, stock exchanges were monopolistic dens of thieves that needed to be closely watched by trustworthy civil servants who would regulate them like old-fashioned water utilities. Regulators often preferred a single monopoly market that they could regulate easily. However, in the later part of the twentieth century it became clear in many industries that extensive regulation did not always produce the best outcomes. In the third era, *Deregulation*, the trend is to give markets a freer hand. The view is that trading platforms are businesses like any other, and competitive market forces, both domestic and international, are used to discipline the trading platforms.

11.2.6 Globalisation

Globalisation, the slow erosion of borders, is another trend. Part of this is a result of the collapse of communication costs, and part of this due to the world-wide trend towards deregulation.

Globalisation has scary implications for regulators. A regulator's power usually stops at the national border. It is much more difficult for all law-enforcement officials, not just regulators, to pursue wrongdoers across borders. Low-cost communications and almost anonymous electronic accounts make it easier than ever before to engage in international shenanigans. Imagine the difficulties faced by a US regulator fighting a case of stock manipulation in which a Chinese national operating through internet accounts based in Singapore allegedly manipulates a stock traded in the USA.

Regulators have few tools to encourage foreign entities to conform to the regulators' wishes. Larger countries such as the USA and the UK can hold out the carrot of access to their capital markets: Their policy has been one of 'If you want access to our capital, play by our rules'. However, this carrot is losing its attractiveness with the further integration of world capital markets. The ability of the largest institutional investors to trade globally increasingly makes the country of registration irrelevant. The fact that Volkswagen is not registered with the US SEC and is not listed on US exchanges is no impediment to Fidelity's trading desk. Instinet now provides its US customers direct electronic access to over 40 markets around the world, regardless of whether the instruments traded on those exchanges are registered in the USA or not.

11.2.7   Falling transaction costs

Not only have communication costs fallen, but so have other transaction costs such as brokerage commissions. This enables trading strategies that were previously too costly, leading to more trading volume in the markets.

11.2.8   Rise of the retail investor

In particular, the amazing reduction in transaction costs is leading to a rise in the retail investor. It is now cost effective for retail investors to run their own mutual funds, and indeed, many are. Brokerage firms such as Foliofn and E*Trade now offer their customers the ability to trade large stock baskets for a fixed monthly charge.

11.2.9   Internalisation and segmentation

The rise of the retail investor highlights another trend. Firms have discovered that different categories of order flow have different levels of information content. For example, I have been a customer of discount-broker Charles Schwab since 1983. Charles Schwab knows from my trading history that I and other retail investors like me are uninformed traders. Schwab can make money by internalising my trades: he buys from me when I want to sell and vice versa. The firm can do this safely because it knows that I don't have any special insight into which way the markets are going. Schwab is not the only firm that does this. Many brokerage firms in the USA and other countries routinely internalise retail orders. Sometimes they fill the customer's order. In other cases, they route the order to a market-maker in return for some kind of *quid pro quo*, such as an explicit payment for order flow, a reduction in other fees, or a gentleman's understanding that the favour will be returned through other lucrative business.

The ability to identify categories of order flow with different information content has a big impact on the structure of this industry. Because it is profitable to trade against certain types of order flow, but not others, we can expect trading platforms to arise that will allow people to take advantage of this. Those platforms that facilitate this type of internalisation will prosper, while those that don't are going to lose business.

11.2.10   Longer trading hours

Exchanges in many countries have also substantially extended their trading hours. By closing their physical floors, exchanges were freed from the human limitations inherent in their systems: traders no longer had to stand on their feet and run around all day. This allowed the exchanges to stay open longer to serve their local investors better. Furthermore, exchanges have also been extending their hours to attract order flow from investors in other time zones as well.

This brings up the question of 'How long will the trading day become?' Will equities turn into an around-the-clock market, like currencies? I do not see this as happening any time soon, because most investors prefer to trade equities during normal market hours, for the reasons that I will enumerate below.

11.2.11   Dematerialisation

Paper stock certificates are costly to process and prone to theft and forgery. Many countries have demobilised the bulk of their paper certificates in central depositories, and some have dematerialised paper certificates entirely. This trend toward total dematerialisation will continue.

11.2.12   Clearing and settlement

As anyone who understands the back office knows, nothing but bad things can happen between the trade and settlement. Or, as the Group of 30 elegantly phrased it, 'TIME = RISK'. In times of financial upheaval, the uncertainty as to whether trades will settle adds further fuel to a crisis.

In the USA, the twentieth century saw a steady lengthening of the equity settlement cycle from $T + 1$ all the way to $T + 5$ in the 1970s. Now the trend is toward shorter settlement cycles, as more countries adopt the Group of 30's recommendation of rolling $T + 3$ settlements. Furthermore, as the industry realises that 'TIME = MONEY' is still true, there will be further shortening of the settlement cycles. It is likely that the USA will move to $T + 1$ in 2004 or 2005.

Eventually, the markets may move to gross real time settlement, in which the settlement takes place at the same time as the transaction.

However, such gross settlement would result in a significantly higher number of transactions through the financial system. The US settlement and depository firm DTCC estimates that the netting system now in place in the USA reduces the number of settlement payments by 95 per cent. It will probably be a long time before the advantages of real time settlement are worth the extensive and costly changes to the infrastructure of the industry.

There is a great need for further efficiencies in clearing and settlement, especially across national borders such as in Europe. There is likely to be further consolidation in clearing and settlement organisations in Europe and other places.

11.3   Why do we have stock exchanges in the first place? Stock markets as financial networks

In order to regulate the industry properly, it is important to ask Ruben Lee's (1998) question of 'What is an exchange?' More broadly, the issue is 'What is a stock market?' In my view, a stock market consists of two basic elements: It consists of one or more trading platforms, in addition to a very thick rule book. Indeed, the rule book is one of the most important aspects that define the market.

Long before there was formal government regulation, stock exchanges created their own rule books. These rule books created a private law that governed trading, complete with penalties and enforcement mechanisms. Why is the rule book such an important part of stock trading, but not other businesses? Why isn't the local version of the Uniform Commercial Code good enough?

Understanding how equity markets differ from other markets helps to answer this question. Note that most markets – including most financial markets–trade naturally over the counter. After all, one does not go to The Paperclip Exchange to buy paperclips. Many financial products such as bonds, currencies, and many derivatives are very liquid without having a large organised, centralised, hyper-regulated market. What is different about the equity business?

This question becomes even more interesting owing to the high cost of establishing an organised market. The cost of a stock exchange is not just the cost of physical facilities such as buildings and computers, but also the substantial costs of rule compliance by participants, and rule enforcement by the regulators. The hardcopy printed editions of NYSE and NASDAQ rulebooks are each over 2 inches thick; the rule books of other markets are likewise quite detailed. It is costly to create these rule books, and it is also costly to comply with all those rules. There are rules about interconnection, systems, licensing of employees, testing of systems, and testing of employees. There are rules about such minutiae as the hours of operation, the tick size, and dispute resolution procedures.

Because of the costs involved, why have stock exchanges at all? Common sense indicates that firms only going to bear the cost of forming or participating in an exchange, are if they are better off as a result. As former NASDAQ Chairman Frank Zarb was fond of saying, 'If there were a flag for the securities industry, it would bear the Latin motto for "What's in it for me?"'

The 'it' for the participants is valuable information about prices and potential trading partners. For most traded goods and services there is very little uncertainty about the price. Any trader who knows the yield curve can calculate the price of a US Treasury bond. Not so for stocks. Nobody really knows what a stock is worth. Therefore, information about what others are willing to pay, as indicated by recent trades and orders, can have a big impact on the prices.

For example, an order to buy 10 million euros in exchange for dollars is not a large trade to a currency dealer. A typical currency dealer would fill the order and probably not even stop yawning in the process. However, an order to purchase 10 million worth of a common equity is a big order that gets a dealer's full attention. Suddenly the dealer is very interested in who is placing the order and why, while thinking about what information is contained in the order. The information in such an order is extremely valuable.

Furthermore, this information is much more valuable, relative to the size of the order, in equities compared with other markets. Because it is easier to determine the prices of most other goods, such as paper clips, there is less need for an organised trading platform with a rule book to aggregate the information.

Most humans do not want to give away valuable things for free, especially if they think that others will use the information against them. Thus traders don't want to reveal any information about the orders they hold, the trades they just completed, or the positions they hold. After all, revealing the existence of a large buy order may run up the price before the order is filled.

However, traders want to know what everyone else is doing, because that is useful for planning their trading strategies. Unfortunately, in order to find the other side of the trade and agree upon price, traders have to reveal some information. However, traders prefer that other traders do the revealing, not them. This is the classic prisoner's dilemma:

every trader has an incentive to hide, but all would be better off if they shared some information.

An organised equity market such as a stock exchange provides a solution to the prisoner's dilemma. An exchange forces participants to disclose some of this information. Most organised trading platforms require traders to reveal the prices and quantities of trades that occur on those platforms, and some require the reporting of trades that take place elsewhere. Most exchanges require some disclosure about the unexecuted orders that participants hold. By joining an exchange, the participant obtains access to the trading facilities (and the resulting information pool) at the cost of partially revealing its own information. Participants, though, still know more about their own customers than others do.

To reinforce the point: by forming an exchange, participants pool their information, and the increased value from the aggregated information more than offsets the cost of participating in an organised and regulated market.

There is another important reason for forming exchanges. In derivative markets, the price discovery aspect of the exchange is relatively less important than in equities. However, the leveraged nature of derivatives along with time delays between trade and final settlement lead to the risk that the final trade will not settle as agreed. The derivative exchanges reduce this counterparty risk through clearinghouse structures in which the central counterparty assumes the risk. This provides an important reason for forming an exchange.

The nature of matching buyer and seller in a trading platform leads to strong network effects. Because of the uncertainty about the price and the effort to find a counterparty, most traders naturally go to the trading platform that they think does the best job filling the order. In tradespeak, this means the platform with the most 'liquidity'. As traders are prone to say, 'liquidity attracts liquidity'. They will go to the platform that has the most liquidity, even if its technology is a little outdated or its fees a little higher, because they want to get the trade done quickly at a good price.

In this respect, an equity trading platform is similar to a dating service. It makes sense for a new customer to join the dating service that has the biggest database of potential mates, even though its fees may be higher than its rivals.' This makes it very hard for new entrants to enter the market for exchange services against an entrenched incumbent in any particular instrument.

The classic example of network economics is that of a telephone network. A telephone is useless if there is no one to talk to. Thus, the value of a phone system is a function of how many people are connected to the system. If there are two rival systems that are not interconnected, the larger network will have an advantage over the smaller one. Indeed, the larger network has a strong incentive to block smaller rivals from accessing its network. Network effects are found in many other industries, including computer operating systems and payment systems.

This brief chapter is not meant to be a complete study of network economics – there are many other good treatments of the subject, such as Shy (2001), and Shapiro and Varian (1998). However, networks are very different from the usual markets that regulators studied when they took a class in Economics 101 long ago. In particular, network markets do not have all of the same 'Laissez-faire is optimal' results that naturally occur in competitive markets without network effects. Regulators are faced with tough choices, and no solution is without drawbacks. Section 11.4 discusses the implications for financial markets and the US experience regulating a 'National Market System'.

11.4 Implications for the evolution of financial regulation

In the old legislative worldview, stock exchanges were natural monopolies run by dens of thieves; they needed to be closely monitored by wise altruistic regulators. In recent decades, there has been a strong trend away from this view and toward the privatisation and deregulation of many industries. The new worldview is that stock exchanges are businesses like any other business, to be disciplined by competition both from other exchanges as well as from other potential entrants.

The question becomes 'What is the role of the regulator in this environment?' First, the most important job of the regulator is to keep the crooks out of the business. Financial markets attract thieves just like banks attract bank robbers, and we are all better off if we keep the crooks out. Thus, it is important to create and enforce rules against fraudulent sales practices, fraudulent accounting, price manipulation, and insider trading.

Second, the shift toward for-profit trading platforms requires a shift in the regulatory attitude of the regulators. In the old way of doing things, the dominant exchange controlled both the rule book and the trading platforms. In a network market of competing platforms, the role of setting the *über*-rule book for trading between platforms falls upon the regulator. Regulators do this either consciously through explicit rules or unconsciously in a *de facto* manner that cements the status quo of the dominant platform.

What kind of rules should the regulator consider for the *über*-rule book?

In the old world, the exchanges were co-operatives that were managed by the industry. The industry participants had strong incentives to make sure that the exchanges functioned efficiently and did not charge monopolistic prices for transaction and data services. In the new demutualised environment, the dominant trading platforms have strong incentives to maximise profits for their shareholders. This raises the potential for charging monopolistic fees for market data, and for taking actions that freeze competing platforms out of the market by denying rivals access to their liquidity. For example, consolidation rules or pricing models that require participants to bring all their business to the dominant exchange make it impossible for competitors to get established.

If regulators are relying upon competition to discipline the players, they need to set up conditions under which competition can flourish. However, this takes some doing because of the strong market position of the historically dominant exchanges, which usually enjoyed *de facto* or sometimes *de jure* monopolies. The huge network effects make it very difficult for competition to flourish unless the regulators take actions to open up the market to competition.

11.4.1 Global competition

One possible solution is to open up the equity business to global competition from foreign exchanges. However, this raises questions about investor protection, and the politically unappealing prospect of business migrating to another country. Furthermore, because it is very hard to unseat a dominant market in an instrument, it is unlikely that other exchanges can provide much real competition for the home market. They do, however, provide a strong spur to innovation out of the fear that the foreigners will steal the market.

11.4.2 Differential regulatory burdens

Providing a lower regulatory burden on competitors is another alternative. In the USA, the SEC has allowed new entrants to register as broker–dealers rather than as more onerously regulated exchanges. For example, Electronic Communication Networks (ECNs) such as Instinet are classified as broker–dealers rather than exchanges. One example of the difference in regulation was the implementation of longer trading hours by ECNs: they just did it, without needing any advance approval from the SEC. However, the Chicago Stock Exchange had to go through a formal rule filing and wait months before the SEC approved its longer trading hours. However, intentionally creating an unlevel playing field that hinders one competitor in favor of another is a crude and unappealing approach. Although it appears to counteract the advantages held by the dominant exchanges, there is no guarantee that the regulators will apply the 'right' amount of disadvantage to the dominant platform, or that such an intentional disadvantage makes any economic sense.

11.4.3 Access to market data

A reasonable solution is to adopt rules that force the dominant exchange to co-operate with the other exchanges, telecoms style. Just as in telecommunications, the classic network industry, the regulator is stuck with regulating the terms and conditions upon which competitor's access each other's networks: the interconnection. How should the regulator do this? Remember that the financial market is fundamentally an information processing engine: it processes the orders that come in, it discovers a price, and it matches buyer and seller. Access to information is the key. Competitors must have access to sufficient information for them to compete. As a result of the 1975 'National Market System' amendment to the Securities Exchange Act, exchanges in the USA are not allowed to deny competitors access to their price and quote data, or to charge unduly discriminatory prices for those data feeds. Prior to the amendments, the NYSE could and did just that.

Nevertheless, this approach reduces the commercial freedom of the exchanges to do what they want with the data that they produce. It is odd that the same US government which is placing an increased emphasis on the protection of intellectual property in software and movies in international trade has quasi-nationalised the best bid and offer data produced by the exchanges. This intellectual disconnect is one that may become increasingly visible in coming years.

11.4.4 Prohibition of anti-competitive practices

Dominant exchanges often desire to implement consolidation rules on the grounds that 'fragmentation' of the market is bad. Such rules basically require that participants bring all orders to the exchange and not fill them internally or elsewhere. However, consolidation rules are also barriers to entry for new players. Thus, the regulator needs the ability to prevent such anti-competitive practices.

11.4.5 Forced linkages

However, even with good access to information, it is still possible for dominant trading platforms to freeze out other platforms just by ignoring them. Even when the new entrant has an order at a better price than the dominant market, the dominant market may trade through that better price because there is no connection to the smaller market. Their justification is usually quite plausible. They see no reason that their market should be held up because of the other market, and they complain, often legitimately, that seemingly better prices on other markets are mirages that cannot be accessed. Because the orders on the smaller platform go unfilled, no one sends orders there and the smaller competitor dies in a death spiral of illiquidity.

Clearly, the dominant market has no incentive to create linkages that would allow competitors to flourish. Regulators have tried to get around this through mandating linkages such as the Intermarket Trading System in the USA, and imposing best execution requirements on brokers.

11.4.6 Pricing rules

However, once competitors are forced to co-operate against their will to aggregate market data, sticky questions arise as to the ownership of the data, pricing of data sales, and the splitting of the data revenue. This issue is closely connected to issues of intellectual property. In particular, when we talk about transparency we have to ask the question: Who owns this information? Isn't trade information the intellectual property of the platform that produced it? Is a regulator who forces disclosure of information expropriating that intellectual property? Similarly, the aggregated information is more valuable than the individual bits of information. Who gets the surplus that is created? The regulators are forced to come up with some type of rules that govern the process. Regulators should never forget that attempting to force competition among rivals is a messy process. The players use every regulatory trick in the book to subvert regulation into a process for stifling rivals. Once again, there is no first-best alternative, and all of the alternative price-setting mechanisms have various disadvantages inherent to a bureaucratically administered price mechanism.[1]

11.4.7 Trust the data vendors?

One could argue that in this internet age with low information costs, that information services naturally spring up to provide the linkages across competing trading platforms. Data vendors can cheaply aggregate the quotes from different markets and display consolidated information to their subscribers. This is appealing in theory, but in practice such voluntary linkages leave much to be desired. Some markets quotes may not be easily accessible outside the market. Such quotes may be 'crossed' in which the bid on one market is higher than the offer on the other. Yet arbitrage activity fails to resolve the situation because markets find creative ways to back away from their quotes. What is the real market at such times? This lack of an unambiguous best bid and offer makes it hard for there to be any type of an enforceable best execution standard for broker dealers.

11.4.8 Foster innovation

The fast and unpredictable changes in technology imply that regulators should not attempt to design the market micro-structure in detail. A few years ago some observers, including myself, thought that a computerised limit order matching system was the ultimate market mechanism. We were wrong. There are many different new trading systems under technological development that go far beyond simple matching of limit and market orders. In its zeal to improve the market, a regulator may overspecify the microstructure of the market in a way that inhibits future innovation.

Regulators should allow as much freedom and flexibility to the trading platforms to innovate and compete as possible, because there's a lot more that technology can bring to us.

11.4.9 Market supervision

One extremely important question is the issue of who monitors trading to enforce the rules. In the Pre-regulation era, it was the job of each exchange. In the Regulation era, regulators often delegated the task to the dominant exchange. However, it is not clear who should do this in a world of competing platforms. If there is a dominant exchange it can be left up to them, but it's unfair to leave such a costly burden on any one exchange when its rivals don't have to pay for it.

Someone has to monitor trading to look for abuses such as insider trading and wash sales.[2] If there are transparency rules that require trades to be reported, what happens with someone who does not report a trade? Who's going to find out about it; who's going to enforce it? One approach is to leave it up to each trading platform, but what about abuses across platforms? This could be left up to the government, but governments often lack the resources and the expertise to do the job alone.

Another feasible alternative is to create an industry-wide body with regulatory powers to enforce trading rules. Many countries adopted the self-regulation model to cut the cost of this regulation by delegating some regulatory powers to a quasi-industry group.

11.4.10 Conclusion

All of these potential rules have advantages and disadvantages, as illustrated by the US experience. In 1975, the US Congress passed the 'National Market System' amendments to the Securities Exchange Act with the explicit goal of fostering competition. As implemented by the SEC, the National Market System (NMS) had the following features:

- SROs, including stock exchanges, had to have their rules approved in advance by the SEC. This was to prevent anti-competitive rules.
- Exchanges were forced to pool their quotations in the Consolidated Quote System (CQS) and their trades in the Consolidated Tape System (CTS).
- A new type of highly regulated SRO, the Securities Information Processor (SIP) was created for the purpose of aggregating and selling the data. The Securities Industry Automation Corporation (SIAC) is the SIP for trades in NYSE-listed stocks. The data revenues were divided up among the exchanges based on the number of trades, leading to all kinds of interesting games known as 'print stealing'.
- The consolidated quote led to a National Best Bid and Offer (NBBO), which became the effective standard for best execution. This allowed regional exchanges and off-exchange dealers to compete with the NYSE by promising to meet or beat the NBBO.
- Exchanges were required to participate in a forced linkage known as the Intermarket Trading System. Exchanges were not allowed to trade through another market's quote without fulfilling the trading interest in the other market. This effectively instituted nation-wide price priority and protected limit orders placed at a regional exchanges.

This approach is worthy of study in other countries that are grappling with the issue of how to switch from a regime of single dominant market to one of competing markets. It has largely achieved its goal of achieving an efficient nation-wide equity market. Americans are rightly proud of the deep, liquid, and low cost US equity markets and their role in the US economy.

However, it is not without some drawbacks. Competitors who do not want to co-operate are forced to co-operate in the ITS, and the SEC is called upon to referee the many squabbles that take place. The SEC is drawn into controversies over the pricing of market data and has still not found a trouble-free mechanism. The requirement for advance SEC approval of SRO rule changes has led to severe micro-management of the regulated exchanges. The exchanges are faced with the regulatory burden of surveilling their markets while their less-regulated competitors lack such a burden.

In the USA, the SROs are no longer really self-regulating in terms of rule-setting. The 1975 amendments severely reduced the 'self' in self-regulation. by requiring every SRO rule change to be pre-approved by the SEC. For example, a few years ago the Pacific Stock Exchange wanted to adopt a rule requiring men to wear neckties on their trading floor. This rule had to be approved, in advance, by the SEC. To the best of my knowledge, stock exchanges are the only businesses in the USA that are required to have their employee dress codes approved in advance by the national government.

Furthermore, the SEC does this in a highly public and politicised environment; proposed rule changes are first published in *The Federal Register*. Then there is a public comment period which provides full employment for lobbyists. The lobbyists from an SRO's competitors attempt to convince the SEC and the US Congress that the proposed rule change would lead to the end of civilisation as we know it, and that a different rule change should be adopted by the allegedly 'self'-regulatory organisation. Meanwhile, the understaffed and underfunded SEC won't approve the SRO rules until the SRO amends the rule filing into the exact form that the SEC wants. For example, NASDAQ's new 'Super-Montage' trading system required nine sets of amendments before the SEC finally approved it. Furthermore, the SuperMontage proposal was NASDAQ's third attempt to put in some type of limit order book. Their previous proposals had been shot down in the regulatory crossfire.

Despite its flaws, the US 'National Market System' (NMS) has helped to foster an equity market that is the envy of the world. The US equity market is a world leader in low-cost execution, liquidity, and the provision of capital to new enterprises. However, one can always debate whether the success of the US market has come as a result of the NMS, or despite it. As other countries re-examine their regulatory systems, they can learn a lot from the US experience. Yet, other countries should not just copy the US system, but learn from it and adapt the good parts of the US model to the unique circumstances within each country.

11.5 Summary

Financial markets are networks of buyers and sellers. As such, they display the peculiar economics of networks in which the usual 'Laissez-faire is best' results don't always hold. Thus, regulators are faced with a tough choice of accepting the potentially non-optimal laissez-faire outcome, or engaging in telecom-like regulation of the financial network. This means regulating the terms and conditions of network access among competitors who don't necessarily want to grant rivals access to their networks. This is done through transparency regulations that permit rivals to access trading system information, regulations concerning the ownership and pricing of market data, best execution requirements that prevent the freezing out of small players, and forced interconnection of competing trading platforms. As Europe transitions from a regime of local monopoly exchanges to one of competing trading platforms, it may wish to study the experience of the 'National Market System' in the USA which was ushered in by the 1975 amendments to US securities laws.

Notes

1   See the SEC (1999) concept release and the 'Seligman Report' (SEC, 2001) for more about this important issue.
2   In the US a *wash sale* occurs when a share is sold to generate a tax loss, and then repurchased. In the UK such sale and repurchase trades are called bed-and-breakfast trades.

References

Abhyankar, A., L.S. Copeland and W. Wong, 1999, LIFFE cycles: intraday evidence from the FTSE100 stock index futures market, *European Journal of Finance*, 5, 123–39.

Abhyankar, A., D. Ghosh, E. Levin and R.J. Limmack, 1997, Bid – ask spreads, trading volume and volatility: intraday evidence from the London Stock Exchange, *Journal of Business Finance and Accounting*, 24, 343–62.

Admati, A.R. and P. Pfleiderer, 1988, A theory of intraday patterns: volume and price variability, *Review of Financial Studies*, 1, 3–40.

Admati, A.R. and P. Pfleiderer, 1991, Sunshine trading and financial market equilibrium, *Review of Financial Studies*, 4, 443–81.

Amihud, Y. and H. Mendelson, 1980, Dealership markets: market-making with inventory, *Journal of Financial Economics*, 8, 31–53.

Amihud, Y. and Mendelson, H., 1996, A new approach to the regulation of trading across securities markets, *New York University Law Review*, 71(6), 1411–66.

Angel, J.J., 1998, *Consolidation in the global equity market: an historical perspective*, Discussion Paper, Georgetown University, 33pp.

ap Gwilym, O., 1999, Bid – ask spreads on stock index futures and the impact of electronic trading, *Derivatives Use, Trading and Regulation*, 5(1), 18–28.

ap Gwilym, O. and J.A. Bennell, 2000, Price clustering under floor and electronic trading, *Derivatives Use, Trading and Regulation*, 5(4), 354–62.

ap Gwilym, O. and M.J. Buckle, 1997, The interrelation of stock index and stock index futures returns and trading volume, *Working Paper*, University of Wales, Swansea.

ap Gwilym, O., M. Buckle and S.H. Thomas, 1997, The intraday behaviour of bid – ask spreads, returns and volatility for FTSE100 stock index options, *Journal of Derivatives*, 4, 20–32.

ap Gwilym, O. and S.H. Thomas, 1998, The influence of electronic trading on bid – ask spreads: new evidence from European bond futures, *Journal of Fixed Income*, 8(1), 7–19.

ap Gwilym, O. and S.H. Thomas, 2002, An empirical comparison of quoted and implied bid – ask spreads on futures contracts, *Journal of International Financial Markets, Institutions and Money*, vol. 12, no. 1, February, pp. 81–99.

Arthur, W.B., 1989, Competing technologies, increasing returns and lock-in by historical events, *Economic Journal*, 99 (394), pp. 116–31.

Bacha, O. and A.F. Vila, 1994, Futures markets, regulation and volatility: the case of the Nikkei stock index futures markets, *Pacific Basin Finance Journal*, 2, 201–25.

Ball, R. and Finn, F.J., 1989, The effect of block transactions on share prices: Australian evidence, *Journal of Banking and Finance*, vol. 13, no. 3, July, 397–419.

Bank for International Settlements (BIS) 2000, *The Global OTC Derivatives Market at End-June 2000*, November, BIS.

Barclay, M.J., 1997, Bid – ask spreads and the avoidance of odd-eighth quotes on Nasdaq: an examination of exchange listings, *Journal of Financial Economics*, 45, 35–60.

Barclay, M.J., W.G. Christie, J.H. Harris, E. Kandel and P.H. Schultz, 1999, Effects of market reform on the trading costs and depths of Nasdaq stocks, *Journal of Finance*, 54, 1–34.

Benhamon, E. and Serval, T., 2000, On the competition between ECNs, stock markets and market makers. LSE Financial Markets Group, *Discussion Paper*, 345, March.

Benveniste, L.M., A.J. Marcus and W.J. Wilhelm, 1992, "What's special about the specialist? Floor exchange versus computerized market mechanisms", *Journal of Financial Economics*, 32, 61–86.

Beny, L.N., 2001, US secondary stock markets: a survey of current regulatory and structural issues and a reform proposal to enhance competition, *Discussion Paper*, 331, Harvard Law School, July.

Bessembinder, H., 1997, The degree of price resolution and equity trading costs, *Journal of Financial Economics*, 45, 9–34.

Biais, B., 1993, Price formation and equilibrium liquidity in fragmented and centralised markets, *Journal of Finance*, 48 (1), pp. 157–85.

Biais, B., P. Hillion and C. Spatt, 1995, An empirical analysis of the limit order book and the order flow in the Paris Bourse, *Journal of Finance*, 50, 1655–89.

Blennerhassett, M. and R.G. Bowman, 1998, "A change in market microstructure: the switch to electronic screen trading on the New Zealand stock exchange", *Journal of International Financial Markets, Institutions and Money*, 8, 261–76.

Bloomfield, Robert and Maureen O'Hara, 1999, Market transparency: who wins and who loses?, *Review of Financial Studies*, 12, 5–35.

Bloomfield, Robert and Maureen O'Hara, 2000, Can transparent markets survive? *Journal of Financial Economics*, 55(3), 425–59.

Board of Banking Supervision (BoBS), 1995, *Report of the Board of Banking Supervision Inquiry into the Circumstances of the Collapse of Barings*, HMSO, London.

Board, J.L.G. and Sutcliffe, C.M.S., 1995a, *The Effects of Trade Transparency in the London Stock Exchange*, January (prepared for the London Stock Exchange and the London International Financial Futures and Options Exchange).

Board, J.L.G. and Sutcliffe, C.M.S., 1995b, The effects of trade transparency in the London Stock Exchange: a summary, Financial Markets Group, *Special Paper*, 67, London School of Economics and Political Science, January.

Board, J.L.G. and C.M.S. Sutcliffe, 1996a, The dual listing of stock index futures: arbitrage, spread arbitrage and currency risk, *Journal of Futures Markets*, 16, 29–54.

Board, J.L.G. and Sutcliffe, C.M.S., 1996b, Transparency and the London Stock Exchange, *European Financial Management*. 2(3), 355–65.

Board, J.L.G. and Sutcliffe, C.M.S., 1997, Inventory-based stock market transparency rules, *Journal of Financial Regulation and Compliance*, 5(1), 23–8.

Board, J.L.G. and Sutcliffe, C.M.S., 1998, Options trading when the underlying market is not transparent, *Journal of Futures Markets*, 18(2), 225–42.

Board, J.L.G. and Sutcliffe, C.M.S., 2000, The proof of the pudding: the effects of increased trade transparency in the London Stock Exchange, *Journal of Business Finance and Accounting*, 27 (7 & 8), 887–909.

Board, J.L.G., Sutcliffe, C.M.S. and Vila, A., 2000, Market maker performance: the search for fair weather market makers, *Journal of Financial Services Research*, 17(3), 255–72.

Board, J.L.G. and Wells, S., 2001, Liquidity and best execution in the UK: a comparison of SETS and tradepoint, *Journal of Asset Management*, 1(4), 344–65.

Bollerslev, T. and I. Domowitz, 1991, Price volatility, spread variability and the role of alternative market mechanisms, *Review of Futures Markets*, 10(1), 78–102.

Bollerslev, T., I. Domowitz and J. Wang, 1997, Order flow and the bid – ask spread: an empirical probability model of screen-based trading, *Journal of Economic Dynamics and Control*, 21, 1471–91.

Booth, G., P. Iversen, S.K. Sarkar, H. Schmidt and A. Young, 1995, Market structure and bid – ask spreads: NASDAQ vs. the German stock market, *Working Paper*, University of Hamburg.

Booth, G.G., J.-P. Kallunki, J.-C. Lin and T. Martikainen, 2000, Internalization and stock price clustering: Finnish evidence, *Journal of International Money and Finance*, 19, 737–51.

Branch, B., A. Gleit, J. Sooy and M. Fitzgerald, 1984, Contract proliferation: a study of the silver futures market, *Rivista Internazionale di Scienze Economiche e Commerciali*, 31, 1058–64.

Breedon, F.J., 1993, Intraday price formation on the London Stock Exchange, London School of Economics Financial Markets Group, *Discussion Paper*, 158, March.

Breedon, F., 1996, Why do the LIFFE and DTB bund futures contracts trade at different prices?, *Bank of England Working Paper*, 57.

Breedon, F.J. and A. Holland, 1997, Electronic versus open outcry markets: the case of the bund futures contract, *Bank of England Working Paper*, 76.

Brock, W. and A. Kleidon, 1992, Periodic market closure and trading volume: a model of intraday bids and asks, *Journal of Economic Dynamics and Control*, 16, 451–89.

Buckle, M. and J. Thompson, 1998, *The UK Financial System: Theory and Practice*, Manchester University Press, 3rd edn.

Burdett, K. and O'Hara, M. 1987, Building blocks: an introduction to block trading, *Journal of Banking and Finance*, vol. 11, no. 2, June, 193–212.

Canadian Securities Administrators, 2000, *Data Consolidation System for a Canadian Consolidated Market*, Canadian Securities Administrators, version 1.0, 25 July.

Chan, K.C., W.G. Christie and P.H. Schultz, 1995, Market structure and the intraday pattern of bid – ask spreads for Nasdaq securities, *Journal of Business*, 68, 35–60.

Chan, K., Y.P. Chung and H. Johnson, 1995, The intraday behaviour of bid – ask spreads for NYSE stocks and CBOE options, *Journal of Financial and Quantitative Analysis*, 30, 329–46.

Chow, E.H., J.-H. Lee and G. Shyy, 1996, Trading mechanisms and trading preferences on a 24-hour futures market: a case study of the Floor/Globex switch on MATIF, *Journal of Banking and Finance*, 20, 1695–1713.

Chowdhry, B. and Nanda, V., 1991, Multimarket trading and market liquidity, *Review of Financial Studies*, 4(3), 483–511.

Christie, W.G., J.H. Harris and P.H. Schultz, 1994, Why did Nasdaq market makers stop avoiding odd-eighth quotes?, *Journal of Finance*, 49, 1841–60.

Christie, W.G. and R.D. Huang, 1994, Market structures and liquidity: a transactions data study of exchange listings, *Journal of Financial Intermediation*, 3, 300–26.

Christie, W.G. and P.H. Schultz, 1994, Why do NASDAQ market makers avoid odd-eighth quotes?, *Journal of Finance*, 49, 1813–40.

Chung, K. H., B. F. Van Ness and R. A. Van Ness, 1999, Limit orders and the bid – ask spread, *Journal of Financial Economics*, 53, 255–87.

Cohen, K.J., Maier, S.F., Schwartz, R.A. and Whitcomb, D.K., 1982, An analysis of the economic justification for consolidation in a secondary security market, *Journal of Banking and Finance*, 6(1), 117–36.

Cohen, K.J., Maier, S.F., Schwartz, R.A. and Whitcomb, D.K., 1986, *The Microstructure of Securities Markets*, Prentice-Hall, Chapter 8, 150–69.

Committee on Financial Services (CFS) 2001a, 14 March 2001, Hearing on 'Public Access to Stock Market Data – Improving Transparency and Competition', Subcommittee on Capital Markets, Insurance and Government-Sponsored Enterprises, US House of Representatives.

Committee on Financial Services (CFS), 2001b, 26 July 2001, Hearing on 'Market Data II: Implications to Investors and Market Transparency of Granting Ownership Rights Over Stock Quotes', Subcommittee on Capital Markets, Insurance and Government-Sponsored Enterprises, US House of Representatives. Both CFS documents are available at *http://www.house.gov/financialservices/testoc2.htm*.

Committee on the Global Financial System, 2001, *The Implications of Electronic Trading in Financial Markets*, Bank for International Settlements, Basle, January.

Commodity Futures Trading Commission (CFTC), 2000a, *A New Regulatory Framework*, Report of the CFTC Staff Task Force, February.

Commodity Futures Trading Commission (CFTC), 2000b, A new regulatory framework for multilateral transaction execution facilities, intermediaries and clearing organizations; exemption for bilateral transactions; proposed rules, *Federal Register*, 65(121), Thursday 22 June, 38985–39008.

Commodity Futures Trading Commission (CFTC), 2000c, *Public Hearing on a New Regulatory Framework*, 1, 27 June, CFTC.

Commodity Futures Trading Commission (CFTC), 2000d, *A New Regulatory Framework for Multilateral Transaction Execution Facilities, Intermediaries and Clearing Organizations*, CFTC, November.

Copeland, T.E. and Galai, D., 1983, Information effects on the bid – ask spread, *Journal of Finance*, 38(5), 1457–69.

De Jong, F., T. Nijman and A. Röell, 1995, A comparison of the cost of trading French shares on the Paris Bourse and on SEAQ International, *European Economic Review*, 39, 1277–1301.

Demarchi, M. and Foucault, T., 1998, Equity trading systems in Europe: a survey of recent changes, *Discussion Paper*, Department of Finance, HEC, France, February.

Di Noia, C., 1999, The Stock Exchange industry: network effects, implicit mergers and corporate governance, *Working Paper*, 33, CONSOB, March.

Di Noia, C., 2001, Competition and integration among Stock Exchanges in Europe: network effects, implicit mergers and remote access, *European Financial Management*, 7(1), 39–72.

Director General of Fair Trading, 1990, *Trade Publication and Price Transparency on the International Stock Exchange: A Report to the Secretary of State for Trade and Industry*, Office of Fair Trading, London, April.

Director General of Fair Trading, 1994, *Trade Publication Rules of the London Stock Exchange: A Report to the Chancellor of the Exchequer*, Office of Fair Trading, London, November.

Domowitz, I., 1990, Mechanics of automated trade execution systems, *Journal of Financial Intermediation*, 1, 167–94.

Domowitz, I., 1993, A taxonomy of automated trade execution systems, *Journal of International Money and Finance*, 12, 607–31.

Domowitz, I., 1995, Electronic derivatives exchanges: implicit mergers, network externalities and standardization, *Quarterly Review of Economics and Finance*, 35(2), 163–75.

Domowitz, I. and Steil. B., 2000, Automation, trading costs, and the structure of the securities trading industry, Paper presented at the Financial Markets Group Conference 'The Future of Exchanges: Strategic Choices Ahead', 19 May. This is a revised version of a paper with the same title published in *Brookings-Wharton Papers on Financial Services*, eds R.E. Litan and A.M. Santomero, Brookings Institution Press, 1999, 33–92.

Dutta, P.K. and A. Madhavan, 1997, Competition and collusion in dealer markets, *Journal of Finance*, 52, 245–76.

Easley, D. and O'Hara, M., 1987, Price, trade size and information in securities markets, *Journal of Financial Economics*, vol. 19, 69–90.

Economides, N., 1993, Network economics with application to finance, *Financial Markets, Institutions and Instruments*, 2(5), 89–97.

Economides, N., 1996, The economics of networks, *International Journal of Industrial Organization*, 14(6), 673–99.

Ellul, A., 2000a, Bid – ask spreads and their components: does market microstructure really matter?, London School of Economics, Financial Markets Group, mimeo.

Ellul, A., 2000b, The market maker rides again: volatility and order flow dynamics in a hybrid market, London School of Economics, Financial Markets Group, mimeo.

Elwes Committee, 1989, *Review of the Central Market in UK Equities: A Consultative Document from the Council of the International Stock Exchange*, International Stock Exchange, London, May.

European Commission, 2001, *Overview of Proposed Adjustments to the Investment Services Directive*, International Market Directorate General, European Commission, July.

Ferris, A.P., T.H. McInish and R.A. Wood, 1997, Automated trade execution and trading activity: the case of the Vancouver Stock Exchange, *Journal of International Financial Markets, Institutions and Money*, 7, 61–72.

Financial Services Authority (FSA), 1999, *The Financial Services Authority: Information Guide*, FSA, August.

Financial Services Authority (FSA), 2000a, The FSA's Approach to Regulation of the Market Infrastructure, *FSA Discussion Paper*, January.

Financial Services Authority, (FSA), 2000b, *The FSA Supervisor Manual*, Consultation Paper 64, August.

Financial Services Authority (FSA), 2001a, Review of the UK Mechanism for Disseminating Regulatory Information by Listed Companies, *FSA Consultation Paper*, 92, May.

Financial Services Authority (FSA), 2001b, *The FSA's Approach to Regulation of Market Infrastructure: Feedback on Discussion Paper*, FSA, June.

Financial Services Authority (FSA), 2001c, Best Execution, *FSA Discussion Paper*, April.

Fishman, M.J. and K.M. Hagerty, 1995, The mandatory disclosure of trades and market liquidity, *Review of Financial Studies*, 8(3), 637–76.

Fleming, J., B. Ostdiek and R. Whaley, 1996, Trading costs and the relative rate of price discovery in stock, futures and option markets, *Journal of Futures Markets*, 16, 353–87.

Flood, Mark D., Ronald Huisman, Kees G. Koedijk, Ronald Mahieu and Ailsa Röell, 1997, Post-trade transparency in multiple dealer financial markets, *Working Paper*, LIFE, Maastricht University, May.

Flood, Mark D., Ronald Huisman, Kees G. Koedijk and Ronald Mahieu, 1999, Quote disclosure and price discovery in multiple dealer financial markets, *Review of Financial Studies*, 12(1), 37–59.

Foerster, S.R. and G.A. Karolyi, 1998, Multimarket trading and liquidity: a transaction data analysis of Canada–US interlistings, *Journal of International Financial Markets, Institutions and Money*, 8, 393–412.

Fong, K., A. Madhavan and P. Swan, 1999, Why do securities markets fragment? *Discussion Paper*, Department of Finance and Business Economics, University of Southern California, Los Angeles, November.

Forster, M.M and T.J. George, 1992, Anonymity in securities markets, *Journal of Financial Intermediation*, 2, 168–206.

Forum of European Securities Exchanges (FESCO), 2001, *Proposed Standards for Alternative Trading Systems*. FESCO, June.

Foster, F.D. and S. Viswanathan, 1990, A theory of interday variations in volumes, variances and trading costs in securities markets, *Review of Financial Studies*, 3, 593–624.

Foster, F.D. and S. Viswanathan, 1993, Variations in trading volumes, returns volatility and trading costs: evidence on recent price formation models, *Journal of Finance*, 48, 187–211.

Foucault, T. and C.A. Parlour, 2000, Competition for listings, Centre for Economic and Policy Research, Discussion Paper, 2222.

Franke, G. and D. Hess, 1996, Anonymous electronic trading versus floor trading, *Chicago Board of Trade Research Symposium Proceedings*, Summer, 101–36.

Franks, J.R. and S.M. Schaefer, 1991, Equity market transparency, *Stock Exchange Quarterly*, April–June 7–11.

Franses, P.H., R. van Leperen, P. Kofman, M. Martens and B. Menkveld, 1994, Volatility patterns and spillovers in Bund futures, *Working Paper*, 16/94, Department of Econometrics, Monash University.

Fremault, A. and G. Sandmann, 1995, Floor trading versus electronic screen trading: an empirical analysis of market liquidity in the Nikkei stock index futures contract, London School of Economics, Financial Markets Group, *Discussion Paper*, 218.

Frino, A., T.H. McInish and M. Toner, 1998, The liquidity of automated exchanges: new evidence from German Bund futures, *Journal of International Financial Markets, Institutions and Money*, 8, 225–41.

Garbade, K.D. and W. Silber, 1979, Dominant and satellite markets: a study of dually-traded securities, *Review of Economics and Statistics*, 61, 455–60.

Gemmill, G., 1994, Transparency and Liquidity: A Study of Large Trades on the London Stock Exchange Under Different Publication Rules, *Research Paper*, 7, Office of Fair Trading, London, November.

Gemmill, G. 1996, Transparency and liquidity: a study of block trades on the London Stock Exchange under different publication rules, *Journal of Finance*, 51(5), 1765–90.

Gilbert, C.L., 1996, Manipulation of metal futures: lessons from Sumitomo, *Working Paper*, Department of Economics, Queen Mary and Westfield College.

Glosten, L., 1989, Insider trading, liquidity, and the role of the monopolist specialist, *Journal of Business*, 62, 211–36.

Glosten, L.R., 1994, Is the electronic open limit order book inevitable?, *Journal of Finance*, 49, 1127–61.

Glosten, L.R., 1999, Introductory Comments: Bloomfield and O'Hara and Flood, Huisman, Koedijk and Mahieu, *Review of Financial Studies*, 12(1), 1–3.

Glosten, L. R. and P.R. Milgrom, 1985, Bid, ask and transaction prices in a specialist market with heterogeneously informed traders, *Journal of Financial Economics*, 14, 71–100.

Godek, P.E., 1996, Why NASDAQ market makers avoid odd-eighth quotes, *Journal of Financial Economics*, 41, 465–74.

Griffiths, M.D., B.F. Smith, D.A.S. Turnbull and R.W. White, 1998, Information flows and open outcry: evidence of imitation trading, *Journal of International Financial Markets, Institutions and Money*, 8, 101–16.

Grossman, S., M. Miller, D. Fischel, K. Cone and D. Ross, 1997, Clustering and competition in asset markets, *Journal of Law and Economics*, 40, 23–60.

Grunbichler, A., F.A. Longstaff and E.S. Schwartz, 1994, Electronic screen trading and the transmission of information: an empirical examination, *Journal of Financial Intermediation*, 3, 166–87.

Hagerty, K. and R.L. McDonald, 1996, Brokerage, market fragmentation and securities market regulation, in A.W. Lo, *The Industrial Organization and Regulation of the Securities Industry*, University of Chicago Press, 35–61.

Hansch, O., N.Y. Naik and S. Viswanathan, 1998, Do inventories matter in dealership markets? Evidence from the London Stock Exchange, *Journal of Finance*, 53, 1623–56.

Hansch, O., N.Y. Naik and S. Viswanathan, 1999, Preferencing, internalisation, best execution and dealer profits, *Journal of Finance*, 54, 1799–1828.

Harris, F.H., T.H. McInish, G.L. Shoesmith and R.A. Wood, 1995, Cointegration, error correction, and price discovery on informationally linked securities markets, *Journal of Financial and Quantitative Analysis*, 30, 563–79.

Harris, L.E., 1990, Liquidity, trading rules and electronic trading systems, New York University, Salomon Centre Monograph Series in Finance and Economics, *Monograph*, 1990–4.

Harris, L.E., 1991, Stock price clustering and discreteness, *Review of Financial Studies*, 4, 389–415.

Harris, L.E., 1993, Consolidation, fragmentation, segmentation and regulation, *Financial Markets, Institutions and Instruments*, 2, 1–28.

Harris, L.E. and J. Hasbrouck, 1996, Market vs. limit orders: the SuperDOT evidence on order submission strategy, *Journal of Financial and Quantitative Analysis*, 31, 213–31.

Hart, O. and J. Moore, 1996, The governance of exchanges: members' co-operatives versus outside ownership, *Oxford Review of Economic Policy*, 12(4), 53–69.

Hasbrouck, J., 1995, One security, many markets: determining the contributions to price discovery, *Journal of Finance*, 50(4), 1175–99.

Henker, T., 1998, Bid – ask spread of the FTSE 100 futures contract, *Working Paper*, School of Management, University of Massachusetts.

Henker, T., 1999, An academic perspective on the trading platform debate, *Working Paper*, School of Management, University of Massachusetts.

Ho, T. and R.G. Macris, 1985, Dealer market structure and performance, in Amihud, Y., T.S.Y. Ho and R.A. Schwartz (eds), *Market Making and the Changing Structure of the Securities Industries*, Lexington Books, Mass.

Ho, T. and H.R. Stoll, 1983, The dynamics of dealer markets under competition, *Journal of Finance*, 1053–74.

Hodson, D., 1994, Equity–derivative linkages, Paper presented at a conference on 'Equity Market Regulation: The SIB's Proposed Changes and their Impact for Market Participants', London, 2 May.

Holthausen, R.W., R.W. Leftwich and D. Mayers, 1987, The effect of large block transactions on security prices: a cross sectional analysis, *Journal of Financial Economics*, 21, 237–68.

Holthausen, R.W., R.W. Leftwich and D. Mayers, 1990, Large block transactions, speed of response, and temporary and permanent stock price effects, *Journal of Financial Economics*, 26, 71–95.

Huang, R.D. and H.R. Stoll, 1996, Dealer versus auction markets: a paired comparison of execution costs on NASDAQ and the NYSE, *Journal of Financial Economics*, 41, 313–57.

International Organization of Securities Commissions (IOSCO), 1993, *Transparency on Secondary Markets: A Synthesis of the IOSCO Debate*, IOSCO Technical Committee Working Party on the Regulation of Secondary Markets, Milan, April.

Jochum, C., 1999, Network economics and the financial markets – the future of Europe's Stock Exchanges, *Aussenwirtschaft*, 54(1), 49–74.

Kandel, E. and L. Marx, 1997, NASDAQ market structure and spread patterns, *Journal of Financial Economics*, 35, 61–90.

Kappi, J. and R. Siivonen, 2000, Market liquidity and depth on two different electronic trading systems: a comparison of Bund futures trading on the APT and DTB, *Journal of Financial Markets*, 3, 389–402.

Katz, M.L. and C. Shapiro, 1985, Network externalities, competition and compatibility, *American Economic Review*, 75(3), 424–40.

Kavajecz, K.A., 1999, A specialist's quoted depth and the limit order book, *Journal of Finance*, 54, 747–71.

Kempf, A. and O. Korn, 1998, Trading system and market integration, *Journal of Financial Intermediation*, 7, 220–39.

Khan, B. and J. Ireland, 1993, The use of technology for competitive advantage: a study of screen versus floor trading, City Research Project Paper, London Business School.

Kleidon, A. and I. Werner, 1993, Round-the-clock trading: evidence from UK cross-listed securities, *Working Paper*, 4410, National Bureau of Economic Research.

Kleidon, A. and R. Willig, 1995, Why do Christie and Schultz infer collusion from their data?, *Working Paper*, Cornerstone Research, New York.

Kofman, P., T. Bouwman and J.T. Moser, 1994, Is there LIF(F)E After DTB? Competitive aspects of cross listed futures contracts on synchronous markets, *Working Paper*, 9/94, Department of Econometrics, Monash University.

Kofman, P. and J. Moser, 1997, Spreads, information flows and transparency across trading systems, *Applied Financial Economics*, 7(3), 281–94.

Kyle, A.S. and Röell, A.A. 1989, Comments on recent developments and proposals concerning dealing practices in the UK equity market, London School of Economics Financial Markets Group Special Paper No. 17, 15 pp.

Lai, M.K., 1996, Market transparency and intraday trade behaviour in the London Stock Exchange, PhD thesis, London Business School.

Lee, C., B. Mucklow and M. Ready, 1993, Spreads, depths and the impact of earnings information: an intraday analysis, *Review of Financial Studies*, 6, 345–74.

Lee, R., 1998, *What Is an Exchange? The Automation, Management and Regulation of Financial Markets*, Oxford University Press.

Lee, S.B. and J.S. Chung, 1998, The effect of market transparency: volatility and liquidity in the Korean Stock Market, *Review of Quantitative Finance and Accounting*, 11(1), 23–35.

Lehmann, B.N. and D.M. Modest, 1994, Trading and liquidity on the Tokyo Stock Exchange: a bird's eye view, *Journal of Finance*, 49, 951–84.

Levin, E.J. and R.E. Wright, 1999, Explaining the intraday variation in the bid – ask spread in competitive dealership markets: a research note, *Journal of Financial Markets*, 2, 179–91.

Levitt, A., 1999, Dynamic markets, timeless principles. Speech at Columbia Law School, 23 September.

Levitt, A., 2001, The national market system: a vision that endures, Speech at Stanford University, 8 January.

Liebowitz, S.J. and S.E. Margolis, 1994, Network externality: an uncommon tragedy, *Journal of Economic Perspectives*, 8(2), 133–50.

Lyons, R., 1996, Optimal transparency in a dealership market with an application to foreign exchange, *Journal of Financial Intermediation*, 5, 225–54.

Ma, C.K., R.L. Peterson and R.S. Sears, 1992, Trading noise, adverse selection and intraday bid – ask spreads in futures markets, *Journal of Futures Markets*, 12, 519–38.

Macey, J. and Kanda, H., 1990, The Stock Exchange as a firm: the emergence of close substitutes for the New York and Tokyo Stock Exchanges, *Cornell Law Review*, 75, 1007–52.

Macey, J. and M. O'Hara, 1999a, Regulating exchanges and alternative trading systems: a law and economics perspective, *Journal of Legal Studies*, 28, 17–54.

Macey, J. and M. O'Hara, 1999b, Globalization, exchange governance and the future of exchanges, in *Brookings – Wharton Papers on Financial Services*, eds R.E. Litan and A.M. Santomero, Brookings Institution Press, 1–32.

MacIntyre, D., 1991, Review of the January 14th Rule changes, *Quality of Markets Review*, April–June, 35–7.

Madhavan, A., 1992, Trading mechanisms in securities markets, *Journal of Finance*, 47, 607–41.

Madhavan, A. 1995, Consolidation, fragmentation and the disclosure of trading information, *Review of Financial Studies*, 8(3), 579–603.

Madhavan, A., 1996, Security prices and market transparency, *Journal of Financial Intermediation*, 5, 255–83.

Madhavan, A., 2000, Market microstructure: a survey, *Journal of Financial Markets*, 3, 205–58.

Madhavan, A.D. Porter and D. Weaver, 2000, Should securities markets be transparent?, *Working Paper*, University of Southern California, Los Angeles, January.

Mahoney, P.G., 1997, The exchange as regulator, *Virginia Law Review*, 83(7), 1453–1500.

Malkamäki, M. 2000, Economies of scale and implicit mergers in Stock Exchange activities, *Working Paper*, Research Department, Bank of Finland.

Martens, M., 1998, Price discovery in high and low volatility periods: open outcry versus electronic trading, *Journal of International Financial Markets, Institutions and Money*, 8, 243–60.

Massimb, M.N. and B.D. Phelps, 1994, Electronic trading, market structure and liquidity, *Financial Analysts Journal*, January–February, 39–50.

McAndrews, J. and C. Stefanadis, 2000, The emergence of electronic communications networks in the US equity markets, *Current Issues in Economics and Finance*, Federal Reserve Bank of New York, 6(12).

McInish, T. H. and R. A. Wood, 1992, An analysis of intraday patterns in bid/ask spreads for NYSE stocks, *Journal of Finance*, 47, 753–64.

Mendelson, H., 1987, Consolidation, fragmentation and market performance, *Journal of Financial and Quantitative Analysis*, 22, 189–208.

Mendelson, M. and J.W. Peake, 1991, Securities trading systems (1): the myth of quote-driven superiority, *Journal of International Securities Markets*, 5, 111–13.

Mendelson, M. and Peake, J.W., 1994, 'Intermediaries or investors': whose market is it anyway? *Journal of Corporation Law*, 19, 443–82.

Miller, M.H., 1990, International competitiveness of US futures exchanges, *Journal of Financial Services Research*, 4, 387–408.

Moessner, R., 2001, Over the Counter Interest Rate Options, *Research Papers in Finance* 1/2001, Centre for Central Banking Studies, Bank of England.

Mulherin, J.H., J.M. Netter and J.A. Overdahl, 1991, Prices are property: the organization of financial exchanges from a transaction cost perspective, *Journal of Law and Economics*, 34(2), 591–644.

Naidu, G.N. and M.S. Rozeff, 1994, Volume, volatility, liquidity and efficiency of the Singapore Stock Exchange before and after automation, *Pacific-Basin Finance Journal*, 2, 23–42.

Naik, N., A. Neuberger and S. Viswanathan, 1994, Disclosure regulation in competitive dealership markets: analysis of the London Exchange, London Business School, Institute of Finance and Accounting *Working Paper*, 193.

Naik, N., A. Neuberger and S. Viswanathan, 1999, Trade disclosure regulation in markets with negotiated trades, *Review of Financial Studies*, 12(4), Supp., 873–900.

National Association of Securities Dealers (NASD), 1983, *Analysis of the Impact of Last Sale Reporting on Market Characteristics of Tier 2 NASDAQ Securities*, Department of Policy Research, NASD, Washington, DC, June.

Neuberger, A.J., 1992, An empirical examination of market maker profits on the London Stock Exchange, *Journal of Financial Services Research*, 6(4), 343–72.

New York Stock Exchange (NYSE), 2000, *Market Structure Report of the New York Stock Exchange Special Committee on Market Structure, Governance and Ownership*, NYSE.

O'Hara, M., 1995, *Market Microstructure Theory*, Blackwell, Oxford.

Pagano, M. and A. Röell, 1990, Trading systems in European stock exchanges: current performance and policy options, *Economic Policy: A European Forum*, 10, 63–115.

Pagano, M. and A. Röell, 1992, Auction and dealership markets: what is the difference?, *European Economic Review*, 36, 613–23.

Pagano, M. and A. Röell, 1993, Shifting gears: an economic evaluation of the reform of the Paris Bourse, LSE Financial Markets Group, *Discussion Paper*, 103, 579–612

Pagano, M. and A. Röell, 1996, Transparency and liquidity: a comparison of auction and dealer markets with informed trading, *Journal of Finance*, 51(2), 579–612.

Pagano, M. and B. Steil, 1996, Equity trading I: the evolution of European trading systems, in B. Steil (eds.), *The European Equity Markets: The State of the Union and an Agenda for the Millennium*, Royal Institute of International Affairs, London, 1–58.

Pieptea, D.R., 1992, Electronic trading and futures market efficiency, *International Journal of Technology Management*, 7, 471–7.

Pirrong, C., 1995, The self-regulation of commodity exchanges: the case of market manipulation, *Journal of Law and Economics*, 38(1), 141–206.

Pirrong, C., 1996, Market liquidity and depth on computerized and open outcry trading systems: a comparison of DTB and LIFFE Bund contracts, *Journal of Futures Markets*, 16, 519–43.

Pirrong, C., 1999, The organization of financial exchange markets: theory and evidence, *Journal of Financial Markets*, 2(4), 329–57.

Porter, D. and Weaver, D., 1998, Post-trade transparency on NASDAQ's national market system, *Journal of Financial Economics*, 50(2), 231–52.

Quality of Markets (1990) The changing structure of the UK equity market, *Quality of Markets Quarterly Review*, January–March, Spring, 15–21.

Rappell, J.R., 1998, Secrets and lies: the battle between OTC market transparency and confidentiality, *Economic Papers [Australia]*, 17(4), 69–75.

Reiss, P.C. and I.M. Werner, 1996, Transaction costs in dealer markets: evidence from the London Stock Exchange, in L.W. Lo (ed.), *The Industrial Organization and Regulation of the Securities Industry*, University of Chicago Press, 125–69.

Reiss, P.C. and I. Werner, 1998, Does risk sharing motivate inter-dealer trading?, *Journal of Finance*, 53, 1657–1704.

Rhodes-Kropf, M., 1997, On price improvement in dealership markets, *Working Paper*, Duke University.

Rock, K., 1991, The specialist's order book, *Working Paper*, Harvard Business School, Cambridge, Mass.

Röell, A., 1990, Dual capacity trading and the quality of markets, *Journal of Financial Intermediation*, 105–24.

Röell, A., 1992, Comparing the performance of stock exchange trading systems, in J. Fingleton and D. Schoenmaker (eds), *The Internationalisation of Capital Markets and the Regulatory Response*, Graham and Trotman, London.

Ross, S., 1992, Market-making – a price too far: the march of technology, *Journal of International Securities Markets*, 6, 109–15.

Sandmann, G. and A. Fremault, 1996, Stochastic volatility, error correction and dual listing in futures markets, London School of Economics, *Discussion Paper*.

Saporta, V., G. Trebeschi and A. Vila, 1999, Price formation and transparency on the London Stock Exchange, *Bank of England Working Paper*, 95, April.

Sarkar, A. and M. Tozzi, 1998, Electronic trading on futures exchanges, *Current Issues in Economics and Finance*, Federal Reserve Bank of New York, 4(1).

Scalia, A. and V. Vacca, 1999, Does market transparency matter? A case study, in *Market Liquidity: Research Findings and Selected Policy Implications*, Committee on the Global Financial System, Bank for International Settlements, Basle.

Schmidt, H. and P. Iversen, 1992, Automating German equity trading: bid-ask spreads on competing systems, *Journal of Financial Services Research*, 6, 373–97.

Schwartz, R.A., 1991, Consolidation of the order flow, Chapter 9 in *Reshaping the Equity Markets – A Guide for the 1990s*, Harper Business, 169–95.

Schwartz, R.A., 1996, Equity trading II: integration, fragmentation and the quality of markets, in B. Steil (ed.), *The European Equity Markets: The State of the Union and an Agenda for the Millennium*, Royal Institute of International Affairs, London, 59–79.

Schwartz, R.A. and B. Steil, 1996, Equity trading III: institutional investor trading practices and preferences, in B. Steil (ed.), *The European Equity Markets: The State of the Union and an Agenda for the Millennium*, Royal Institute of International Affairs, London, 81–112.

Securities and Exchange Commission (SEC), 1994, *Market 2000: An Examination of Current Equity Market Developments*, Division of Market Regulation, SEC, Washington, DC, January.

Securities and Exchange Commission (SEC), 1999, *Regulation of Market Information Fees and Revenues*, Release No. 34–42208, SEC, 17 December.

Securities and Exchange Commission (SEC), 2000a, *Self-Regulatory Organizations: Notice of Filing of Proposed Rule Change by the New York Stock Exchange, Inc. to Rescind Exchange Rule 390: Commission Request for Comment on Issues Related to Market Fragmentation*, Release No. 34–42450, SEC, 23 February.

Securities and Exchange Commission (SEC), 2000b, *Comments on NYSE Rulemaking: Notice of Filing of Proposed Rule Change by the New York Stock Exchange, Inc. to Rescind Exchange Rule 390: Commission Request for Comment on Issues Related to Market Fragmentation*, Release No. 34–42450, SEC.

Securities and Exchange Commission (SEC), 2000c, *Report Concerning Display of Customer Limit Orders*, Office of Compliance Inspections and Examinations, Office of Economic Analysis, SEC, 4 May.

Securities and Exchange Commission (SEC), 2000d, *Electronic Communication Networks and After-Hours Trading*, Division of Market Regulation, SEC, June.

Securities and Exchange Commission (SEC), 2000e, *Disclosure of Order Routing and Execution Practices*, Release No. 34–43084, SEC, 28 July.

Securities and Exchange Commission (SEC), 2000f, *Comments on Proposed Rule: Disclosure of Order Routing and Execution Practices*, Release No. 34–43084, SEC.

Securities and Exchange Commission (SEC), 2000g, Advisory Committee on Market Information: Minutes, 10 October 2000, SEC, Division of Market Regulation.

Securities and Exchange Commission (SEC), 2000h, *Disclosure of Order Execution and Routing Practices*, Release No. 34–43590, November, SEC.

Securities and Exchange Commission (SEC), 2001, *Report of the Advisory Committee On Market Information: A Blueprint For Responsible Change* (the Seligman Report).

Securities and Investments Board (SIB), 1994, *Regulation of the United Kingdom Equity Markets* (the Agnew Report), Discussion Paper, Securities and Investments Board, London, February, 60 pp.

Securities and Investments Board (SIB), 1995, *Regulation of the United Kingdom Equity Markets*, Report by Securities and Investments Board, London, June.

Securities and Investments Board (SIB), 1996, *A Review of the London Metal Exchange: Summary and Conclusions*, December, SIB.

Securities and Investments Board (SIB), 1997, *Securing Enhanced Market Liquidity*, Report by Securities and Investments Board, London, July.

Semkow, B.W., 1989, Emergence of derivative financial products markets in Japan, *Cornell International Law Review*, 22, 39–58.

Senate Banking Committee (SBC), 1999, 27 October 1999, Hearing on The Changing Face of Capital Markets and the Impact of ECNs.

Senate Banking Committee (SBC), 2000:
  29 February 2000, Hearing on the 'Financial Marketplace of the Future'.
  22 March 2000, Subcommittee on Securities, Hearing on 'Trading Places: Markets for Investors'.
  13 April 2000, Hearing on the 'Structure of Securities Markets'.
  26 April 2000, Subcommittee on Securities, Hearing on 'Competition and Transparency in the Financial Marketplace of the Future'.
  8 May 2000, Hearing on 'Maintaining Leadership in the Financial Marketplace of the Future'.
  21 June 2000, Hearing on 'Commodity Futures Modernization Act'.
  All available at <http://www.senate.gov/~banking/hrg00.htm>

Shah, A., 2000, A natural experiment in market transparency, *Working Paper*, Indira Ghandi Institute for Development Research, Bombay.

Shapiro, C. and H.R. Varian, 1998, *Information Rules : A Strategic Guide to the Network Economy*, Harvard Business School Press.

Shy, O., 2001, *The Economics of Network Industries*, Cambridge University Press.

Shyy, G. and J.H. Lee, 1995, Price transmission and information asymmetry in Bund futures markets: LIFFE vs. DTB, *Journal of Futures Markets*, 15, 87–99.

Shyy, G., V. Vijayraghavan and B. Scott-Quinn, 1996, A further investigation of the lead–lag relationship between the cash market and stock index futures market with the use of bid/ask quotes: the case of France, *The Journal of Futures Markets*, 16, 405–20.

Silber, W.L., 1981, Innovation, competition and new contract design in futures markets, *Journal of Futures Markets*, 1, 123–55.

Snell, A. and I. Tonks, 1995, Determinants of price quote revisions on the London Stock Exchange, *Economic Journal*, 105(428), 77–94.

Snell, A. and I. Tonks, 1998, Testing for asymmetric information and inventory control effects in market maker behaviour on the London Stock Exchange, *Journal of Empirical Finance*, 5, 1–25.

Stoll, H.S., 1992, Organization of the Stock Market: competition or fragmentation?, in K. Lehn and R.W. Kamphuis (eds), *Modernizing U.S. Securities Regulation: Economic and Legal Perspectives*, Irwin Professional Publishing, 399–406.

Stoll, H.S., 1992, Principles of trading market structure, *Journal of Financial Services Research*, 6(1), 75–107.

Stoll, H.S. 2001, Market fragmentation, *Financial Analysts Journal*, 57(4), 16–20.

Stoll, H.R. and R.E. Whaley, 1990, The dynamics of stock index and stock index futures returns, *Journal of Financial and Quantitative Analysis*, 25, 441–68.

Tonks, I., 1996, The equivalence of screen based continuous-auction and dealer markets, London School of Economics, Financial Markets Group, *Special Paper*, 92.

Treasury, 2000, *The Financial Services and Market Act 2000 (Recognition Requirements for Investment Exchanges and Clearing Houses) Regulations 2001*, December, HM Treasury, <http://www.hm-treasury.gov.uk/fsma/recognition_req/index.html>

Tse, T., 1999, Market microstructure of FTSE-100 index futures: an intraday empirical analysis, *Journal of Futures Markets*, 19, 31–58.

Umlauf, S.R., 1991, Information asymmetries and security market design: an empirical study of the secondary market for US government securities, *Journal of Finance*, 46(3), 929–53.

Viswanathan S. and J.J.D. Wang, 1998, Market architecture: limit-order books versus dealership markets, *Working Paper*, Fuqua School of Business, Duke University.

Wang, J., 1999, Asymmetric information and the bid – ask spread: an empirical comparison between automated order execution and open outcry auction, *Journal of International Financial Markets, Institutions and Money*, 9, 115–28.

Wang, G. H. K., R. J. Michalski, J. V. Jordan and E. J. Moriarty, 1994, An intraday analysis of bid – ask spreads and price volatility in the S&P500 index futures market, *Journal of Futures Markets*, 14, 837–59.

Wells, S., 1993, Transparency in the equity market: the publication of last trades, *Stock Exchange Quarterly*, January–March, 13–16.

Werner, I. and A. Kleidon, 1996, US and UK trading of British cross-listed stocks: an intraday analysis of market integration, *Review of Financial Studies*, 9, 619–64.

Williamson, C. 1999, Structural changes in exchange-traded markets, *Bank of England Quarterly Bulletin*, May, 202–6.

Witt, U., 1997, Lock-in versus critical masses – industrial change under network externalities, *International Journal of Industrial Organization*, 15(6), 753–73.

Yagil, J. and Z. Forshner, 1991, Gains from international dual listing, *Management Science*, 37(1), 114–120.

Yamori, N., 1998, Does international trading of stocks decrease pricing errors? Evidence from Japan, *Journal of International Financial Markets, Institutions & Money*, 8, 413–32.

Index